FRUITS
AND
BERRIES
FOR THE
HOME
GARDEN

◆◆◆◆◆◆◆

by Lewis Hill

A Garden Way Publishing Book

STOREY

Storey Communications, Inc.
Schoolhouse Road
Pownal, Vermont 05261

Cover and text design by Wanda Harper
Edited by Gwen Steege
Illustrations by Alison Kolesar
Indexed by Kathleen D. Bagioni

The name Garden Way Publishing is licensed to Storey Communications, Inc. by Garden Way, Inc.

Printed in the United States by The Book Press
First Printing, March 1992

Library of Congress Cataloging-in-Publication Data

Hill, Lewis, 1924-
    Fruits and berries for the home garden / Lewis Hill. — Completely rev. and updated.
        p.   cm.
    Includes bibliographical references and index.
    ISBN 0-88266-764-5 — ISBN 0-88266-763-7 (pbk.)
    1. Fruit-culture.   I. Title.
SB355.H65   1992   91-55508
634—dc20   CIP

Table of Contents

Author Notes

Lewis and Nancy Hill live in northern Vermont, where the Hill family settled in 1791. For many years, they operated a retail nursery that Lewis started in 1947, specializing in hardy fruit trees, berry plants, and ornamental shrubs. Now, although fruit-growing remains an important part of their lives — each summer they fill two freezers with home-grown fruits and vegetables — their nursery efforts are devoted to growing and selling over 500 varieties of daylilies.

During the long Vermont winters when the plants are sleeping, they write books and magazine articles; they contributed entries for *The Wise Gardening Encyclopedia.* Both speak frequently to garden clubs and civic groups.

The Hills have conducted hardiness tests on hundreds of plants for universities and experiment stations. They are active members of the Vermont Plantsmen, which Lewis helped organize in 1968. He is active in community affairs, and as Justice of the Peace, married over 100 women in addition to his wife, Nancy.

Nancy, also a Vermont native, worked for *House Beautiful Magazine* and an advertising agency in New York City, and taught English in Thailand as a Peace Corps Volunteer before her marriage and return to the Green Mountain State. She recently completed eight years as a commissioner of the regional District Environmental Commission and is a member of the local planning commission. One of her hobbies is collecting fruit recipes and experimenting with new ways to use their fruits and berries. Hiking, especially in England, is another interest, but she does it without Lewis, who prefers to stay at home. A true Yankee, he says, "Why should I travel when I'm already here?"

Preface

Cultural methods in horticulture do not change as fast as in medicine or physics; they do change, however, so the time has come to update this book. Recommended varieties, fertilizers, and pest controls undergo continual evolution as more information appears and old methods are discontinued. Most deadly pesticides and fast-acting nitrates once used by orchardists have been replaced by safer methods. Even aluminum sulfate, long recommended as a way to acidify soil for blueberries, is now on the "beware" list of most gardeners.

Even the language changes. As more becomes known about plants, botanists reclassify them, and new terms have come into common usage. An example is the word "cultivar," which designates the registered name for a plant. The word "variety" is now reserved for the names of different but closely related plants of the same species. Thus *Jackii* is a variety of the *Malus baccata* species, a Siberian crab apple, while Dolgo is a cultivar of the same species. Both were formerly called varieties, as were fruit names like McIntosh and Yellow Delicious. Cultivar is just coming into common use, however, so you can expect to see the word variety used interchangeably with it for some time to come. Many new fruit and berry cultivars, most from North America, but others from Europe, the Orient, and Australia, have become available since the first edition of this book.

We are enjoying many of these advances in horticulture, and I know that they will also make it even more pleasurable and worthwhile for all of you who want to grow your own fruit.

Preface to First Edition

One of the best things about walking the mile to our country school when I was six was cutting through our old and rather decrepit orchard and picking pocketsful of apples to eat on the way. The early Yellow Transparents and Tetoskys were ready on the first day of school, and even a child could eat a lot of them without feeling stuffed. Later came the "heavier" apples — the zippy-flavored Duchesses, the Astrachans with their waxy red skins, golden Peach apples with rosy blooms, and the Wealthys, which ripened a week or so later. The Bethels, Pound Sweets, and Tolmans ripened even later, and we stored those in the cellar for winter eating.

Lots of other apples grew in the orchard, too. We didn't even know their names, so we called them by their flavor or appearance: the pear, pumpkin, banana, sugar, or whatever. All the kids in the neighborhood knew where the best apples in each orchard grew, and when they were at their best. Like the raccoons that stole them at night, we could go unerringly to the choicest trees.

Even with all those wonderful kinds to choose from, we continually heard the old-timers speak fondly of other varieties they had grown long ago. They remembered the Alexander, Baldwin, Fameuse, Pearmain, Seek-No-Further, and many others. They would tell of cellars stashed with barrels of cider and boxes of apples that would keep all winter. "Can't seem to grow fruit anymore," they said sadly.

Our old orchard gradually died, and it fell apart within a few years. Soon not a tree was left, and most other nearby farm orchards disappeared too. Only here and there an occasional tree stayed alive and bravely produced fruit. Like home gardening, interest in backyard fruit growing had faded. Few people planted new trees in our neighborhood and those who did seemed to pay little attention after they stuck the trees in the ground. It was easier to buy fruit in bags or cans from the local store or go to a nearby commercial orchard. Most people failed to notice that the highly colored, uniform-sized fruits were tough skinned and not nearly as tasty as the old homegrown ones, and the sauce and preserves made from them was far less flavorful.

As I became older, I remembered how much better I had liked the homegrown fruits and was already sentimental about the stately old orchard and the heaps of apples that fell on the ground there each fall. Why couldn't we grow fruit anymore? The soil was still there and still good. The weather wasn't any worse, and maybe it was even better, to hear the old folks reminisce.

So, without having any idea of how to go about it, I decided to plant some apple trees. I couldn't find any of the old favorites that I remembered or had heard about, so I had to order new kinds from tantalizing catalogs sent by faraway nurseries. Their assortment in the 1940s was small, consisting mostly of the same varieties as those that were displayed in our local stores each fall: Red and Yellow Delicious, Rome Beauty, Jonathan, Winesap, and Grimes Golden. I planted a few of each, and soon, just as my neighbors had predicted, every one of them died.

"'Course, we always grafted our own," my elderly neighbor told me one day. "We never bought fruit trees. There was always somebody who traveled around and sold grafts. We'd have him stick them on some of the seedlings coming up all over. Next year we'd move them into the orchard, and most of them grew. That way you knew both the top and the root were hardy." Here was the first clue to what I was doing wrong. Right away, I bought a book about how to graft and care for fruit trees, and soon things began to look up.

After some friends noticed my beginner's luck with the first grafts, they began to show more interest in the project. Soon people were telling me about old trees here and there that were still bearing the good old kinds I remembered.

I learned that when I bought fruit trees it was wise to study the catalogs carefully, because a tree suitable for Oregon might not be happy in New England. When a catalog promised that something was hardy in the North, it might mean northern Missouri, North Carolina, or northern California. Only by buying or grafting the kinds that were actually suitable for our area did I finally get my orchard going.

One reason for the success of those early orchards was the kind of care the old-timers gave their fruits and berries. The orchard, a century ago, was as important to people as their grain, animals, poultry, woodlot, or vegetable garden. They never neglected the annual fertilizing, pruning, and insect control, even though the latter might consist only of flinging wood ashes through the trees now and then, or perhaps an occasional spray of soapsuds and water. They fenced out the farm animals except in late fall when pigs or cattle were let in for a short time to pick up any unused fruit in which insects and disease could spend the winter.

Growing apples was my stepping stone to trying other fruits, and a few years later we were harvesting plums, pears, grapes, cherries, and a large assortment of berries, just as our ancestors had done. We no longer need to depend on the small selection of varieties in the supermarket, because the dozens of different kinds of fruits growing in our backyard give us an exciting variety of good eating. Unlike Grandpa and Grandma, we have the advantage of a home freezer that lets us enjoy our produce all year. It seems good not to have to wash a raft of sprays and waxes off our fruit and berries before we eat them, or worry about whether our apple pie contains more preservatives than vitamins.

In fact, just about everything connected with fruit growing is a pleasure, especially the harvest. When I pick the first red strawberry of the season, or the first juicy, ripe raspberry, or the first crisp, tangy apple, any battles with insects or weeds are quickly forgotten. Instead, my boyhood memories of the majestic old orchard return, and I am filled with hopeful anticipation of all the fabulous harvests ahead. It took me about twenty years to learn how to grow good fruit. I hope this book will help you accomplish it in less time — a whole lot less.

CHAPTER 1

Getting Started with Fruits

"As the twig is bent, so the tree is inclined." The old saying is very true. Several fruit trees on our place lean badly and will eventually topple over. Other trees suffer from being too close to large maples, and a few are struggling where the soil is far too thin or too wet. One large crab apple in the front yard even started to grow up into the telephone wires. All are sad monuments to my early days of planting and pruning, when I had little idea of how to do either one properly.

No one ever told me about tree nutrients, and how grass and weeds were likely to steal them all while the poor tree suffered from malnutrition. I just kept heaping on the wrong combinations of fertilizers, awaiting the amazing results that didn't come. Nor did I know that winter's sun could be as responsible for frost injury as winter's cold, or that pollination was necessary to get fruit and that I could even help the bees, if necessary. It took a while to learn that when a tree looked sick it wasn't always bugs or disease but sometimes a physiological difficulty that sprays couldn't help. I found there are ways to get trees to yield larger fruit, to bear at an earlier age, and even produce a good crop *each* fall instead of every other year. I finally began to grasp that the way you start is terribly important, because the first years in the orchard set the course for the next fifty or more.

Many people hesitate about getting involved in what they consider such a long-term project. Every spring the same couple used to come to our nursery to buy vegetable and flower plants. They always looked longingly at the little trees and said, "If only we weren't so old, we would put in a few fruits and berries." They repeated that same line for over fifteen years, and I had trouble not pointing out that if they had planted their orchard the first year, they could already have harvested a dozen crops!

Others hesitate to grow fruits because they have planted a few trees at one time or another, watched them die, and decided not to try again. Still others think fruit trees are expensive or that they take a lot of room. I also meet a surprising number who feel that fruit growing is the pinnacle of gardening, requiring a higher level of expertise than they care to attempt, and that such

1

▲ **A country home and a fruit tree seem to go together.**

gardening should be left strictly to the experts. Many have been frightened, too, by tales of twice-a-week spraying with deadly poisons. Some Extension Services in the past even advised gardeners that it would be more practical to buy fruit than to bother with a small orchard.

All of this is most unfortunate. The truth is, if you choose the right kinds of fruits (and many beginners don't), give them a suitable place to live and a little attention (and again, many beginners don't), fruit trees and berries require no more — and often less — care than most other growing things.

You can plant and enjoy your own produce even if you are along in years or you have no plans to let your descendants inhabit the same spot for generations. Dwarf fruit trees begin to bear within two or three years, many small fruits produce big crops within three years, and you can pick everbearing strawberries even the first year. If you sell your property, your fruit orchard and berry patch will add tremendously to the sale value.

Our orchard and berry patch is small, but each year we put hundreds of packages into the freezer, in addition to all the fruits we store in our root cellar or preserve in other ways. All summer and fall we eat pies and shortcakes, drink lots of juice, and give away quantities of fruit. We won't even mention the amount we eat right off the trees and bushes while we are picking. Naturally, it would cost a tidy sum to buy all this food in the local market, even if it were available. Increasing prices and lack of availability of many fruits makes us appreciate our orchard and berry patch more each year.

The plants are not a large initial investment in light of all the future dividends you get from them. A fruit tree can cost as little as a bushel of fruit, and strawberry plants are only a few cents each. By raising its own vegetables, fruits, and berries, a family can easily save over $1,000 a year on its food bill. Why buy tropical fruit drinks when you can make your own? Why spend hard-earned money on commercial wines? In addition to the amount you save on your food bill, your homegrown food can give you extra savings in taxes, too. Except for seed, plants, and fertilizer, it doesn't cost you anything but labor, so it is tax free. If you had shelled out the $1,000 for food, you would have needed a sizeable addition to your income not just for the food, but also to pay the federal, state, and city taxes on it.

If you have only a small lot, you can still grow fruit. Many dwarf trees grow to full size within an 8-foot circle. Strawberries thrive in crocks, hanging baskets, pyramids, and barrels. A short row of raspberries will produce quarts of fruit every year. When landscaping, why not use blueberries, currants, and gooseberries as substitutes for ornamental foundation plants and hedges around your house? Fruit trees can replace flowering trees and shrubs, and nut trees are good substitutes for shade trees. Although our plantings bear little resemblance to those in Kew Gardens, we find pleasure and satisfaction in growing things that are beautiful in all seasons and also produce a product that can be put into a tasty pie or a tantalizing jug.

Choosing the Right Kinds of Fruit

Begin with a tree that is not only healthy, but also right for your location. If you're going to buy a dog, you're not likely to select a Mexican hairless Chihuahua to romp with you in the snow of upper Alaska, or an English sheepdog for your tropical island retirement. Yet each spring post offices and United Parcel depots in the northern states are filled with peach, fig, apricot, walnut, pecan, and sweet cherry trees that have no more chance of survival than a walrus caravan crossing the Sahara.

Gardeners in the South can have trouble, too. In order to survive, most temperate zone trees need a period of cool temperatures so they can rest completely for a few hundred hours each year. If you live in a frost-free or nearly frost-free area, plant only those cultivars that can survive without long periods of chilling.

Because so many plants are not right for the climate where they're planted, thousands of dollars, tons of fertilizer, and hours of work are wasted each year, not to mention the shattered dreams of would-be backyard orchardists. Many disappointed gardeners never try again. Others keep at it year after year, thinking they did something wrong; but the cards are always stacked against them.

So get things in your favor by choosing trees that are suitable for your climate. The chapters on specific fruits suggest cultivars for each planting zone.

Getting Acquainted with Your New Tree

One day, when I spotted a novice orchardist at our nursery, I inquired about his planting plans and made some suggestions. He exploded, "Why don't you just come right out and make us file adoption papers when we buy a tree!" Come to think of it, maybe that's not a bad idea. Anyone who has raised a tree from infancy to adolescence hates to send it out into the world to be treated with no more attention than one would give a newly set birdbath or flagpole.

Everyone wants trees that grow and produce, but a surprising number of people seem to forget that a tree is a living, growing thing and needs care. Many times along country roads you've probably seen abandoned farms where there are dozens of sturdy old apple trees growing miles from civilization. They obviously get no care whatsoever, yet they appear to be growing well and producing fruit. Still, it is very likely that sometime, long ago, someone helped those trees get off to a good start. You'll want to do the same for your fledgling fruit trees, too. It's easy. All you have to do is think from the tree's point of view.

When your new tree arrives, treat it like the living infant it is. No one would buy a puppy and dump him in the backyard to shift for himself; yet gardeners often buy a helpless little tree, plant it far too quickly and carelessly, and promptly lose interest in it. Unlike the pup, the poor tree can't go hunting for food and water, or even howl to remind you it is being neglected. Plant it carefully and make certain that the roots never lack moisture.

What a Tree Needs

Your tree has the same basic requirements as any living thing:

A place to live. The earth around the tree will be its permanent home, so be sure it is to its liking. Can the soil accommodate the huge root system of a mature tree and, with a little help from you, properly nourish it? Is the soil well drained, not too dry, but certainly not too wet? Fruit trees detest wet feet and get sick if water ever covers their roots for more than a few days at a time.

Air to breathe. Instead of breathing oxygen, trees "breathe" in carbon dioxide and give out oxygen, so they freshen our air. Remember how nice the woods smell!

Food and water. Like any living thing, a tree needs water and nourishment, and both should be available, especially in early summer when the tree makes most of its growth. The roots take in nitrogen, phosphorus, potassium, and a sprinkling of other minerals from the soil, but since soils alone are seldom well supplied with all these nutrients, you will probably need to provide additional amounts. Chapter 5 on soils will tell you how.

Sunlight. Most plants need light, and fruit trees need a great deal of it throughout most or all of the day. Sunlight is necessary for photosynthesis—the process by which plants convert energy from the sun into the carbohydrates necessary for plant growth. If buildings or large trees block out sunlight, your tree will not grow well.

Room to grow. No tree should be crowded. Be sure not to plant it too close to other trees, highways, overhead wires, paths, or buildings. And make sure there are no young shade trees nearby that will crowd it in the future. Not only can the tops of trees present a problem, but the roots of large trees can steal valuable nutrients and moisture from your young tree. There is as much of a tree underground as there is above, and in areas where the soil is not deep, the roots of a large shade tree often reach out 60 or more feet in every direction.

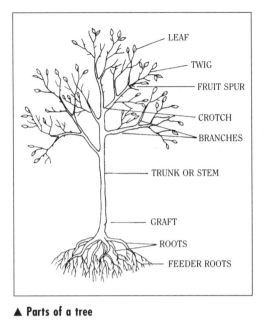

▲ Parts of a tree

Protection. Although a grown tree can stand a little neglect, you must give a young tree careful protection. Animals, insects, machinery (especially lawn mowers), children, and weather all take their toll of newly planted trees each year. Keep an eye on your young acquisition and be ready to spring to its rescue whenever danger threatens.

Two Trees for the Price of One

Unlike shade and forest trees, fruit tree cultivars will not, if they are propagated from seed, be like the parent. Even seeds from the best apples, plums, peaches, and pears are likely to grow into trees that produce poor fruit. The fruit from Johnny Appleseed's famous trees wasn't good for much except cider.

Your new little Jonathan apple tree that you may have ordered by mail or picked up at a nursery is likely to be two trees joined together by a surgical operation called a *graft*. The part that grows above ground and produces fruit was started from a tiny piece of branch called a *scion* (pronounced SĪ on), which was taken from a large Jonathan apple tree. The scion determines the shape of the tree, and what the size, color, and quality of the fruit will be. The rootstock, or underground portion of your tree, may have been grown from a seed, or it may have been started from a division of a larger clump of roots. A rootstock greatly influences the size of the tree, its vigor, its hardiness, and its ability to grow in various types of soil. Grafting is common in horticulture. You are probably already familiar with such grafted plants as tea roses, two-colored cactus plants, red-leaf maples, and copper beech trees.

◀ The graft of this fruit tree is very obvious. Most are not quite so distinctive. *(University of Illinois)*

You can easily locate the graft on your young fruit tree. It will be a good-size bump or bend in the stem either at ground level or a few inches above or below it. As the tree grows, the bump gradually disappears, but if the graft was made above ground the different kinds of bark are often noticeable years later.

Since everything growing below the graft will produce poor quality fruit if it is allowed to grow, cut off any sprouts from that part of the tree immediately. If mice or rabbits should chew the bark and kill the tree above the graft, any growth coming from below will be a wild tree. Unless you re-graft one of these wild sprouts with a scion from a good variety, it is better to dig up the roots and replace them with a new tree.

Your new grafted fruit tree is the result of centuries of improvement over the fruits that the early Greeks cultivated. Now it is ready to enrich your life with its beauty and bounty, asking only a little care and attention in return.

CHAPTER 2

Planning Your
Fruit Garden or Orchard

When you become involved in a project like growing fruit trees that will quite likely last a lifetime or longer, you'll naturally want to do it right. Mistakes made early have ways of coming back to haunt us. If you plant your vegetable garden with the seedlings too close together or in the wrong spot, or if you choose the wrong varieties, you will lose only one season. But if you make similar mistakes with fruit trees, it may be years before you find out there's a problem and decades before you can get new trees into full production. That's why I like first planting our fruits on paper, then putting the trees in the ground.

Even if you can't plant everything you want the first year, a plan will help you put each kind of tree in the most favorable location. Keep your plan up-to-date, because labels invariably get lost, and whenever a tree begins to bear, you'll want to know what it is. Also, if a tree does poorly or dies, you'll want to replace it with one that is similar.

If you have only a small lot, you don't have much choice about where to plant the trees. But within the boundaries you have, try to find a place where they will have good, deep soil, full sun, and plenty of room to grow.

Before you choose the exact location of your future orchard, investigate anything that goes on there that might affect its growth, now or in the future. Is the spot a neighborhood trail for motorcycles, snowmobiles, or hikers? Will you or someone else in the future have to dig to repair a cable, water pipe, or sewer line? Will the orchard block off an area where you may need service vehicles to drive through someday? Will your neighbor's row of little oak trees grow to powerful heights and shade your trees, or will his horse get loose and graze them to the ground? Do heavy rains or melting snows form pools of water that could drown them? Or will road salt drain onto them?

Sometimes it seems as if the whole world is out to get a newly planted tree, so it's good insurance to plant it near your home where you can keep a watchful eye on any troubles before they get too serious. Probably George Washington wouldn't have cut down his father's cherry tree if it had been where his mother could have kept a better eye on it! Fruit trees planted close to a busy sidewalk

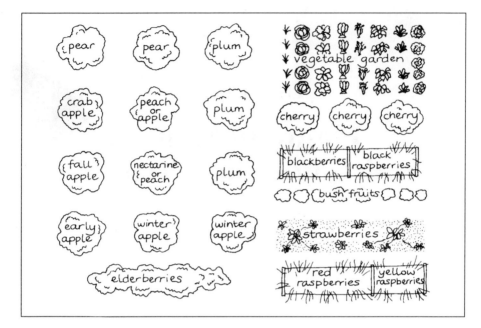

▲ Suggested planting plan for a small orchard

may be tempting to passersby, and you'll likely have competition for your bounty from all the neighborhood kids. To better reduce temptation, plant your apples, pears, and peaches in a less convenient place.

Keep in mind that certain fruit trees are susceptible to disease and insects, and will need spraying from time to time. Don't plant them near a pool, birdbath, dog run, clothes line, water supply, or near the vegetable garden or berry patch. Be pessimistic and consider all the possibilities so that you can avoid trouble in the future. A large tree is difficult to move and a disappointment to lose.

Before you make a blueprint of your future orchard or berry patch, decide roughly how many trees and berries you will plant. Resist the temptation to crowd in too many if the space is limited, and even if you have a large lot, don't let enthusiasm get the best of you. In the quiet of winter too many of us succumb to colored catalog pictures and tantalizing descriptions of fruits and berries. Soon we have made out quite an order, and only when the trees arrive in the spring do we realize that we overestimated not only the space available, but also our time, energy, and needs. A few trees and plants, well cared for, are far more productive and satisfying than a larger orchard partially neglected.

It is impossible to suggest the precise number of trees that would be right for every family, since each has different needs and tastes. It makes a difference, too, whether all the fruit will be consumed fresh or if much will be preserved. I suggest the following list to serve only as a guide, for no two gardeners are likely to choose the same assortment of trees. Any that are not suited to your climate should be omitted, too.

For a family of four who will do some preserving:

Apples (full size or semi-dwarf) 3–6
Apples (dwarf) 4–10
Apricots 2–4
Cherries..2–3
Nectarines 2–3
Peaches..2–4
Pears 2
Plums 3–5
Quince 1

From time to time I'll mention fruit trees and berries that are disease resistant. These are particularly good choices, even though they, too can have problems. I feel that fruit gardening, like every other form of agriculture, is a legal way to gamble, and you can stack the odds in your favor by planting disease-resistant cultivars.

Try to plan the spacing of your orchard so that no tree will touch any other tree, even when all are full grown. Be certain, too, that they won't eventually rub against buildings or overhang highways, sidewalks, or property lines. Allow enough room between the trees so that sunlight will reach all of the leaf surface of each tree.

Since not all kinds of fruit trees grow into the same shapes, it is difficult to say how wide each will grow. Some, like the Yellow Transparent apple and the Dolgo crab, grow upright; others are more spreading, the McIntosh, for instance. Trees also may grow differently in varying soils and climates. The following are therefore only approximate diameters of mature fruit trees in feet:

FRUIT TREES

Apple (standard size) 25–35
Apple (semi-dwarf) 15–20
Apple (dwarf)..7–10
Apricot (standard) 18
Apricot (dwarf) 8
Peach (standard) 18
Peach (dwarf) 8
Pear (standard) 20
Pear (dwarf) 8
Plum (standard) 18
Plum (dwarf) 8
Quince 12

Nut Trees

If you plant standard (full-size) trees, for the first few years you can use the space between them for growing vegetables such as carrots, until the fruit trees begin to bear and need spraying. As long as you provide enough fertilizer for both crops, it will not harm the fruit trees.

Some people plant extra fruit trees (fillers) in their home orchards, intending to take them out as soon as they begin to crowd each other. It is difficult for most of us to cut down a healthy, producing tree, however, so unless you can be very ruthless I don't recommend this technique. Filler trees must definitely be removed when the time comes.

Shopping for Trees

Fortunately, the current assortment of fruit trees and berry plants offered by nurseries and garden centers is much larger and better suited to the home gardener's needs than the choices of a half century ago. Even so, many supermarkets and garden shops have little knowledge of local conditions, and their suppliers are as likely to ship the same assortment of fruit trees and plants to northern Maine as they do to southern Kentucky.

If possible, buy your trees at a nearby nursery that grafts and raises its own trees. Unfortunately, this may not be possible, so look for well-established nurseries or mail-order houses that are able to recommend plants for the different climatic zones.

When shopping for fruit trees, you may wonder what size and age to select. Bare-rooted trees come in all sizes, from a few inches tall to 10 feet and more. They may be either one, two, three, or four years old, and are priced accordingly. It seems logical to think that if you were to plant a large tree you would be guaranteed a full-size crop sooner, but that isn't always true. In fact, commercial orchardists seldom buy the large-size trees. Bare-rooted trees, one or two years old, lightly branched, and from 4 to 6 feet tall, tend to be the best choice for planting. They become established sooner, grow faster, and usually bear earlier than a large tree, which may need some time just to get its big root system re-established. On the other hand, small trees can be difficult to protect from lawn mowers and other hazards. You may also need to devote more care to train them into a single stem, because some will try hard to grow into ill-shaped bushes.

If you buy a tree growing in a large pot, or one with its roots intact and wrapped in burlap or plastic, almost any size is practical. When you plant it, there is no setback, because you have every root, and the tree can get off to a fast start. Just be sure it is in fresh, healthy condition and not dried out.

Although nurseries are much more reliable now than many once were, there are still a few that tend to exaggerate in their descriptions, using superlatives such as *biggest, sensational, tremendous crops,* and *astonishing* in a generous way, along with enhanced-color photos of trees that only Madison Avenue could grow. I suspect that those catalog writers once worked for P. T. Barnum and his circus.

Trees for Summer Places

Many home orchardists spend summers in the country and must care for their fruit trees only during vacation months. If you are an absentee orchardist for most of the year, it is even more important for you to choose the most reliable, easiest to grow, and most disease-resistant cultivars you can find. Also choose cultivars that will ripen before you have to return to town. Early apples, pears, and peaches, most plums and cherries, and berries are ideal.

Since fruit trees need attention at other times of the year, perhaps you can find a year-round resident to help you out if you aren't able to manage working weekends at your place. Successful orcharding requires late winter pruning, early spring feeding, and usually some dormant spraying.

5-in-1 Trees

Color nursery catalogs sometimes display photos of gorgeous "orchard-in-one-trees" with several cultivars grafted on a single tree. A beginning orchardist should probably avoid these 3-in-1 or 5-in-1, multiple-grafted fruit trees. The different cultivars seldom grow at the same rate and are difficult to prune. We used to have a large tree in our backyard with several kinds of apples growing on it, and each year I grafted a few more branches. By late winter pruning time, I could never remember where all the various kinds were and I invariably cut off a few each year, so I never gained anything. Except for being a local curiosity, it had no practical use.

On the other hand, if you want something really unusual or if you have only a small space, and if you're willing to give it the special care it needs, the multiple graft tree may be ideal for your backyard.

Patented Trees

Sometimes in catalogs you will find a fruit tree listed with U.S. patent number thus-and-so. Most new gardeners are surprised to find that trees can be patented, but over the years quite a few thousand plants have been developed that were unusual enough to be registered and given a number. A patent does not mean that a plant is superior in every way to any other named cultivar, but that it is unique and that only the person or firm holding the patent, or those licensed to do so, can propagate it.

Shade and flowering trees, roses, and fruit trees are the plants most often patented. Perennials, shrubs, and small fruits are not as likely to be patented. Because they can be started so easily, a patent on them is difficult to enforce.

Over the years some great fruits have been patented. Stark Brothers has pioneered in the introduction of many outstanding fruits, and they sometimes pay handsome prices for new discoveries. They have been known to build a huge iron cage over the tree to prevent damage or theft. Then, to ensure their exclusive right to start trees from it, they take out a patent.

Some nurseries, especially Stark Brothers, Millers, and the C & O Nursery (see addresses in the Appendix) list in their catalogs patented fruits that you may want to consider for your orchard. Many patented fruits, however, have been developed especially for the lucrative commercial growers' market, and may not always be the best choices for a home orchardist. Better choices may be fruits that have been popular for years, as well as some of the newer unpatented kinds recommended for the home orchard.

Choosing Cultivars

If you are growing trees for the first time, choose cultivars that are easy to grow. Although it may be tempting to plant French wine grapes, sweet cherries, Japanese plums, and English walnuts, it makes more sense to start with kinds that need less painstaking care. Start with some easy-to-grow apples, for instance. Avoid the familiar McIntosh, Delicious, and Rome that are commonly seen in the markets, because they require so much spraying. Better not choose Northern Spy or Macoun either, even though you like the flavor. They require far too careful pruning. Bypass another favorite, the late-ripening Granny Smith, unless you live where there is an extra-long growing season. Of course, if you have been successfully raising outdoor plants for years, go ahead and try plums, pears, grapes, blueberries, peaches, and anything else that will grow well where you live.

Most small fruits are ideal choices for a beginning gardener. Raspberries, strawberries, currants, gooseberries, and elderberries are all easy to grow, have few pests, and need no special skill in pruning.

After you have decided on the fruits you want to grow, pick out the cultivars of that fruit best suited for your geographical region. The chapters on the different fruits and berries will offer help, and you may also want to consult your Extension Service or Agriculture Canada. Talk with local fruit growers who have been at it long enough to know what they are doing, too. They are often better sources of helpful information than all the books, extension pamphlets, and fruit magazines ever written. They not only know which trees are best for your climate but also what insects and diseases you are likely to encounter.

One word of warning, however: avoid advice from any know-it-all neighbor, relative, or friend who doesn't garden much but is an "authority." Listen politely to those people who have just read a good article, had an ancestor with an exceptionally green thumb, or known of someone who always had wonderful success by doing thus-and-so, but let common sense be your guide. I have met many otherwise intelligent people who dumped unreasonably large quantities of borax, Epsom salt, alcohol, kerosene, sawdust, superphosphate, ammonium nitrate, and even hot coffee on their trees just because someone told them it was a good idea.

If you are unable to find good local advice in choosing easy-to-grow cultivars for your area, the following list may be helpful, although it is in no way complete. If you don't know your growing zone, spot it on the map on pages 26–27, keeping in mind that conditions sometimes vary widely within each zone.

For instance, if you live on a mountain in zone 5, you may be getting zone 3 type weather. Likewise, a sheltered spot near a large lake in zone 4 can make your growing conditions resemble those in zone 5.

FRUIT CULTIVARS SUGGESTED FOR BEGINNING GROWERS

Zone 3

Apple:	Astrachan, Beacon, Connell, Dolgo Crab, Duchess, Lodi, Prairie Spy, Wealthy, Yellow Transparent
Cherry Plum:	Compass, Sapalta
Peach:	None
Pear:	Golden Spice, Mendell, Parker, Patten
Plum:	La Crescent, Pipestone, Redcoat, Waneta
Sour Cherry:	Meteor, North Star, Richmond
Sweet Cherry:	None
Nuts:	Butternuts

Zone 4

Growers in this zone should be able to grow everything listed for zone 3, plus

Apple:	Freedom, Honeygold, Liberty, MacFree, Northwest Greening, Regent, Yellow Delicious
Peach:	Reliance (in favored spots)
Pear:	Flemish Beauty, Kieffer, Seckel
Plum:	Green Gage, Monitor, Stanley
Sour Cherry:	Richmond
Sweet Cherry:	None
Nuts:	Black walnuts, hardy filberts

Zone 5

Growers in zone 5 should be able to grow everything listed for zones 3–4, plus

Apple:	Gravenstein, Prima, Priscilla, Rhode Island Greening
Peach:	Stark Frost King, Stark Sure Crop, Sunapee
Plum:	Burbank, Damson, Earliblue, Italian, Santa Rosa, Shiro
Sour Cherry:	Montmorency
Sweet Cherry:	Bing, the Dukes, Stella, Windsor
Nuts:	Carpathian walnut, filbert, hickory

Zones 6-8

Some cultivars that will grow in the colder zones do not grow as well here, because they need a longer chilling period during the winter.

Apple:	Adina, Granny Smith, Grimes Golden, Stayman, Winesap
Cherry:	All sweet and sour cherries should do well.
Peach:	Candor, Elberta, Halehaven, Madison, Redhaven
Pear:	Anjou, Bartlett, Bosc, Clapp's Favorite, Oriental kinds
Plum:	All except American hybids should do well.
Nuts:	The chestnut hybrids, walnut, and the hardiest pecans

CHAPTER 3

Fruit Gardening on a Small Scale

The word "orchard" may stir up visions of acres of well-spaced trees, or at least a dozen big, old, gnarled specimens around Grandpa's house in the country, but a modern orchard can consist of three or four dwarf fruit trees, a few grape vines, and a small berry patch on a half-acre lot. Such mini-gardens have, in fact, become very popular in recent years. Intensive gardening has always been necessary in tiny, backyard city lots, and it is now common in suburban and even rural areas, because lot sizes have become so much smaller. The size of the lot isn't the only reason people plant on a mini-scale. You may prefer to limit the size of your plantings because you have only a small family or because you lack time to spend gardening.

Whatever the space of your gardening area, you'll find that although neighbors or the local zoning board might raise a ruckus if you were to keep a few pigs in your backyard, no one is likely to find an ordinance prohibiting a few trees. In fact, planting a tree almost anywhere is encouraged.

Dwarf and Semi-Dwarf Trees

For years, gardeners have planted dwarf peas and midget sweet corn in backyard plots, and landscaped small front lawns with miniature roses and dwarf evergreens. It was inevitable that someone would develop dwarf and semi-dwarf fruit trees. This development has opened up exciting possibilities for home orchardists, since from four to sixteen of these trees can grow in the same space that one full-size tree would require. Not only can backyard orchardists now grow a variety of fruit, but older folks and those suffering from acrophobia can prune, spray, thin, and harvest while standing firmly and safely on the ground.

Many dwarf cultivars of apples, cherries, pears, plums and peaches are now available. The sizes of the trees vary. Dwarfs grow only 6 or 8 feet tall and spread about the same width, but semi-dwarfs get from 8 to 12 feet in height. Nearly all dwarfs have the nice habit of growing quite rapidly when they are young and then slowing down, which means that not only is pruning easier on these trees

▲ Dwarf trees are practical not only for small lots but also for country places and even commercial orchards.

but less of it is required. Dwarfs usually bear at an earlier age than standards, but their fruit is the same size. Of course, a dwarf tree produces considerably less fruit than a full-size tree, but since so many more trees can grow in the same space, the total yield per acre compares favorably.

The size of the tree is determined by the rootstock on which it is grafted. Some catalogs now give customers a choice of trees grafted on dwarf, semi-dwarf, or standard rootstocks. See Appendix for a list of those rootstocks most commonly used, with their hardiness and other characteristics, to help you make a better decision when ordering trees.

Unfortunately, dwarfs have some disadvantages, especially if you live in a cold or windy area. The most common dwarfing rootstocks are the Mallings, shrubby trees of English origin that are not as hardy as the seedling rootstocks ordinarily used for standard trees. For this reason, check the recommendations of your local Extension Service or Agriculture Canada to see what is best for your area before ordering.

Some dwarf trees are rather brittle and tend to break in high winds. Also, since they are shallow rooted, the wind may tip them unless they are firmly

▲ Dwarf fruit trees can be planted in large tubs, planters, pots, or boxes for use on terraces.

▼ Comparative sizes of dwarf and full-size fruit trees: Twelve or more dwarf trees can be grown in the space it takes to grow one standard, full-size tree.

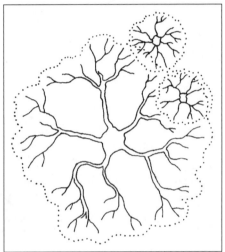

▼ Espaliered trees take little room and are very attractive.

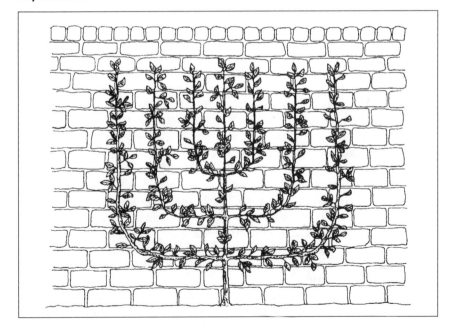

staked. Deep, heavy snow can cause problems when it settles in spring, possibly tearing the buried lower branches from the tree and devastating most of the tree. In some areas, dwarfs appear to be more susceptible, too, to diseases and insect damage than trees grown on native rootstocks. Despite these drawbacks, dwarf fruit trees may be the perfect choice if you have the right conditions for growing them.

Espaliered Trees

Remember how I cautioned you not to plant trees too close to buildings? You can disregard that advice if you grow espaliers. They not only grow well in close quarters but provide decorative landscaping, and when well cared for, produce an abundance of fruit.

The word *espalier* comes from the French word for *shoulder,* but to gardeners it has come to mean a tree grown as a vine — flat against a building, wall, or fence. Espaliers are widely used in Europe where gardens are small and land is scarce. In America, gardeners use them more for their ornamental value. I know a farmer with several hundred acres of land who delights in the beautifully espaliered trees on his fences and buildings.

You might guess that espaliers are a little more difficult to train than regular fruit trees, since it means forcing a tree to grow in a completely different manner than it otherwise would. Naturally, an espalier requires some extra care, but the training isn't at all complicated and not nearly as exacting as bonsai.

You can save a great deal of time and effort by buying a tree with the shaping already started. Since the difficult preliminary work has already been done, it is quite easy to continue the training. Nurseries that specialize in espaliers often advertise in garden magazines (see Appendix.) It is challenging and fun to create your own espalier, however. Pear and apple trees are good choices, because they are easiest to train. We once espaliered a red-flowering crab apple on our white barn, and enjoyed it immensely until we finally had to remove it to repair the barn.

Peaches, nectarines, and apricots are only a bit more difficult to espalier. It is possible to use cherries, plums, and quinces, too, but their bushy habit of growth makes training them much more difficult. I have seen blueberries, trailing blackberries, and even the taller growing varieties of currants and gooseberries espaliered in small, cottage-type gardens where a large tree would be impractical.

The first step is to decide on the kind of design you want. The candelabra is one of the shapes most commonly used, but there are countless others. Your design can range from a simple cordon — a tree with a single unbranched stem, in a bean pole shape — to complicated forms that only a mathematician could devise. After you decide on a design, go to a nursery that has a good choice of trees, so you can find one that you can train with the least trouble.

Unless you are gardening in the North or intend to plant your tree against a house that is two or more stories tall, choose a dwarf or semi-dwarf tree, because it will need much less pruning. If you decide to create an impressive-looking espalier against a large white barn, however, choose a standard tree, and plan on doing most of your pruning and harvesting from a ladder.

Select a small tree with branches that are already growing in the right directions if possible. For a candelabra, a U-shaped tree that would be totally unsuited for an orchard may be perfect, because you can spread out the two tops to start the design. If you find nothing like this available, choose a tree with two branches that are nearly opposite each other. Prune back the center stem, leaving only the two branches and start with that. (See drawing on page 16.)

Avoid planting an espalier under a wide roof overhang, since the tree will need both skylight and rain. Choose a place where it can get at least a half day of sunshine and full skylight all day, and, of course, plant it at the proper time, with all the necessary fertilizer and watering (see Chapter 6).

Set the tree so the trunk is about 18 inches from the building or wall. Drive nails into the building or wall (if you don't mind doing that) and use plastic ties, rawhide, or cloth strips to secure the tree to the nails. Add more fasteners as the tree grows. Avoid the use of string or wire that will cut into the tender bark.

A more attractive way is to train the tree along wires, and on a brick building or stone wall, this is the only practical way. After planting the tree, install a post 7 or 8 feet high at each end of where the espalier will ultimately grow; posts should be set 2 feet deep. Staple strands of 9-gauge wire to run between the posts to make a "fence" of four or five strands. Place the bottom wire about 2 feet from the ground, and the top three wires each about a foot apart. Make them taut and securely anchor them to the posts so they won't sag, and be sure the posts are well braced so they won't tip upward.

As the branches begin to grow, snip or pinch off all those that are growing in the wrong directions. When the lateral branches are long enough, pull them down and fasten them to the bottom wire. Allow branches to grow upward from this bottom branch and fasten them to the upper wires as they grow with one of the materials mentioned above.

It may take two or more seasons before the espalier becomes well established, so don't be discouraged if it doesn't look like much the first year. Check it every few days to make sure the branches are growing the way you want and not sneaking out toward the yard. After your tree is sturdy and well shaped, remove the wire trellis.

Pruning Mature Espaliers

Whether you buy trees already espaliered or create your own, the pruning process must go on forever since it will always be the tree's natural tendency to grow branches in all directions, just as nature intended. You must do most pruning of espaliers in the summer, even though fruit trees are not usually pruned at that time. Perhaps pruning isn't the best word to use, since for the most part you need only to prevent growth in the wrong places. When you are cutting off all this new growth, watch for the fat flower buds that are forming. Don't clip off too many of them, or there will be no fruit the following year.

When espaliers are planted under the eaves in snow country, you may need to protect them from ice and snow falling from the roof. Also, trees under eaves will need lime and fertilizer more frequently, since the rain falling from the roof leaches nutrients rapidly from the soil.

In addition to using espaliers against buildings and walls, you can plant them in a row to make a living, fruit-producing "English fence." Train them along two or three wires just as if they were planted against a wall, except that you graft the ends of the limbs of each tree to the limbs of the next to form one continuous unit. (See Chapter 13 for how to graft.) English fences are a beautiful, productive novelty, but they take a lot of time to create and maintain. So far we have chosen to enjoy them in formal public gardens instead of our own.

Two-Story Gardening

You may be familiar with two-level, or two-story, gardening — the growing of a crop of berries or vegetables beneath fruit trees. In some cases this may be practical, but I feel it usually is not. It is difficult to fertilize the soil so that both the tree and the crop beneath it are properly fed, and the trees are likely to provide too much shade for good growth of the undercrop.

A further danger in growing plants under a fruit tree is that often it is necessary to spray to control tree fruit pests. This spray may have to be applied at the time when berries or vegetables growing beneath the trees are ready for use. It is far better to give both trees and other crops all the space they need for best growth, and to plant them a good distance apart.

Landscaping with Fruit

One nice way to enjoy fruit, especially on a small lot, is to landscape with fruit trees and bushes instead of ornamentals and shrubs. If you are planting around your home for the first time or replacing existing landscaping, why not substitute fruits for the more traditional evergreens and flowering bushes? Most fruit trees are just as lovely as flowering trees. Not only do they bloom, but their crop gives the effect of a second flowering. We have a Dolgo crab apple in the front yard that thrills us with a profusion of white blossoms each spring and is covered with gorgeous, bright red apples every fall—plenty for us, our friends, the freezer, and even a flock of mi-

▲ Everbearing strawberries can be planted in barrels, window boxes, hanging baskets, or flower borders to make use of limited space.

grating Canadian robins who include us on their route south each fall.

In addition to fruit trees, small fruits such as blueberries, currants, and gooseberries all make attractive foundation plants around the house, and some provide good fall color. Put the sun-loving blueberries on the east and south sides, the currants and gooseberries on the west and north. The tall-growing elderberries can serve as a screen, and still provide good fall eating and an invitation to birds. They are good choices for soils that are too moist for other fruits, and will even grow on the north side of a building.

Strawberry plants make charming edgings for flower beds and are useful in other ornamental ways. I've seen them in hanging baskets, window boxes, jars and pots, barrels with large holes drilled in them, and pyramids. The everbearing kinds are most commonly used for edible landscaping, because they begin to produce fruit the first year.

CHAPTER 4

Outwitting Jack Frost

A friend visiting us from Mexico commented, "You spend lots of time talking about the weather. We hardly ever mention it at home." We realized that she was right. The weather plays an important part in our lives because it constantly affects our plans, as it does those of most gardeners. About forty years ago, I began to keep a daily record of weather and temperature, hoping that the information would help us better plan our growing program. Two decades later, all I really knew for sure was that New England weather is cussedly unpredictable, which any Yankee could have told me in the first place.

Our weather may change several times a day, or get bogged down and stay the same every day for six weeks. The last frost of spring hits our crops any time from late April to late June, and the first fall frost may come as early as late August or as late as early November. Snow might arrive first in mid-September or in mid-December, and snowstorms of a foot or more have descended upon us in late May.

Nearly every part of North America has similar surprises on the weather scene. Each year we hear of crop failures in one area or another due to unusual weather conditions. Whether in New Jersey, Idaho, Minnesota, or even the Deep South, sudden temperature changes occasionally ruin the fruit crop. Few areas can be absolutely certain of a good harvest every year. Predictions for the future vary. We are told that fewer trees, more people, and increased pollution will either bring about global warming through the greenhouse effect or usher in a new glacial age through excessive cloudiness. It all depends on who is forecasting.

There are many ways in which cold weather can affect trees, and even the experts are baffled by some forms of winter injury. Extremely low temperatures can cause damage, but, surprisingly, it isn't always the frigid temperatures that do the most harm. Injury is sometimes most severe during mild winters, because sudden fluctuations can cause as much damage to trees as low temperatures. A long January thaw may induce the tree to start growing, or a warm sun in March may quickly heat its brown bark. In both cases the return to below-freezing is a severe shock and can even be fatal to the tree.

Any long duration of cold can hurt a tree, too, as can extended periods of

▲ **Frost cracks open wounds that can cause trouble later on.** *(University of Illinois)*

wind chill. Like animals and humans, a hardy tree can stand considerable cold for a short period but it will suffer if the situation continues for days.

You may not discover winter damage until spring, when whole limbs may fail to leaf out. Or you may notice large cracks where the bark of the trunk has split open, loosened, and started to come off. These open wounds create ideal conditions for fire blight, cankers, rots, and other infections. Inspect your trees in late winter and promptly seal up any openings with tree paint (available at nurseries and garden centers) to keep out fungi and bacteria. Choose a warm day when the wood isn't frozen, and cut off all damaged limbs that cannot be repaired.

Weather also often causes stress and subsequent damage to trees and plants that may not show up immediately. One spring following a dry summer and hard winter, many of our young trees leafed out beautifully, only to wither and die within a few weeks. The long period of stress had weakened them enough so they didn't have the stamina to continue to grow.

What Trees Are Hardy in Your Area?

When buying new trees, select kinds that are acclimated and can stand the weather expected for your region. If you have extra room, it is always fun to experiment with a few that are intended for a warmer zone, but for most of your planting you'll want to stack the odds in your favor.

To be successful in your orchard, a fruit tree must meet several requirements. It must be able to make its growth during the first half of the growing season, then stop growing and harden up all new growth before the first frost. Some people assume that a tree's hardiness is determined only by the cold temperature it can stand. Actually, a short growing season may limit your choice of fruits more than the lowest temperatures. Certain peaches, plums, and nuts are often advertised as being hardy to -20°F. What is left unsaid is that the trees need a long growing season to properly harden the wood so that it can stand those low temperatures. Some tree fruits, as well as many grapes, nuts, blackberries, and blueberries that were developed in warm zones are still growing when the first fall frosts hit in certain areas of zones 3, 4, and 5. Since their new wood is still green and soft, the moisture-filled cells freeze and rupture. Native plants have become adjusted to local conditions, and the shortening days trigger their growth mechanisms to stop growing and harden their wood before frost. Imported trees are often not able to do this, and not only continue to grow late in the fall, but may also start to grow during the first warm week in early spring.

Your tree should also be able to ripen its fruit before the first killing frosts of autumn, and many late-ripening apples, such as Granny Smith, cannot do this and therefore are completely unsuited for northern gardens.

Finally, during the winter the entire tree — fruit buds, branches, trunk, and roots — should be able to withstand the most likely coldest temperatures. It should also stay completely dormant all winter, and not begin to grow during a midwinter thaw.

Southern gardeners, too, must be careful to choose the right plants for their climate. Plants grown in temperate zones need a certain period of chilling during their dormant period, and can't grow in the tropics. The length of winter chill needed varies from a long period for gooseberries to a far shorter one for pecans.

In addition to the other factors that determine hardiness, different parts of a tree may have different tolerances to cold. Often the roots and tops of some plants are perfectly hardy but their blossom buds are tender. Peach, plum, and pear trees all tend to bloom early, which makes them a special target of Jack Frost, but even later-blooming fruits like apples and grapes can be hit in areas that are prone to late spring frosts.

Although the requirements for a specific fruit tree might seem to limit your chances for growing it successfully, each planting zone has a large number of fruits that will thrive there, and you have only to discover which do best in your area. See the chapters describing each fruit for help in making your choices.

I sometimes hear older gardeners complain that the trees they buy these days don't grow as well as they used to. In the good old days, the soil might have been better and fewer insects and diseases have appeared, but a more likely reason is that trees grew better several decades ago because they came from a nearby nursery that grew them on the spot; or they were grafted by a local horticulturist who specialized in joining acclimated cultivars to native wild seedlings. By planting trees that had originated in the same neighborhood, the grower had just about everything going for him or her.

Now, many of us have to plant trees that originated hundreds of miles away. Northern nurseries and garden centers often buy their stock from huge whole- sale nurseries in the South and Southwest, where a tree can be grown to selling size in only one of their long growing seasons. Northern nurseries, meanwhile, now concentrate on growing the more profitable ornamental shrubs.

People disagree over whether it really matters where a tree was grown. Is a McIntosh tree grafted on a Malling rootstock in Alabama really different from a McIntosh grafted on a Dolgo seedling in Quebec? I feel that the ones grown closest to home always do better, and whenever possible, these are the ones to buy. We once saw some Tennessee-grown sugar maples planted in Vermont as an experiment. The southern-grown trees held their leaves for a month after their Yankee companions had lost theirs. Likewise, a few years ago some Christmas tree growers in northern New England planted some balsam fir seedlings grown in other states. They were surprised the following spring when the imported trees started to grow much earlier than the native ones, and were considerably upset when a June frost killed all the new growth.

Trees from one zone can acclimate to another zone if they are able to survive long enough. Both the maples and the firs imported from warmer areas are becoming more like their northern cousins each year. Trees that are vastly unsuited for another climate, however, have little chance of adaptation. Nectarines may never adjust to North Dakota, and the McIntosh will probably never grow well in Louisiana.

We gardeners love to experiment and keep right on trying new kinds that are marginal in our zone, as you probably will, too. It's part of the joy of fruit growing.

Microclimates

Although knowing your growing zone helps a great deal when choosing plants, every gardener soon finds out that within each zone there are many microclimates where a small area may be a zone or two warmer or colder than the surrounding area. Varying elevations, air drainage patterns, fog, frost pockets, prevailing air currents, proximity to bodies of water, and many other conditions cause these variances. It frustrates gardeners who bemoan the fact that while they can't seem to grow a certain plant, the Joneses who live ten miles away can grow the same cultivar with no trouble whatsoever.

Artificial Climates

In Iceland, Alaska, and parts of northern Europe, many fruits and vegetables are grown in glass or plastic houses. Since North America has a generous supply of land and an excellent transportation system, fruit growing in greenhouses is seldom done commercially. Some home gardeners use such houses as a hobby, however, and enjoy raising fruits and berries that wouldn't ordinarily grow in their zone. We have friends who have cultivated dwarf peaches, pears, cherries, boysenberries, and grapes near the Canadian border in small greenhouses attached to their home.

One of these greenhouses consists only of a wooden frame, which our friends cover with plastic in late summer and then uncover in late spring after all danger of frost. There is a small, above-ground swimming pool in the greenhouse to help maintain more even temperatures and provide humidity. The ground and pool soak up the daytime heat in early spring and fall, and release it during the cold nights, so artificial heat is seldom needed. During the winter the ground and even the pool freeze slightly, but since the inside temperatures are greatly modified, the widely fluctuating outside temperatures have little effect on the trees. With the longer growing season, the dwarf peach trees are able to complete their growing cycle and harden their new growth. As a result our friends pick a few dozen delicious peaches each year.

Greenhouse fruit growing is demanding. In a tight building, the trees need extra water, and, on sunny days in midwinter, the inside temperature may rise to over 100°F. It is necessary to provide ventilation by opening a window or installing an outside fan that works on a thermostat. The artificial climate can also provide good conditions for diseases and insects, since natural outdoor controls are missing, and this may require extra spraying. Also, unless there are plenty of bees in the neighborhood that you can let into the greenhouse at the time the trees are blossoming, you will probably need to pollinate by hand.

All in all, however, fruit growing in a greenhouse can be an interesting hobby. Whether or not it is worth the considerable money and work involved is your decision. Most of us will probably choose to do our gardening outdoors, facing the weather head-on. Whether we live in Bismarck or Tallahassee, Bangor or Spokane, nothing is guaranteed, but with planning and care there should be enough successes to far outweigh the failures. That makes it all worthwhile.

Outwitting the Weather

To sum up, I can't overemphasize the fact that you shouldn't make any large plantings of fruits for yourself or as a commercial venture until you have grown a few of them successfully in the same area for several years. This advice comes from past experience — my own failures and those of many other gardeners I've known.

You can use various schemes to protect your trees from frosts and you can repair winter damage, but the best way to outwit the weather is to choose cultivars that are suited to your climate. If you live in the Deep South, this means searching out plants that have the proper chilling requirements for your climate. If you are a northern gardener, you need ones that are hardy to the likely lowest temperatures and that are also able to complete and harden their growth during your growing season.

USDA
ZONE MAP

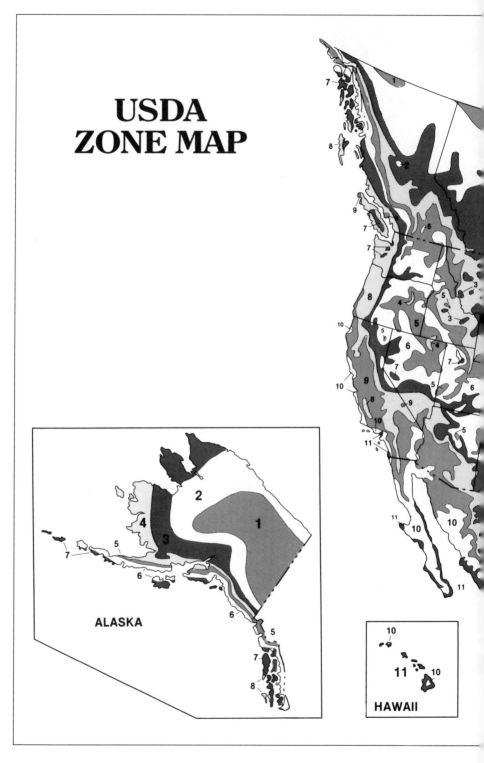

ALASKA

HAWAII

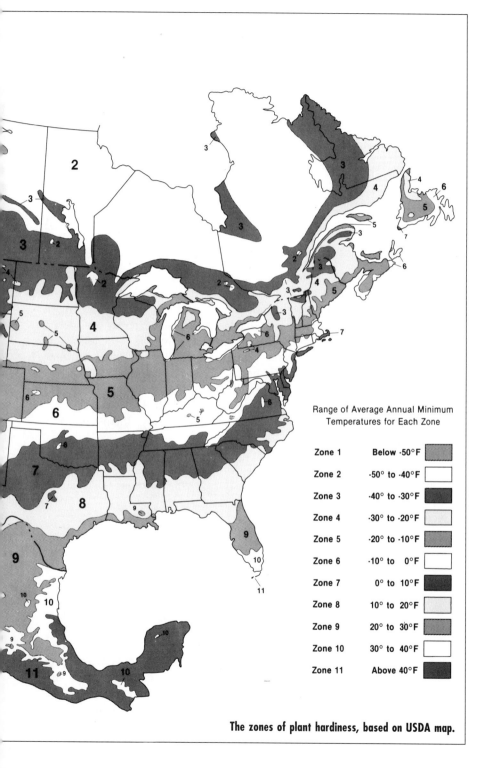

Range of Average Annual Minimum
Temperatures for Each Zone

Zone 1	Below -50°F
Zone 2	-50° to -40°F
Zone 3	-40° to -30°F
Zone 4	-30° to -20°F
Zone 5	-20° to -10°F
Zone 6	-10° to 0°F
Zone 7	0° to 10°F
Zone 8	10° to 20°F
Zone 9	20° to 30°F
Zone 10	30° to 40°F
Zone 11	Above 40°F

The zones of plant hardiness, based on USDA map.

CHAPTER 5

Orchard Soils and Soil Improvement

How was your diet last week? If all you had was a little weak tea, chances are you don't feel too much like an evening of vigorous square dancing or painting the spare bedroom. If you had three healthy meals each day, you're much more likely to be feeling energetic and ready to take on anything. Nobody considers a steady diet of weak tea as sensible, but a great many would-be gardeners act as if their fruit trees can get by nicely on even less. Often, people tell me their trees are looking poorly and ask what could possibly be wrong. "What do you use for fertilizer?" I ask. "Fertilizer?" they say, looking puzzled. Though there are gardeners who overfeed their trees and frequently give them a shot of something or other, many more neglect feeding altogether or give them a preparation that is of little nutritive value.

When you plant a fruit tree, keep in mind that with proper care and a little luck with weather, it will provide you with many tons of fruit in its lifetime. Since the soil around your tree is the repository for the nutrients that the tree needs, you'll want to understand that soil.

What Is Soil?

Years ago I mentioned to a group of gardeners that they should mix manure or compost with the dirt before planting their trees. A lady immediately protested. "Dirt is something you sweep off the floor," she said indignantly. "Soil is what you are talking about."

She was right. Dirt farmers would be more accurately called soil farmers, because soil is definitely not the same as dirt. And good soil is something special. It is full of life and provides the right conditions for plants to grow and thrive. It contains mineral nutrients, clay, sand and other rock particles, and humus formed from decaying plant life, plus moisture and air. Good soil also has an abundance of beneficial bacteria that break down the organic matter, and it contains earthworms that loosen the soil and add fertility.

If you have ever gardened, you already know that soil is found in several

28

layers. Most of the action takes place in the topsoil layer, and that is the most important to gardeners. Good topsoil contains humus and fertility and is loose in texture. Subsoil, the next layer down, is usually quite hard. It contains mostly minerals and possibly traces of organic material from long ago. Often it is filled with lumps of clay, veins of gravel or sand, and large rocks. Roots of trees, particularly deep-rooted trees, penetrate this subsoil and absorb many mineral nutrients from it. Farther down is the hardpan, which is a thick layer of clay and bedrock. Roots cannot penetrate these, except for spots where breaks or faults occur, and water cannot move through it freely.

The depths of both soil and subsoil vary greatly from place to place. Very few spots on the earth are still blessed with deep fertile topsoil of just the right texture, moisture-retaining ability, and alkalinity for good plant growth. Most of us have to doctor up our soils in some way, and it is very important to diagnose soil problems and correct them, not only when you plant your trees, but frequently thereafter.

Organic and Chemical Gardeners

Some gardeners regard soil as something that holds up a plant and acts as a temporary repository for nutrients and moisture. They find out what nutrients a tree needs, mix the chemicals in correct proportions, then pour the concoction over the soil to feed the tree.

Organic gardeners have a different viewpoint and consider the soil a living thing — loose, spongy, and full of earthworms. They believe it should contain an abundance of decaying organic matter as well as additional minerals in natural form. To protect it, they cover it with mulch, or a living crop such as grass. They believe that when soils contain an abundance of nutrients in natural form, the plant will select the kinds and amounts it needs for best growth. They suspect that gardeners who rely on synthetics force their plants to absorb highly soluble plant foods whether they need them or not, causing flashes of growth that are susceptible to insect and disease attack. Since disease and insects tend to strike weak plants, they feel those grown in a "natural" environment are more pest-resistant. It follows, they insist, that people who eat food grown on healthy plants are healthier people.

These gardeners also point out that organically managed orchards have a better chance of continuing to produce good fruit if, for any reason, they must be neglected for a season or two. Under the same circumstances, a planting that depends entirely upon chemicals for sustenance suffers badly if the treatments are discontinued for any length of time.

Since chemical and organic gardeners are kilometers apart in their thinking, there is a third group who feel that the best way to garden falls somewhere in between. The middle-of-the-roaders don't think of ammonium nitrate spreaders as mad scientists out to destroy the world with test tubes. Nor do they see the smelly compost makers as narrow-minded activists armed with pitchforks and standing in the four-lane highway of progress. Instead, they pragmatically use the best methods of both groups. They believe in good, healthy, organic soils, deep mulches, and in recycling garden wastes, but they feel no guilt about adding a little chemical fertilizer if a plant seems to lack nutrients. A great many gardeners, including myself, belong to this group.

Your Soil and How to Improve It

If your soil is good enough to grow a nice lawn, it can usually be put in shape for berries and fruits. Even if it is not deep enough for the large root systems of full-size trees, dwarf trees may do very nicely there.

To help understand what is going on beneath the surface of your orchard or berry patch, let's divide the properties of soil into three important parts: structure, pH, and fertility.

Soil structure can be loosely defined as the general makeup of the soil, whether it is sandy, clay, rocky, marshy, or worn-out powdery dust. Because trees need considerable room to freely spread out their roots, neither rocks, heavy clays, nor wet mucky soils provide good growing conditions. Neither does sand nor gravel, since these dry out so fast.

Soil structure is more difficult to improve than pH or fertility. If you are stuck with a thin layer of soil over solid rock, there is little you can do short of hauling in many loads of topsoil. New home owners may have a problem because builders usually scrape off all the good topsoil and later put back only a few inches for a lawn.

Nevertheless, you can often take measures that will enhance poor soil. Sandy soil can be given more moisture-holding capability if you till in shredded bark, manure, leaf mold, peat moss, or compost. Heavy loam soils can be lightened in the same way, or by adding sand. You can break up clay subsoils by deep plowing or dynamiting, although neither of these methods are feasible if you own only a small piece of land.

Mulches, too, can perform miracles when you are trying to improve your soil, but they take time. In addition to enhancing the structure of the soil, they prevent erosion from sun, wind, and rain, and add nutrients and humus. Another way to improve soil is to plow under crops of growing plants, such as clover, oats, or winter rye, a process called *green manuring*.

Soil pH indicates the alkalinity or acidity of the soil, and is caused by the breakdown of water molecules in the soil into positive and negative ions. The soil's mineral and organic materials affect the breakdown. If the parent material for the soil is calcium limestone then the soil is likely to be alkaline, for example; the presence of large amounts of sphagnum moss, sulfur, or aluminum usually leads to an acid soil. Soils with adequate amounts of organic matter such as compost and manure are less likely to have pH problems than those with smaller amounts of organic matter.

All plants and trees have a certain pH at which they can best utilize fertilizer. When soil becomes too acid ("sour") or too alkaline ("sweet"), the plants' roots cannot absorb the fertilizer and the nutrients remain locked within the soil. The plant is like a hungry man with his hands tied to the chair at Thanksgiving dinner.

Some plants — certain weeds and grasses, for instance — can grow over a wide range of soil pH, but others are very fussy. Most cultivated soils range from 4 to 8 on the pH scale, with 7 being neutral — neither acidic nor alkaline. Anything below 7 is acid and anything over it is alkaline. Blueberries will not grow at all well unless the soil is extremely acidic (4½ to 5). Plums and peaches prefer about 6; apples and pears like 6½ to 7. Strawberries and blackberries grow best at the 5 to 6 range, while raspberries, elderberries, currants, and gooseberries grow well in a pH from 5½ to 7. pH shouldn't cause you great concern because, except for blueberries, most fruits and berries grow well in ordinary garden soil if it is well supplied with organic matter. If you are in doubt about your soil's pH, you can purchase an inexpensive, simple-to-use soil acidity test kit in a garden store. For somewhat more money you can get a complete testing kit that will also show your soil's fertility; and for a bit more you can get an electronic tester that will analyze soil pH instantly. We have used one in our nursery for many years, but for most small gardens the chemical kits are adequate.

Soil pH is easy to improve. Acid soils can be made more alkaline by adding lime or wood ashes. You can spread lime evenly on top of the soil and let rain dissolve it, but since it moves through the soil slowly, for fastest results, rototill it in. Soil pH can be raised one point by applying 10 pounds of lime per 100 square feet (a square area 10 feet by 10 feet or a circle about 12 feet in diameter). Because it is cheap, it may be tempting to add large amounts, but avoid overdoses, because too much lime, like too little, locks up the fertilizer and stops plant growth. A surplus of lime can also cut off the flow of nutrients to a tree just as the fruits are nearly ready to ripen, and cause large numbers of them to drop before they mature.

Lowering the pH is seldom necessary since overly acidic soils are far more common than those that are overly alkaline. But if it must be done, 3 or 4 pounds of powdered sulfur per 100 square feet will lower the pH 1 point on ordinary soils. Aluminum sulfate is an old remedy used to acidify soils, but most gardeners feel that it is poisonous to the soil and spoils the flavor of fruits such as blueberries. They prefer to use quantities of cottonseed meal, composted oak leaves, peat moss, and mulches of pine needles for creating and maintaining acidity.

Soil fertility is determined by the amount of readily available nutrients. Despite what you may hear, it is difficult for anyone, even an expert, simply to look at a soil and know how rich it is. It is safe to assume that most soils are depleted both by erosion and use, so orchard and berry crops are likely to need at least some additional fertilizer every year. The essential elements needed for plant nutrition are nitrogen, phosphorus, and potassium, plus calcium and sulfur.

Nitrogen. This element is necessary for good fruit tree growth and is lacking in most soils. Organic gardeners who use vast quantities of greensand, wood ashes, granite dust, and rock phosphate, sometimes do not realize that none of these supply much nitrogen. Nitrogen is absorbed from the air in small amounts by the soil, and thunderstorms provide larger amounts. You have probably noticed how plants spruce up after a summer storm. You can add nitrogen by using certain nitrates and other chemicals, manures, or butcher shop wastes such as blood meal, bonemeal, and tankage. Since nitrogen in its pure form is a gas, it can be volatile, and in some of its nitrate forms, it can burn plants if used in excessive amounts. The organic forms provide safer feeding for longer periods than the chemical ones.

Phosphorus. Rock phosphate, bonemeal, manures, superphosphate, compost, and other organic and chemical fertilizers supply phosphorus.

Potassium. Organic gardeners use greensand, granite dust, and wood ashes to supply this element. Chemical-minded growers rely on potash salts of various kinds.

Trace Elements. Plant life utilizes dozens of other elements, from boron to zinc, in minute amounts. Home gardeners seldom have to be concerned about these because most soils already contain the small amounts that plants need. Manure or compost (especially composted leaves) are good additional sources. Trace elements are also available commercially, often fused onto small particles of glass to ensure a slow release. Because they are needed in such tiny amounts not much is known about their effects on plant life, but if you use them, apply them sparingly. If they are present in the soil in more than small amounts, some can be poisonous to plants.

How to Feed a Tree

You can apply slow-acting organic fertilizers and mulches to the soil around trees and plants almost any time and get good results, but I believe early spring, as soon as the ground thaws, is the best time for all feeding, chemical or organic. Fertilizers spread early in the season can permeate the soil quickly while it is still moist, so the tree's roots can absorb it readily just when the nutrients are most needed for fast growth. The second best time to use organic plant foods is in late fall, just before the ground freezes.

Since there is approximately as much of a tree underground as above, the area covered by the tree's root system is at least the same size as the spread of the branches, and likely much wider if the topsoil is shallow. The largest

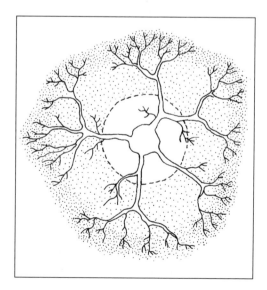

▶ **How to feed a tree: Fertlilizer is spread in the shaded area where the feeder roots of the tree are located. Heaviest feeding should be toward the outside of the circle.**

roots are near the trunk of the tree, and the small, fibrous hair roots that absorb the soil nutrients are farther away. The roots that feed a young tree are in a circle beginning a foot or two from the trunk and continuing to the outside spread of the branches. With older trees, the feeder roots will all be further from the trunk, and any fertilizer placed close to the trunk or much outside the branch area is likely to be wasted (see drawing on page 32).

Bulky fertilizers such as compost, manure, and animal tankage should be spread on top of the soil and under the mulch, but dry commercial fertilizers work more effectively if they are put into the soil, because they can lose nitrogen easily if exposed to air. Cut a slit with a spade, or punch a hole with an iron bar and put the fertilizer a few inches into the soil. Do not spread lime, manure, compost, or any kind of fertilizer on frozen ground unless it will be covered with mulch. Otherwise, melting snows and rains will wash it away before it has a chance to work.

If you mulch your trees, pull off the mulch and spread the fertilizer directly over the soil beneath the outer rim of branches. Then replace the mulch and add to it if necessary. Mulched soils need less fertilizer and lime than those that are unmulched or cultivated, because they are better protected against erosion. Don't overdo mulches, however. Mulches that are more than 2 inches deep after they settle can have the same effect as burying the tree too deep, and can also make it hard for rains and waterings to reach the roots. Deep mulches also encourage the shallow rooting of plants, and provide a convenient nesting place for rodents.

Choosing Fertilizers

Each gardener has his or her favorite plant foods. Many fertilizers can be easily acquired for free, and garden magazines advertise many commercial preparations. We organic gardeners use large quantities of farm manure when it is available, and faithfully compost all kitchen and garden wastes. Some even go so far as to collect hair from the local barber, or stale bakery products from stores and restaurants to make into compost.

When you buy commercial fertilizer, whether chemical or organic, the analysis is printed on the bag as required by law. It is listed in numbers, such as 5–10–10. The first number indicates the percentage of nitrogen (N), the second of phosphorus oxide (P_2O_5), and the third of potassium oxide (K_2O). Thus a 50-pound bag of 5–10–10 fertilizer contains 2½ pounds of nitrogen and 5 pounds each of compounds of the other elements that are able to break down readily to furnish nutrition to the plants. Most of the other weight is filler consisting of inert ingredients, sometimes lime.

A complete fertilizer contains at least some of each of these three prime nutrients, but one that is incomplete includes only one or two. Thus, rock phosphate could be listed 0–30–0, superphosphates as 0–20–0, and bonemeal as 4–20–0. The actual analysis of the product may be slightly higher than that listed on the package since most companies do not want to get into trouble by listing their formulas too high.

In selecting an orchard fertilizer, choose one that contains all three ingredients, plus any others your Extension Service may recommend. Because there are so many kinds available to collect or buy, you may be tempted to overfeed your trees to get faster growth and more fruit. Like overfeeding ourselves, it isn't a good idea and twice as much is never twice as good. Feeding late in the season encourages growth that is susceptible to winter injury.

The following list contains some common fertilizers and the approximate analysis of each. The "amount to apply" listed here is intended for one application per year, unless otherwise stated. Naturally, these amounts are to serve only as a guide. As you gain experience, you'll probably decide to use more or less than the suggested amount, depending on your soil and the size and demands of each fruit tree.

Organic Fertilizers

Animal tankage. A byproduct of the meat industry. 8 percent nitrogen, 20 percent phosphorus. Rather smelly, even when dried, but it does make things grow. Use 3 pounds per 100 square feet.

Blood meal. Dried animal blood. Good fertilizer and deer repellent. Use with wood ashes or greensand in combination with bonemeal or rock phosphate for a complete fertilizer. Use 1 or 2 pounds per 100 square feet.

Bonemeal.   Finely ground animal bones. Use with greensand or wood ashes. Steamed bonemeal is sometimes available and works faster. Use 3 pounds per 100 square feet.

Cottonseed meal.   Good for acid-loving plants such as blueberries.   7 percent nitrogen, 3 percent phosphorus, 2 percent potassium. Use 5 pounds per 100 square feet.

Cow or sheep manure (dried). Pure dried manure contains about 5 percent nitrogen, 3 percent phosphorus, 5 percent potassium. Use 10 pounds per 100 square feet. Unfortunately, much dried manure is diluted with varying amounts of peat moss, and the percentages may be much less. Check the label carefully before buying.

Greensand. Material from ocean deposits. Contains about 2 percent phosphorus, 6 percent potassium, and many additional trace elements. Use 5 pounds per 100 square feet.

Poultry manure (dried). So strong smelling that some gardeners think trees grow just to get away from it. It is more powerful than cow and sheep manure, so use only 6 pounds per 100 square feet.

Raw manure. Dairy farmers used to give this product away, but no more, and some won't even part with it for a price. Horse stables and chicken and rabbit farms may be better bets because they seldom have a use for it. Apply fresh manure on top of the ground under the mulch around trees or berries in early spring or late fall after the fruit is harvested. Use cow, sheep, horse, and pig manure at the rate of 100 pounds per 100 square feet; poultry manure at 30 pounds per 100 square feet.

You can till well-aged manure into the soil before planting berries, but fresh manure should be composted before putting it near plant roots. Rabbit and bat manures (guano) are safe to use in the soil without composting.

Leather meal. Leather scraps ground fine provide a good source of nitrogen over a long period.

Rock phosphate. Natural phosphate rock that has been ground very fine. 30 percent phosphorus. It becomes available to trees extremely slowly, but should last for three years. Use 5 pounds per 100 square feet.

Wood ashes. Ashes make soil more alkaline. 7 percent potassium. Combine with fertilizers that contain nitrogen and phosphorus. Use 5 pounds per 100 square feet.

Liquid Organic Fertilizers

Fish emulsions, liquid seaweed, and various other commercial products are available to give your plants a quick start. If you have manure, you can make a fast-acting manure tea (sometimes called manure tonic water). Just mix manure — either fresh or dried — and water in a large garbage can, and then pour the "tea" over the soil.

Dry Chemical Fertilizers

5–10–10. The most commonly used commercial fertilizer. It is sold under many trade names. Start with 1 or 2 pounds per 100 square feet each year.

5–10–10–2. The first three numbers represent the same ingredients used above; the 2 percent is an additional ingredient, one that is recommended for certain crops or soils. Boron, magnesium, and manganese are most often added. Use the formula recommended for your soil type and crop.

10–10–10 or 15–10–10. Fertilizers with two or three times as much nitrogen as the 5–10–10 formula. These should be used very sparingly, since over-fertilizing induces excess foliage growth and may delay bearing on young trees, and causes poor fruit color on mature ones. Excessive amounts "burn" plants.

Liquid Chemical Fertilizers

Liquid fertilizers such as Peters, Miracle-Gro and Rap-id-Gro can be useful to help newly transplanted trees get established, and to get them growing quickly. As with all chemicals, use them according to directions, and never after mid-season, so you won't encourage late summer growth.

Slow-Release Fertilizers

Slow-release chemical fertilizers such as Osmocote and others have some of the advantages of organic ones. They release their nutrients slowly over a period of weeks or months, assuring a long season of even feeding for the tree. They also reduce the likelihood of burning plants from excess fertilizer. Slow-release products are less likely to leach away in rains than ordinary chemical fertilizers. Some are available in a pill form that orchardists can bury near their trees or plants.

Although slow-release fertilizers give long-term, even feeding under ordinary conditions, when the temperature goes unusually high, the release is faster. For this reason, in warmer climates it is better to apply two smaller feedings per year, rather than one heavier one in the spring.

You can create your own slow-release fertilizer by putting half a cup of 5–10–10 fertilizer in a plastic bag and punching two or three holes in it with a pencil. Place two bags — one on each side of the tree and near the outside spread of the branches — to feed a mature dwarf fruit tree all season. Six or more bags would be required for a mature full-size tree.

Mulches

Mulches offer such great advantages it would be a mistake not to use them on your orchard and berry plants. Organic mulches suppress weeds and grasses that steal soil nutrients, control moisture by preventing evaporation, and protect against soil erosion. They also encourage earthworms and guard against rapid freezing and thawing of the ground, and as they rot, they add humus and fertility to the soil.

My favorite way to mulch fruit trees is to spread a layer of manure or compost around each tree from the trunk to the outside spread of the branches, and cover this with a layer of newspapers or magazines. This smothers the grass

MULCH MATERIALS

Decomposing	Nondecomposing
Citrus pulp	Black plastic
Coarse shavings	Commercial landscaping fabrics
Cocoa shells	Crushed rock or gravel
Composted bark	Flat rocks or slate
Evergreen needles (pine are best for blueberries)	Marble or granite rock chips
Farm wastes (spoiled ensilage, straw, hay, etc.)	Paving blocks
Lawn clippings (let dry slightly before using to keep them from heating)	
Leaves (maple, birch, etc.; use oak leaves for blueberries)	
Magazines	
Newspapers	
Peanut shells	
Peat moss	
Shredded bark	
Wood chips	

and weeds very effectively. Then I add a layer of wood chips, shredded bark, or old hay several inches deep to hide the not-too-attractive paper and keep it from blowing away. Each year I renew it and add a little fertilizer.

Mulches are also good for berry bushes, but avoid using shavings, wood chips, or other slow-to-rot ones on strawberry beds, if they will be plowed back into the soil within a year or two. Straw, leaves, cocoa hulls, or similar products make better mulches for them. Besides all the other advantages, mulches keep rains from spattering dirt on the ripening berries.

Nonorganic mulches may be the best choices for berry plants and trees that are part of your home landscape. Gardeners often choose the clean appearance of crushed rock, flagstones, marble chips, or slate around their plantings, and blueberry and strawberry growers often spread black plastic between the rows, too. Nonorganic mulches last for years, and offer many of the advantages of organic ones except the all-important one of adding humus and nutrients to the soil.

Leaves as Fertilizer

One of the best fertilizers I have ever used is also one of the cheapest: leaves. If you are lucky enough to live in an area where they lie in large heaps on the ground every fall, consider them a gift from nature and scoop them up. Leaves are an excellent soil conditioner. The roots of large trees reach far into the subsoil, and bring up nutrients and trace elements that shallow-rooted trees and plants never reach.

There are three different ways to use leaves. Shred and add them immediately to the soil, compost them for a year or more before use, or use them intact as a mulch around fruit trees or berry plants. They will compost into leaf mold, one of the best fertilizers there is.

▶ A mulch suppresses weeds, helps retain moisture, and helps prevent frost heaves.

Check under it in a year, and you will find earthworms galore and hundreds of little root hairs exploring the composted leaves for nourishment.

Some people feel that leaves make the soil acidic, and it is true that oak leaves will, but a little lime or wood ashes can neutralize them, if you don't need an acid soil. Maple and most other leaves are not acidic.

Gather leaves not only from your own or neighbor's trees, if they are willing, but also from forests and along country roads, where they often lie in great heaps. Municipal crews are often thankful for a place to dump their leaf collections, too. Since the leaves of one mature maple tree are estimated to contain about $30 worth of fertilizer, rake on and expect your trees to grow lavishly.

Compost

Composting does in a faster and more manageable way what nature does all the time in gardens, fields, and forests. The rotting of trees and plants over millennia has provided us with the humus in the soil that makes it possible to grow our plants and trees. Gardeners and orchardists can speed up the natural process by building compost piles. Piling waste material in heaps increases the heating process and speeds decomposition. It works best to alternate layers of soil 1 or 2 inches thick with layers of manure 2 or 3 inches thick and layers of green material (leaves, garbage, garden wastes) 5 to 8 inches thick. (See drawing on page 39.)

Build your pile in the open, or enclose it in a commercially made box or bin or one constructed from stones, boards, or cement blocks. Some towns forbid

---

Possible Sources for Low-Cost Fertilizers and Mulch Materials

Manures
Farms
Packinghouses
Racetracks
Stables
Zoos

Vegetable and Fruit Wastes
Processing plants
Restaurants
Stores

Shavings, Bark, Chips
Furniture factories
Paper mills
Wood plants and sawmills

Leaves
Country roads
Parks
Street departments

Paper and Cardboard
Newspaper offices
Rubbish collectors
Recycling centers

Hay and Straw
Farms
Seashore for seaweed
Marsh hay

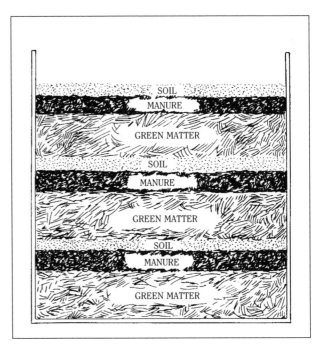

SOIL
MANURE
GREEN MATTER
SOIL
MANURE
GREEN MATTER
SOIL
MANURE
GREEN MATTER

▶ A compost pile is made of alternate layers of manure, soil, and green waste matter. Keep the pile moist and covered to hasten decomposition.

open compost piles, so check your local laws. If necessary, you can make compost in covered garbage cans in a garage or basement.

Compost heaps should stand about 2 to 3 feet high after settling has taken place. Keep the top of the pile flat or slightly concave so rain will soak in. If a pile is properly made, there will be no unpleasant smell either when the compost is rotting or while it is being used. Turn the heap occasionally to speed up decomposition.

Most gardeners like to have three compost piles: one which is being made, a second in the process of rotting, and a third being used. In areas with normal precipitation it takes a full year to rot an outdoor compost heap properly, but keeping the heap wet during dry weather speeds up rotting. You can also use activators, available at garden stores, for even faster decomposition.

It is possible to develop good orchard soil, even if nature presented you with something less. With all the possibilities for free and low-cost fertilizer, soil building needn't be expensive, and will make all the difference between puny, struggling fruit plants and thriving, healthy specimens.

CHAPTER 6

Planting the Tree and Getting It Off to a Good Start

Each spring, we observed Arbor Day at our little one-room country school. If every tree planted over the years had survived, the schoolhouse would now stand in a forest. Instead, none of them ever lasted a season.

The tree-planting ceremony was quite impressive. After a salute to the flag, someone especially chosen for the honor would dig the hole, a decree that had gone out from the Governor would be duly read, and a child always recited "Trees" by Joyce Kilmer. The ritual went on and on, and finally the group sang an appropriate song, quite off key. Then we would plant the tree. The ceremony was well organized and the poetry more than adequate, but we were all deficient in our planting ability. Although most of us were from farm families experienced in growing vegetables, grains, and hay, few of us had ever planted a tree, and our ancestors had spent years clearing the land of trees.

Looking back on those days, I'm not surprised that none of our Arbor Day trees survived. No one considered that the tree might be planted too shallow or too deep. No one thought it might be suffering more than we were, as the poems and readings went on, and both they and the tree were getting drier and drier. No one ever thought to cover the little tree's roots or to bring a pail of water.

Although I have since planted thousands of trees of all kinds, I often meet people who feel that ceremony is more important than proper planting. Some folks check the phase of the moon, or worry about whether the tree should face in the same direction it originally grew, or if perhaps it should be planted before sunup for the best results. When ritual means more than good soil, fertilizer, and water, planting success can never be assured. Instead of bowing thrice toward the fruit goddess Pomona, it's a good idea to tend to some seemingly minor details.

A deep, fertile soil is important for the future health of your tree. If you hit a rock ledge or hard clay when you dig the hole for it, seek out another location.

The tree's roots can find their way around small rocks, but if the soil is too shallow, your planting will be doomed from the start. Attempts to break up subsoils are usually so frustrating that you resort to it only if no other location is available. Use iron bars, pickaxes, or tractor subsoilers. In the past we occasionally used a quarter stick of dynamite in each hole to break through the hard subsoil, but I don't recommend that in a suburban neighborhood!

Sometimes gardeners hurry the planting operation too much. When trees they've ordered in the leisure of winter arrive during the spring rush, their new owners often unwrap them hastily by pulling away the strings and packing, scraping off bark in the process. They let the defenseless tree lie in the sun and wind while they dig a hole that is too small. Then they cram the roots in the hole as best they can, heap the soil over part of them, and leave the tree to its own devices. "Why did my tree die?" the owner puzzles. "Must be it wasn't any good to begin with."

If the tree comes bare-rooted — that is, without being wrapped in a ball of soil or in a pot — treat it like a fish. It can't live long without lots of moisture. Never allow potted or balled trees to dry out, either.

Most mail-order trees are shipped bare-rooted, packed in some sort of moisture-retaining wrap. The trees you purchase at a local nursery or garden center may also be bare-rooted, or they may be potted or balled. You can set out balled or potted trees successfully at about any time of the year when the ground isn't frozen, but it's best to plant bare-rooted trees in the spring before growth starts in northern areas, so the trees will have a full season to get established and well rooted before winter. If you live in zone 6 or warmer, however, you can safely plant in the fall.

▶ A common mistake in planting is to dig too small a hole. The roots should not be crowded and should have plenty of loose soil to get started in. This hole needs to be three times larger.

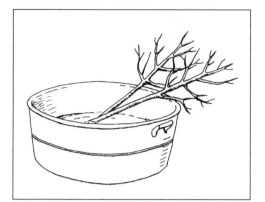

▲ **Bare-rooted trees and bushes should be soaked in a tub of water for several hours before being planted.**

Bare-rooted trees are the least expensive. Nurseries dig them in the fall, store them in controlled temperature and humidity sheds during the winter, then wrap and ship them in the spring. They are likely to be quite dry when they reach your doorstep, so your first, and very important, step should be to unwrap them at once upon arrival, and soak the roots in a pond or tub of water for four or five hours. Don't worry if the trees arrive on a cold day. Even if the roots are frozen, there is no problem as long as you let them thaw slowly by leaving the package in a cool basement or garage for half a day before soaking.

Remove any plastic wrapping or container from a balled or potted tree, but keep intact the soil ball surrounding the roots. If you disturb it, you will break all the little feeder roots that make a balled or potted tree superior to one that is bare-rooted.

Presumably you've already chosen a good location with plenty of sun, room to grow, and good garden soil that is not wet, so the next step is to dig a hole and plant. Dig the hole much larger than you really feel is necessary — one the size of a bushel basket should be adequate for a 6-foot tree. Put all the soil that you remove in two heaps, the good topsoil on one side and the poorer subsoil on the other.

Mix generous amounts of compost or manure with the topsoil. Half soil and half organic matter is a good proportion. Don't use any dry, granular chemical fertilizer at this point, because it is much too strong for a tender new tree.

Put enough of this mix in the hole so you can set the tree at about the same level as it grew in the field or pot. On a bare-rooted tree you can find this level easily on the bark just above the roots. If you plant a tree too deep, the roots will be smothered, which is likely to kill it; if you set it too shallow, the roots will dry out.

Hold the tree straight, spread out the roots (if it is bare rooted), and put back enough of your soil mix to barely cover them. Then fill the rest of the hole completely with water. Allow the water to soak into the soil mix and drive out any pockets of air that could dry out the roots.

With the remaining soil mix, finish filling the hole to nearly ground level. Be careful not to damage the tree with your shovel during the process, because the bark is tender and can't stand rough treatment. It may be necessary to use a little of the subsoil you've dug up to fill the hole completely, but most of it should be discarded. Pack the soil firmly.

Leave a slight depression in the soil around the tree trunk to catch rain and future waterings. Unless it rains hard, water your newly planted tree thoroughly two or three times a week, using a 3-gallon pail full of water each time. Pour slowly so all of it will reach the bottom of the roots, and continue this thrice a week watering for about a month, or until the tree is well established. This watering cannot be emphasized too heavily. It is the least expensive and most dependable way to help your little tree get off to a fast start. One nursery I know of furnishes a packet of tablets with each tree and tells the customer to dissolve a tablet in a pail of water and pour it on the tree every other day. The tablets, like the doctor's sugar pills, do nothing, but they remind the customer to water.

To get your tree off to an even better start, add some manure or a small amount of liquid fertilizer such as fish emulsion or Miracle-Gro to the water once a week.

Don't overdo either the watering or the fertilizing, though. One of our neighbors accidentally left the hose running on a small tree for an entire weekend. Not only was this hard on his well, but by Monday morning his poor tree had drowned.

▶ **(A) When planting, dig a hole more than large enough to contain all the roots without crowding. Put the good topsoil on one side of the hole, and the poorer subsoil on the other. Mix compost or manure and peat moss with the good soil and put enough of this mixture back into the hole so that the tree can be planted at the same depth at which it grew previously. Pack the soil firmly. (B) Slowly pour a whole bucketful of water into the hole. (C) Fill the hole nearly to the top with the remaining soil-compost mix. Leave a slight depression around the trunk to catch rain and future waterings. Stake the tree.**

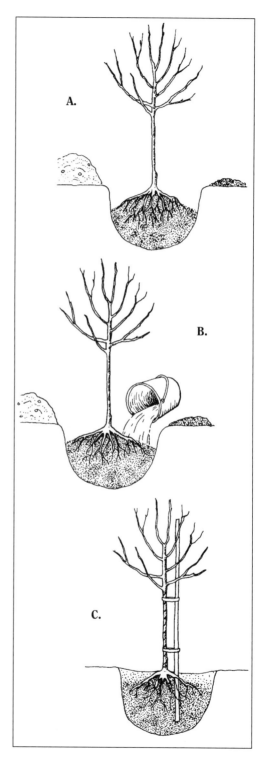

Pruning

If you buy a bare-rooted tree through the mail, it may have already been cut back before being shipped. If not, it is a good idea for you to do it right after planting. When the tree was dug most of its small feeder roots were lost, so a corresponding amount of top should be cut back to compensate. Otherwise, there will be too much top for the small amount of roots to support. Even though your tree will look butchered, if you do it right, by delaying too fast top growth you will help the roots keep ahead. The tree can then start growing sooner, rather than take weeks to get over the transplant shock.

Some orchardists like to prune severely and cut the tree back to a stub, as shown in A, below. Others remove only the weakest branches, leaving the rest. I prefer to trim out all the weak and broken branches, cut back the strong ones by at least half, and then cut back the top to about three-fourths of its original height, just above a strong, fat bud. The tree will look pretty well chopped up, but it will grow and thrive far better than if you planted it with its branches intact (see B, below).

If cutting off a third of your tree makes you too unhappy, you can omit that, and instead water your tree every day and feed it a weak solution of liquid fertilizer twice a week, so the roots will have an extra supply of nutrients. This doesn't always work, but some people swear by it.

Of course, if you plant a balled or potted tree, no pruning is necessary, except to remove any branches that are growing in the wrong directions. Just make sure that the tree has a strong central stem, with branches coming out from it at wide angles like a Christmas tree (A, page 45). If there are extra tops, or limbs growing at close angles (B, page 45), remove them or cut them back to prevent the formation of bad crotches that will eventually split under heavy loads of fruit. If tree has two equal-size tops (C, page 45), cut off the more

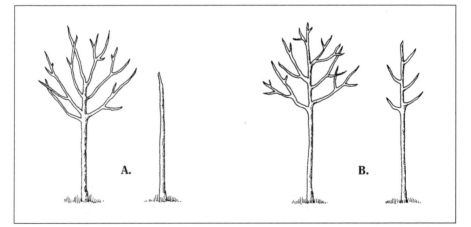

▲ Prune all bare-rooted trees at planting time. Tree A is cut back to a whip. Tree B has all limbs partly cut back.

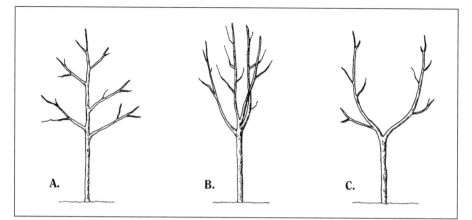

▲ Training the young fruit tree is important. (A) is a tree growing in a strong, sturdy shape. (B) is developing too many tops, which will result in a weak tree. (C) has a wide crotch that is likely to split under a load of heavy fruit.

crooked of the two and stake the remaining limb so it will grow into a straight new top.

Staking

Newly planted, standard-size fruit trees seldom need staking if you set them in carefully. However, in a windy area the trees may lean with the prevailing winds unless you give them some help in their early years. Young dwarf trees, which are extremely shallow-rooted, will need staking unless they are in a sheltered location. Drive a sturdy post in the ground near the tree, wrap a protective covering of burlap, cloth, or panty hose around the tree. Then secure the wrapped part of the tree to the post with strips of cloth, or wire enclosed in pieces of garden hose. (See C, page 43.) After the tree is three or four years old and well anchored, remove the stake.

Mulching

Unless you planted your fruit trees in a well-manicured lawn, spread a layer of mulch around them after the planting. As I explained in Chapter 5, a mulch helps hold moisture, suppresses grass and weeds, and as it rots, feeds the tree. The depth of the mulch should not be more than 2 inches. More than that may smother the roots, as well as prevent rain and waterings from reaching them.

Make a Chart

Labels soon fade and fall off, so record plant names, dates, and any other pertinent information, such as where you bought them. Paste your chart inside this book, or in some other easy-to-find place. A record of your plantings will not only identify the fruits when they start to bear, but will help you if you need to replace any trees. Remove any labels that are wired to trees to prevent them from girdling the tree as it grows.

The First Years

After the initial cutting back, your young tree should need only minor pruning until it begins to bear. Continue to train it so it has only one central leader, and make sure all the side branches are coming from that. Remove any new growth that may develop into a bad crotch later and take off branches that are growing too close to the ground. Although a gnarled, spreading, twisted old fruit tree can look very picturesque, if you want maximum fruit production, this early shaping is essential. Usually this means only some early summer clipping or pinching off of any new growth that is starting in the wrong direction.

Some fruit cultivars grow naturally into a nice shape with little care. The Dolgo crab apple, for instance, shapes itself beautifully. On the other hand, trees such as the Yellow Delicious apple and most pears seem bent on growing as many tops as possible. On such trees, cut back all but one central leader to encourage a spreading tree. Many plum trees grow so wide that the outer branches hang on the ground unless they are snipped back occasionally.

I carry a pair of small, hand-held pruning shears whenever I am walking through the orchard. Frequent light pruning is ever so much better for the tree than cutting off large limbs later. It also conditions the orchardist to the pruning habit and helps develop both the right attitude and skill.

Overbearing

As a beginning fruit grower anxiously awaiting my first crop, I was always delighted to find a tree blooming the first or second year after planting. As the little fruits grew, it was even more exciting to see how many of them the tree was producing. Actually, as I found out later, it wasn't at all good for the young tree.

If your tree is growing extremely well and is in good rugged condition, it probably won't hurt it at all to bear a fruit or two the second year after planting. But some cultivars have a tendency to bear far too early and too heavily, which weakens them so much that they may not produce another crop for several years. Such a tree can easily get infected with a disease and die an early death.

Whenever a precocious tree begins to bear when it is still too small, you can curb its ambition by picking off most of the small fruits as soon as they appear. How many you leave, if any, should depend on the number of fruits you think your tree can safely mature and still make good growth for the years ahead.

Even after your tree is mature, you should control overbearing by annual pruning and by thinning out the small fruits (see Chapter 8). Otherwise, the tree will tend to bear large crops of small fruits every other year.

CHAPTER 7

Pollination

Despite the legendary childhood lectures about the birds and the bees, pollination is still a mystery to many would-be fruit gardeners. People ordering trees usually know they should take it into consideration, but some are unsure about whether they will get the best pollination by selecting two trees of the same cultivar or two completely different kinds. Others are not positive whether pollination will change the variety of fruit, or if planting several kinds of berries near each other will result in a grand mix-up of them all at some future time. People have asked me whether a plum can pollinate a cherry; or if European plums can cross with Japanese cultivars; if apples will mate with stone fruits or pears; and if all the thousands of apple cultivars are compatible with each other. One new gardener thought that the year-old plants in his raspberry patch might be male and the young, new plants, female.

Years ago, tree salesmen, either from lack of knowledge or outright dishonesty, sometimes took advantage of an amateur's ignorance and sold him trees he neither wanted nor needed. Today, most nursery catalogs and garden centers do a far better job of informing their customers, but even so, before you order your trees, it makes sense to know something about pollination.

Like all other living things, a fruit plant's biological duty is to reproduce itself. It does this by blooming and bearing fruit that contains seeds. As in the animal world, both genders are involved. The male and female parts of blossoms must join together if offspring — fruit and seed — are produced.

A perfect flower is bisexual, with both male and female organs. Some plants, such as holly, bittersweet, and certain tropical trees, including dates, have imperfect flowers; that is, each plant produces either all-male or all-female blossoms. A date orchard is usually planted with each male tree surrounded by dozens of females, like a sultan and his harem. Only female plants produce fruits, but males must live in the same neighborhood to produce the necessary pollen. These all-male and all-female plants are not common in the plant world, and the flowers of most fruit-bearing plants grown in temperate zones are bisexual.

Sex and the Single Tree

Even with perfect flowers, nearly all fruit trees do better with a mate. Although a few are self-fertile, which means that a single tree can bear fruit by itself, most need what is known as cross-pollination and require a partner nearby.

This is how it happens: In a perfect flower, the male portion is the cluster of several little upright projections in the center called stamens (see illustration below). These are covered with pollen, a brown, red, yellow, or orange powder, that you get all over your nose when you sniff a flower up close. The female part of the blossom, the pistil, is the long, slender, green tube slightly taller than the stamens and in the midst of them. The pollen from the stamens on one flower must be moved to the pistil of the same flower (if it is a self-pollinating cultivar) or to the pistil of a flower on another tree or plant, if those particular plants require cross-pollination (cross-fertilization.) In other words, for most fruit trees and many small fruits to bear fruit, pollen from the stamens of Plant A must move to the pistil in Plant B.

In order to cross-pollinate each other, the trees must be in the same family group. Apples cannot pollinate pears, nor can pears pollinate plums. You therefore need at least two of each species of the fruit tree that you plant. If you want to grow pears, you should plant two pear trees. If you want to grow apples, you need two apple trees, and so on.

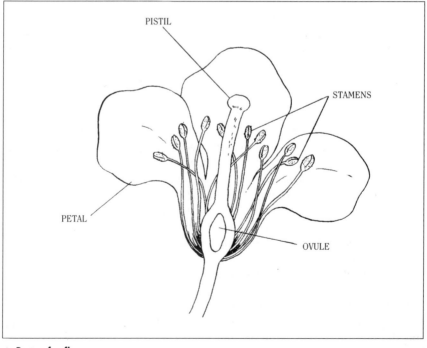

▲ **Parts of a flower**

There is one more catch. The trees have to be two *different* cultivars of the same species, because two alike won't cross-pollinate. Every true Jonathan tree in the world came originally from one tree, so each Jonathan is really part of the same tree divided millions of times. Since a tree cannot fertilize itself, if you have two trees that are just alike it is no different from having only one tree. You need to plant two separate kinds — a Jonathan and a Delicious, for instance. Likewise, if you want to grow plums, you should plant two different kinds of plums. If you want to grow pears, you need two different kinds of pears, and so on. Only then can you be sure of true cross-pollination.

How does all this pollen get around? Forest trees — pines, maples, oaks, and so forth — are pollinated by the wind, as are most grasses and grains, such as corn. Most ornamentals, vegetables, and fruit trees, however, are pollinated by insects, primarily bees. Although bees can and do travel much farther, as a rule the busy little fellows should not be forced to fly more than 500 or 600 feet to bring about the mating of two blossoms.

The bee is, undoubtedly, an innocent party to these goings-on and accidentally fertilizes the flower as she goes about her business of gathering nectar to take to the hive. In reaching deep into the throat of the flower for the sweet stuff, she has to wiggle past the stamens, and in the process her fuzzy body picks up lots of the abundant pollen. As she goes from tree to tree, a great quantity of

▲ Peach blooms, with the pistil and stamens clearly visible. *(USDA)*

pollen gets moved from the stamens of one flower to the pistils of others. On a good day one busy bee may visit 4,000 to 5,000 blooms.

When a grain of the proper pollen hits the head of the pistil, it is absorbed in a tiny opening and moves down the tube to the ovary. There it joins with the ovules to produce a growing cell which, in a short time, develops into fruit and seed. Fruits with a single seed or pit need only one grain of pollen. Apples, which have ten seeds, need ten grains. If the pistil of an apple receives only one or two grains, the developing fruit will fall off soon after it forms. If it takes in only five or six pollen grains, an apple may still develop but it will be lopsided.

You might question whether the quality of your fruit will be affected by the pollen of your tree's partner, and worry that pollen from a sour wild tree might produce sour apples. Don't be concerned. The mating tree's pollen influences only the genes in the seed and therefore any plant grown from that seed. The fruit is merely the host for the seeds and will stay the same whether the bees bring pollen from a sour crab apple or a high-quality grafted tree. The trees grown from the seeds, however, will vary widely, each producing fruit quite different from its parents and from each other.

For more information on the pollination requirements of various kinds of fruits, nuts, and berries, see the chapters on specific fruits. Even though in some cases, two plants of the same species are not needed for pollination, it is common knowledge that they produce far better if several are planted together. It is possible that not only the extra available pollen, but also the companionship of the others may be beneficial!

Apples. Two or more different cultivars are recommended for pollination. Northern Spy and Baldwin are poor pollinizers, so a third kind should always be planted with them to ensure that they have fruit. If several apples all belonging to the same family group — such as Delicious, Starking, and Starkspur—are planted together, you should plant another cultivar nearby that is not closely related to them, such as Rome, Dolgo, Greening, or others. Otherwise, cross-pollination may not take place, unless your neighbors have apple trees nearby.

Peaches. Although many peach cultivars are self-fertile and can bear by themselves, several of the most popular kinds do not. Mikado, J. H. Hale, and Elberta, are among those that need a mate. In any case, it is a good idea to plant two different cultivars for insurance.

Pears. Two or more different cultivars are recommended for good crops. Bartlett and Seckel do not get along well together pollenwise, so a third kind is needed if you plant those two.

Plums. More gardeners have trouble with plum pollination than with any other fruit. Often they complain that even though the trees bloom heavily they set no plums. One reason is that plums bloom so early that sometimes bee colonies have not yet built up to full strength, and as soon as the more fragrant apple blossoms burst open, the few bees available often ignore the plum blooms and go to them. Equally important is that there are several families of plums, and two different cultivars of plums within the same family are necessary for pollination. See Chapter 16 for more information about the various plum families.

Sour cherries. Sour cherries are one of the few fruits that nearly always self-pollinate well, so one tree is all you need.

Sweet cherries. Two or more different sweet cherry cultivars are necessary. Sour cherries are not good choices as pollinators for sweet cherries because they seldom bloom at the same time.

Small fruits. The named cultivars of blueberries and elderberries bear better when you plant more than one kind. There are seldom any pollination problems with wild blueberries and elderberries, or the cultivars of currants, gooseberries, blackberries, raspberries, and strawberries.

Nuts. Most nuts are pollinated by the wind, and two or more trees are necessary for them to bear. The exceptions are butternuts and black walnuts, which seem able to go it alone. When you plant named cultivars, two different ones are necessary; or one cultivar and a seedling tree of the same species will do.

Helping Out the Bees

We are always delighted as we walk through the orchard when it is in bloom and we hear a loud buzzing coming from each tree. A hive of bees is good fruit insurance, because wild bees are often in short supply in early spring. If you keep bees, don't place the hives near the trees, because you may have to spray, and you don't want to endanger them. Commercial orchardists often rent hives of bees for the peak of bloom, and return them just before they apply the spray they use directly after the petal drop.

Orchardists who live where late spring frosts are a problem especially appreciate a strong colony of bees in the neighborhood. If the flowers are pollinated soon after they bloom they can resist a light frost better than virgin blooms. The pistil, which carries the pollen into the ovule, is delicate and easily damaged by cold. After pollination has already taken place and the pistil is no longer needed, the bloom can stand a lower temperature.

When only one kind of fruit tree is blooming and there appears to be no suitable partner blossoming anywhere in the neighborhood, you can still get fruit. Here's how we do it: When only one of our pear trees is in bloom, we drive across town to an abandoned farm where a big, ancient pear tree always blossoms at the same time as ours. We cut off a few branches, bring them home, and put them in a bucket of water under our tree. The bees take over from there.

Some gardeners who have no room to plant more than one kind of tree of each species graft another variety on the limb of their tree for pollination. This method, like the bouquet-in-a-bucket, is a last resort. Two different trees, yours or those of a nearby neighbor, are a more reliable way to get consistently heavy crops.

Artificial Pollination

To supplement the sometimes unreliable work of the bees, orchardists have experimented with do-it-yourself methods of gathering and spreading pollen. Some have used a type of vacuum cleaner to gather pollen, which they then spread over the trees by airplanes, motor-driven dusters, or even shotguns.

To ensure the best pollination, commercial orchardists sometimes buy pollen from companies that gather and sell it. They either blow it over their trees or put it in inserts that they place in a beehive. The bees, on their way out of the hive pick up generous amounts of pollen and spread it around the trees. See the Appendix for some companies that supply pollen and inserts.

Although the idea may at first seem silly, a method that is more practical for small orchardists is hand pollination. When bees are scarce, we sometimes pollinate a few of our fruit trees ourselves. If we consider the cost of fruit, the time is well-spent, and fun as well. We take a small artist's paintbrush and gently dust the pollen from the flowers into a teacup. Then we brush it carefully onto the blossoms of an adjoining tree.

If you do this, mark the limbs to show which ones you have treated, or, if you have the energy, you can pollinate the entire tree. It takes only a short time to pollinate a small orchard of dwarf trees, since you need to dust only one bloom in a cluster. There's no need to start a big crop of fruit that will need thinning later.

Obviously, this system is impractical on a large scale, but if a home orchardist finds few bees among the blossoms, he or she can often salvage part of the fruit crop by personally buzzing around the trees with a camel's-hair brush. The bees, though well organized, apparently have no strong labor unions, and we have not yet run into difficulties by usurping some of their duties.

CHAPTER 8

Spring and Summer in the Orchard

Although the harvests of autumn may be what fruit growing is all about, I enjoy the rest of the year in the orchard, too. Watching the trees gradually come to life in the springtime is exciting. First comes the swelling of the buds as the sap begins to move in the spring, and not long after, the leaves appear. Still a bit later come the flower buds and finally the flowers.

A stroll through an orchard when it is in bloom is one of the most delightful of experiences. The rich, sweet fragrance of the blossoms is a perfume no chemist could possibly capture, and it is delightful to the eyes, whether you are looking at small new trees bravely blooming for the first time, or a gnarled, ancient specimen now well into its second century. The birds also seem to enjoy the fragrant beauty, and their songs and chirps blend cheerfully with the humming of thousands of bees. No matter how much there is to do on a spring day, a fruit grower should never become too busy to pause for a few minutes and enjoy springtime.

This is the time we hope for a week of warm, sunny weather, so no frost will harm the tender blooms, and the bees will have a chance to gather the nectar and spread the pollen among the trees. Rainy, cold days or frosty nights when the trees are flowering means a poor crop, and sometimes none. Soon the petals will fall and new fruits must begin to form before they do.

It is a busy time. The birds have already started their nests, and insect eggs laid last fall will soon begin to hatch. Every creature is at work and so, too, must be the orchardist. It is the time to check the orchard frequently to see that insects, disease, animals, or any other dangers are not threatening it. Insects tend to increase rapidly when the weather is warm, and diseases abound in cool, humid conditions. Some springs, unfortunately, provide an abundance of both! Scavenging animals, too, can swiftly pass the word to their friends to join them to feast on your young succulent twigs and forming fruits.

Trees need a good supply of nutrients, because they should be growing their fastest at this time, especially if you garden where the growing season is short. In the North, trees have to grow rapidly during the long days of spring and early summer to make the same growth they would during a longer period further south.

Not only should you make sure that plenty of fertilizer and moisture are available, but be certain that your trees get first chance at that nourishment. A grower asked me one day if I could help him figure out why his little fruit trees were doing so badly. As we walked through his backyard he said, "Just a minute, I'm sure they're in here somewhere." Some minutes later among rank-growing weeds and grass that stood nearly up to our waists, we located several puny little trees. I mentally compared those trees to a small boy at a family reunion where everyone is outreaching him at the table. He'd like a plateful of the food, but by the time his relatives stop grabbing, everything is gone. There's not even a glass of water left for him. Likewise, no new little tree is going to be able to compete with healthy, green-blooded, all-American weeds. After all, they were probably there first. The only way to deal with weeds and tall grass is to be firm and demand that they leave. Dig them out, keep them mowed, spray them with an herbicide, or smother them with a heavy mulch.

Early spring is the time to encourage birds in your fruit grove. Birdhouses, hedges, windbreaks, and a few evergreens offer all sorts of protective nesting places for birds, and they will reward you by feeding their new broods on the thousands of hungry larvae busily hatching everywhere, and anxiously waiting to feast on your leaves and young fruits. Although birds can be your best ally in the battle with the bugs, some other controls are usually necessary. Chapter 9 will help you plan your pest management program.

As I said before, early summer is the time to begin shaping your new trees. By keeping them growing in the right directions, and preventing extra tops, you can save much corrective, heavy pruning later. Remove all the little sucker plants and branches that spring from the roots and the lower part of the trunk. These are all parts of the wild rootstock, and because they sap the energy of the tree, they should be removed as soon as they sprout.

Thinning

Here's a trick that will help your tree produce those big, perfectly shaped, catalog-picture fruits that will make you the "envy of all your neighbors," as they used to say. It will also encourage your tree to bear every year instead of every other year: simply thin the little fruits as soon as they reach marble size.

Thinning can be a difficult task for some people. They think it is wasteful or contrary to nature. If you stop to think about it, though, Mother Nature herself thins even wild fruits. Immediately after the fruit sets, a mature tree usually drops many of its tiny fruits, and a few weeks later, when the fruits are a bit larger, it often drops another batch. These fruit falls are known as the May drop, June drop, or July drop, depending on where you live. Although it may seem alarming the first time you witness it, the tree is merely getting rid of the extra fruit it can't mature.

Since the aim of a fruit tree is to produce a big crop of seeds by maturing a large number of fruits, filling up your pantry shelves doesn't enter into its

Top: Apples in need of thinning

Bottom: Apples after thinning, with each now having room to develop to its fullest.

plans. Because good fruit rather than seeds are your main interest, you simply continue what nature has started and thin out more of the small fruits that are left after the natural drops. The tree's strength and energy are thereby diverted to the remaining fruits, which will then grow much larger.

The seeds contain the potential of all future trees, and it thus takes more of the tree's vitality to produce the tiny seeds than the large flesh. Therefore, cutting down on seed production saves a tremendous amount of a tree's energy. Suppose, for example, your apple tree has 1,000 small fruits on it. Each one contains ten seeds. If you pick off 800 small fruits, your tree will bring to maturity only 2,000 seeds instead of 10,000, a big difference. Naturally, it will be more likely to try again next year.

Try not to feel guilty about thinning. It is a perfectly nice thing for you to do for your tree, like disbudding your roses for bigger blooms or thinning your carrots. Always clip or pick the small fruits carefully, however, so you don't damage the limbs and remaining fruits. If it is hard for you to pick and throw away so much of your crop, do as I do and spread the operation over several days, so it will be less painful. After you see the results, it will become easier each year, and you may be tempted to thin more heavily to get even larger fruits. Each fruit cultivar has a built-in size limit, however, so overthinning will not increase its size beyond this limitation. If a large tree bears only one fruit, that fruit will be no larger than its built-in potential.

We have found that peaches, apples, pears, and large-fruited plums all benefit from thinning, but we never bother to thin cherries, crab apples, small canning pears, or small fruits, with the exception of large-fruiting gooseberries and clusters of grapes when too many are present. How many should you pluck off? We like to leave only one fruit in a cluster and about 6 or 7 inches between each fruit. In years when a tree bears heavily, this culling can mean that we pick off 70 or 80 percent of the crop, which can be a real shocker. If you have ever heard that a Yankee gardener is so tight-fisted he has to bring in a neighbor to thin his turnips, you should see us squirm when we have to thin our fruit crop. Painful as it is to throw away perfectly good apples, pears, and peaches, you won't mind doing it after you see how much bigger and better the remaining fruit is, and when you find that you actually have more bushels of usable fruit than you would have picked otherwise. And almost all of the fruit will be topnotch, with few culls, since as you thin you naturally remove any that are imperfect or insect-damaged.

Some apples, such as the McIntosh, do a good job of thinning themselves by early summer drops, if they have been properly pruned. On the other hand, many apples, such as the Wealthy, Lodi, and Yellow Transparent, have a tremendous desire to overproduce. Heavy thinning of such trees is usually necessary, not only to ensure large fruit but sometimes even to save the tree from bearing itself to death.

In addition to producing larger and better fruit, thinning provides other benefits. One of the frustrating things about fruit growing is the bad habit of many trees to bear only every other year. This seems to be a normal tendency of some trees, such as Macoun and Baldwin apples, and even severe pruning and

▲ Small apples result if the fruit set is too heavy.

thinning doesn't completely correct it. Most trees, though, will bear nearly every year, if you prune them annually, and thin the fruit heavily.

Commercial growers often thin their fruits by using chemical sprays that cause the excess fruits to drop early in the season. Most home orchardists, however, will prefer to do it in the safe, reliable, old-fashioned way.

Late Summer Care

Toward the end of summer, fruits begin to increase in size rapidly. Insects and disease may still be a problem, especially in years that are unusually wet or dry, so keep a watchful eye out for them. Check trees that are bearing to be sure the crop is not overloading the branches. In a good year, a large tree may produce nearly a ton of fruit, and even lighter loads may put a strain on weak branches. Place wide boards or planks of the proper length upright under sagging branches to prop them up until the fruit is harvested.

Resist any temptation to use fast-acting fertilizers in late summer to increase the size of the fruit. Feeding the plants at that time will stimulate the tree to grow just when it should be getting ready for its long winter nap. Instead, fertilize only in spring or very late fall.

Getting the feel of the orchard is best accomplished by actually being there to observe what takes place from week to week. When you get in tune and begin to feel the extraordinary cycle of a fruit tree, what you might have once considered a difficult chore and performed nervously will become a delightful experience, and your trees will thrive. "The footsteps of the owner are a garden's best fertilizer," according to an old proverb. The same applies to one's orchard.

CHAPTER 9

Disease and Insect Control

Quite often I hear someone say, "I'd love to plant a few fruit trees, if they weren't so much work." This usually comes from someone who seldom complains about other garden chores, and I soon realize that what they are worried about is spraying. Many people suspect that commercial orchardists spend much of the summer spraying one chemical or another on their trees, and they think this has to be a fruit grower's way of life. They also fear that all orchard pesticides are poisonous, and even opening the package may be risky.

This assumption used to be true, but in recent years there has been a shift away from the separate-chemical-for-every-pest craze. The arsenic, DDT, dieldrin, parathion, and chlordane that gardeners used so carelessly only a few years ago are now banned or severely restricted. Scientists have discovered natural pest controls that work and many of the trees now being sold are surprisingly disease-resistant. With good sanitation, you will be able to get by with very little spraying, especially if your plantings are located some distance from a neglected orchard or infected wild fruit trees. If spraying is necessary, you can now buy many pesticides that even organic gardeners can use with a clear conscience.

I tell prospective growers that it is far better to raise your own fruits and berries and have control over what materials you use, than to buy fruits that have almost certainly been heavily sprayed to give them that great appearance.

Small home orchards consisting of a mixture of apples, pears, and stone fruits are not as inviting to epidemics of bugs and diseases as are plantations consisting of acres of all the same kind of fruit. Still, if you grow fruit year after year, sooner or later there is a good chance that a few pests will locate your trees and decide to make them a summer project. Fruits have been grown for so many centuries and in so many places they have accumulated a huge number of enemies.

Diseases and insects are not the most pleasant subjects to read about, and I don't mean to overwhelm you by listing every possible pitfall your trees may encounter. Like a medical reference, it is here to help you cope with those little surprises nature occasionally tosses at us to make life more interesting, and to keep gardening from becoming too boring.

▲ Sunscald injury has developed into a large wound.

Determining What's Wrong

Fruit trees and berry plants can look sick for a variety of reasons and the trouble is not always caused by insects or disease. Many times it is physiological and created by environmental conditions. If a tree is unhappy with its climate, moisture, soil, fertilizer, or light conditions, or if it is starved because of weed and grass competition, it will not do well, and no amount of orchard spray or dust will help. Likewise, if a tree has been damaged by animals, chemicals, salts, or machinery, it is almost certain to look less than thrifty. Diagnosing the problem correctly is the most important first step.

After you have determined that your tree's problems are not caused by its environment or by mechanical damage, check for insects on the leaves and bark. Some you can spot easily, like tent caterpillars and Japanese beetles; others, such as mites and scale, are very small and hard to identify, even though their damage can be recognized. Other insects spend the daylight hours out of sight and do all their mischief at night. Some moths lay their eggs inside the blossom or under the skin of the fruit. The eggs then hatch, and the larvae work inside the fruit where they are invisible until you take that fateful bite.

Every insect you see in your orchard is not an enemy, of course. Most are quite harmless, and some even beneficial, so it is important to know friend from foe before you load up that sprayer.

Diseases are easier to identify. Whoever named many of them used terms so descriptive that anyone seeing the problem for the first time can often recognize them. How could you not identify brown rot, powdery mildew, leaf curl, scab, sooty blotch, fire blight, black knot, rust, or leaf yellows? Others may not be quite as obvious. Chapters on the specific fruits list particular problems that may bother each species, but a list of the common physiological ailments, diseases, and insects that could arise in your orchard is included here for ready reference.

Before deciding that a lethal disease is invading your fruit patch, spend some time trying to determine which problem you have. If the leaves are yellow, for example, it could mean any number of things might be wrong, and occasionally you may need to call in an expert for help.

Physiological Problems of Trees

Lack of sun. Fruit trees need to get almost full sun to grow well and to produce good fruit. Don't plant them too close to buildings or large shade trees.

Too much sun. Sometimes in the South, certain temperate zone fruits and berry plants can get stressed by more heat than is good for them.

Too much water. Fruit trees need good soil drainage. Their roots should never stand in soil that is constantly wet or where pools of water stand for hours after heavy rains.

Too little water. In dry seasons trees can suffer from thirst, especially in poor or sandy soils.

Over limed. Too much lime locks up nutrients in the soil and causes fruit drop and poor growth. Test your soil every few years to determine the pH, and take steps to make any necessary corrections.

Under limed. Too little lime has the same effect as too much lime.

Over fertilized. Fertilizer burn shows up as a brown, scorched appearance on leaves and may even kill a tree. Moderate over fertilizing can cause a young tree to grow too fast and not bear for many years. It can also cause a mature tree to produce fruits with poor color and with less flavor.

Under fertilized. When a tree makes weak growth and the leaves appear yellowish or pale green, lack of nutrients may be the problem. Check your feeding schedule.

Weed and grass competition. You'll find the same results as when the plant is under fertilized. The roots of nearby large trees can have the same effect.

Late frost injury. If buds fail to open or blooms fail to set fruit, the cause may be frost injury.

Animal damage. When bark is rubbed or chewed, or twigs snapped off, wild or domestic animals may be the culprits.

Mechanical damage. When bark is scraped from the trunk, suspect the careless use of mowers or other equipment.

Road salt. Melting snow and salt runoff from roads and driveways can cause drying out of leaves and weakening of the tree.

Soil compacting. Good growth cannot take place in soil that is packed hard. Compacting can be caused by heavy machines or by excessive foot traffic through the area, and is most common in worn-out soils and those lacking in humus.

Too little soil. When large rocks or subsoil are close to the surface, poor growth results since roots can't grow well enough to properly feed the tree.

Electrical leakage. An underground cable sometimes ruptures and heat "cooks" the tree.

Sewage burn. Leaking sewage pipes sometimes allow chemicals and sewage to "burn" a tree. Bad fruit flavor can also result when trees are planted too near a septic drainage field.

Excessive suckering. Some rootstocks send up lots of little plants below the graft. Cut these off regularly to direct the energy into the grafted part of the tree.

Water sprouts. Remove any water sprouts — clumps of new growth that tend to grow upright around a recently pruned limb. Do a moderate amount of pruning annually rather than severe pruning every two or three years, to help prevent water sprouts.

Winter injury and sunscald. In both North and South, low temperatures and sudden temperature changes can cause serious problems, especially to young trees. Sunscald results when warm sunshine strikes dark-colored bark, raising the temperature of the wood. The sudden drop in temperature as night falls or a cloud covers the sun can cause rupturing of the plant cells in the bark, making it split. A similar injury may result even in the South during the hot days of summer. Orchardists spray a diluted white latex paint on the east and south side of the trunk of young trees to reflect the sun and prevent this injury.

Organic vs. Chemical Pesticides

When it comes to spray, orchardists tend to split along organic-chemical lines, just as they do with fertilizers. The chemical users believe that modern chemicals have been thoroughly tested, and are safe when properly used. Natural or organic gardeners feel that many of today's insect infestations and diseases are the result of overuse of chemicals in the past, and that the use of more natural cultural methods will result in fewer problems. They point out that chemicals do not discriminate, but kill good as well as bad insects, and poison the birds that eat the sprayed bugs. In addition to the ecological reasons for not using chemicals, organic-minded folks do not want to eat fruit that has been sprayed with materials that might be toxic.

As with fertilizers, there is a third group taking a somewhere-in-between position. These growers are organic-minded and far from spray-happy, but are willing to rely occasionally on modern chemistry rather than put up with wormy or scabby fruit — just as they might reject a penicillin shot for a common cold, but would snap it up fast if they had double pneumonia.

Integrated Pest Management

You have probably heard about IPM, the technique of controlling pests by using a combination of sanitation methods, natural controls, and, when necessary, some of the safer pesticides. IPM is less expensive than relying completely on chemicals and, if you plan carefully, no more work. The results last longer, too, and the fruit produced is far less likely to have harmful residues.

Orchard Sanitation

Whether you prefer chemical or natural pest control, or a combination of both methods, to decrease problems from orchard pests, it helps to follow certain sanitation practices:

1. Pick up all unused fruit. Bury it in the compost pile or destroy it. Many bugs and diseases overwinter in old fruit.

2. Prune the trees regularly. Burn the prunings or take them to the landfill.

3. Thin out the branches to allow more sun to enter and permit better air circulation. This will help control mildew and scab.

4. Rake up and compost dried fallen leaves since these are favorite overwintering spots for scab and other diseases. The heat from the composting process will destroy fungus and insect eggs.

5. Pull loose bark from older trees so insects can't overwinter there.

6. Keep your planting as far away as possible from wild fruit trees or neglected orchards. Make it difficult for bugs and disease to find you. If there are other small orchards in your area, try to organize your pest management programs together.

7. Mix up your plantings. Like isolation, it's another way to make things tough for bugs and discourage disease. Large growers need all the same cultivars together for convenient picking and spraying, but we small growers don't. As one of our friends put it, "If a bug finds one of my plum trees, I'm not going to make it easy for him to hop to the next one."

Natural Controls

Plant resistant cultivars. It is one of the best pest controls. (See lists in the chapters on individual fruits.) Many of these are of superior quality, but are not yet well known or widely planted.

Electric bug traps work well for trapping flying insects, particularly those that move at night. Hardware stores and garden supply companies sell them (see Appendix), or you can make your own by shining a light bulb with a re-

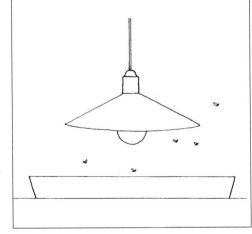

▲ **A homemade bug light**

flector on it into a shallow pan of water that is covered with a layer of kerosene. The light attracts the insects and they'll subsequently die in the kerosene.

Some people feel that electric bug traps kill good bugs as well as bad ones and that they also attract more insects than they kill. Also, insects such as the apple maggot that are more likely to be abroad in the daytime may not show any interest in them at all.

Gallon glass jugs with a pint or so of vinegar in them can attract and trap large numbers of fruit flies.

Paper cups with a bit of molasses in the bottoms, hung among the limbs of apple trees, trap egg-laying codling moths in the spring.

Red artificial apples (available commercially), covered with a sticky material, attract and trap egg-laying apple maggots in early summer.

Black paper loosely tied around tree trunks can be used to provide a shelter for some harmful insects. Remove the paper at intervals and kill the insects hiding there.

A hedgerow provides protection and nesting places for insect-eating birds. Birdhouses, feeders, and bird baths also encourage residency.

Keep the grass mowed to discourage field mice and voles and to eliminate breeding places for insects and disease.

Toads eat vast quantities of those insects that spend part of their life cycle on the ground. Encourage these beneficial and friendly fellows by laying out inverted clay pots with a hole broken on one side and providing pans of drinking water.

Beneficial Insects

Organic orchardists rely on several insects that are good guys. Because the use of toxic sprays might kill them, as much as possible avoid spraying and urge your neighbors to avoid spraying, too. Some beneficial insects are:

Ground beetles. These large, iridescent brown or dull black insects have bodies ridged lengthwise. They run rapidly but do not fly. Both the beetle and its larvae eat caterpillars of all types.

Lacewing flies. These pale green flies with lacy, netted wings lay eggs on other insects; the eggs hatch into larvae and consume the insect hosts.

Ladybugs. Ladybugs are aphid eaters and are often advertised in magazines for that purpose. Unfortunately, imported ladybugs may not stay around all summer unless you have a large supply of aphids, although they usually stick around long enough to be helpful. Encourage the ones you already have by keeping spraying at a minimum.

Praying mantis. The large size and strange appearance of these creatures makes them a little frightening at first glance, but they, too, are well-known consumers of aphids and other unfriendly insects. Their huge, brown egg cases are a welcome sight to the gardener in the fall. Mantis do not survive the winter well in cold areas, but thrive in regions where they are most needed. Like ladybugs, they are often listed for sale in the classified columns of garden magazines.

Tachinid flies. Horseflies, as these insects are often called, have iridescent wings and are gray-black in color. They attach their eggs to other insects where they hatch and subsequently consume their host.

The Case for the Messy Orchard

I don't want to leave the subject of insects and disease without a word about a completely different cultural method—the messy orchard. It is not a new idea. Old-time growers had little time for the niceties of orchard neatness. They left the prunings that were too small for firewood on the ground to rot and return to the soil. Farmers spread thick layers of manure under the trees in early spring, and often kept a hive of bees and let the geese roam in the orchard. They often allowed their pigs to pick up any unused fruit in the fall. They did no spraying and mowed the grass only once a year to control the weeds and brush. Some farmers planted a special hay called orchard grass to help repel fire blight. In any case, disease and wormy fruits were seldom serious problems.

It's true that pests weren't as widespread in the old days, but some "natural" gardeners suspect that earlier cultural methods helped keep out insects and disease, and the years of not mowing that turned the orchard floor into a thick, mulch-like thatch added natural fertility to the soil. It also provided safe living quarters for bug-eating, ground-nesting birds, mice-eating weasels, and wild bees.

The lazy man's orchard, as it is sometimes called, is not a good description, because in no way is the orchard neglected. Any wounds and broken limbs should be promptly treated. New trees need a heavy mulch to suppress competing grass and weed growth. Fertilizing is essential, and should actually be increased, since both trees and thatch need to be fed. Trees still should be pruned, but if possible the prunings should be cut fine or chipped and left to rot, and the small fruits must be thinned.

I mention this method of growing because in many cases it appears to work, but in no way do I recommend it over the conventional method, especially if your orchard is on a city lot or in the suburbs. If you have plenty of room in the back country, however, and want to pioneer in the old style it may be worth a try.

Orchard Diseases

Diseases are caused either by a fungus, bacteria, or a virus. Most of the ones I list are *fungus diseases,* commonly spread by wind, rain, and insects, and are controlled by fungicides. *Bacterial diseases* are less common than fungus diseases, but hard to control. Fire blight and root gall are good examples. *Virus diseases* are spread in the same way and are often also passed on through an infected scion or rootstock. Most virus diseases greatly shorten the life of a tree or plant and are very hard to control. About the only way to cope with them is to start with virus-free plants and isolate them from infected ones.

I won't list any specific products to use for disease control because the list

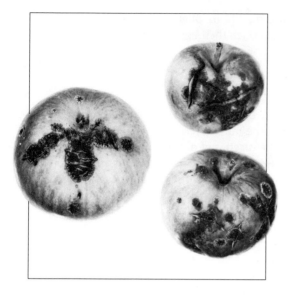

◄ **Apple scab attacks leaves, twigs, and fruit.** *(Gertrude Catlin)*

changes frequently as old ones are discontinued and new ones come on the market. Ask your Extension Service, Agriculture Canada, or a local farm store for the treatment that is currently being recommended for any problems in your area.

Most home orchardists prefer the convenience of a ready-mixed, commercial home orchard spray containing both a fungicide and insecticide, so one spraying will control most common orchard diseases and pests. When diseases or insects are especially bad, preventative spraying may be necessary, because by the time symptoms appear, considerable damage may already have occurred.

Apple scab, the most common apple disease, is a fungus, *Venturia inaequalis*. It attacks both leaves and fruit, forming olive-colored splotches on the leaves, often making them warped and curly. Infected fruits are covered with dark, hard, unsightly blotches and cracks. Fruits that become diseased early in the season may fall before maturing, and those contaminated later are often unfit for use. Scab may not be a problem at all if the year is dry, but in rainy summers, you may need to continue spraying until a few weeks before harvest to get perfect fruit. Dormant oils sprayed early help to prevent early infestations of apple scab, but fungicides are likely to be the only way to control it throughout the season. Since scab overwinters in apples and in leaves on the ground, careful orchard sanitation helps prevent the disease.

Black knot is easy to recognize by the thick, fleshy, black excrescences on limbs of cherry, plum, and other stone fruits. It begins in summer as sticky secretions but is most noticeable in winter when the leaves are gone. Spraying is largely ineffective, so remove all diseased limbs in summer as soon as you spot them, and cut down all infected wild plums and cherries that are nearby.

Brown rot attacks the growing fruit of all stone fruits, but plums and peaches are most affected, and the fruit becomes a mass of mushy rot just before it ripens. Like scab, it overwinters in decaying fruit on the ground and is worse in wet summers. Regular spraying with a fungicide controls it.

Canker in its many forms can be caused by either a virus or bacteria, and one or more forms occasionally infect fruit and nut trees as well as small fruits. **Apple blister canker, bleeding canker, blueberry canker, butternut melanconis dieback, camellia canker, currant canker, grape dead-arm disease,** and **nectria canker** are only a few of them, but fortunately probably none will ever bother

▲ Black knot, a disagreeable disease on plums and cherries *(USDA)*

▲ Cherries badly infected with brown rot *(Gertrude Catlin)*

▲
Top: Canker on an apple twig *(Gertrude Catlin)*

Bottom: Canker on a peach tree *(Gertrude Catlin)*

your orchard.

Canker manifests itself as a very noticeable, diseased section of the woody part of a tree or bush, and may show as an open wound. In some cases it may spread around the entire circumference of the trunk and kill the tree. Canker usually results from injuries that have been left untreated.

The best method of canker treatment is to cut out all the diseased wood and seal the cavity with a tree sealer or cement. Then sterilize all the tools you used with a chlorine bleach solution (see page 70.

Cedar apple rust is the worst of several rusts that infect apple trees, and it attacks both leaves and fruit. To complete its life cycle the disease needs to have wild junipers, *Juniperus virginiana* (red cedar) nearby, so elimination of that plant controls it completely. If this is impossible, you can control it with one of the fungicides recommended for that purpose.

Cherry leaf spot, as its name implies, attacks cherries. Overwintering on fallen leaves, it is spread by spring winds and rains. Rake and compost the leaves each fall as a preventative, and spray with a fungicide if necessary.

Fire blight is a deadly disease that attacks pears, apples, and quince, with certain cultivars being especially vulnerable. If you are strolling through your orchard and see some sick-looking leaves hanging on branches that look as though someone had held them in a fire, fire blight bacteria are probably at work. It is a mysterious disease because it can be bad during certain years and then disappear entirely with no treatment.

If fire blight is common in your locality, plant disease-resistant kinds of fruit cultivars (listed in their respective chapters), and at the first sign of the

▲
Top: Cedar apple rust lesions on apple leaves and an apple *(Gertrude Catlin)*

▶
Right: Fire blight injury on an apple twig *(Gertrude Catlin)*

disease prune away all infected parts and seal the wounds with a tree compound.

Fire blight bacteria are spread by wind, insects (including bees), and pruning tools. The first two are hard to control, but you can prevent infection by the latter. Each year, prune all your uninfected trees first. Then, after pruning the infected ones, immediately disinfect all tools with a chlorine bleach solution.

Commercial orchardists sometimes use antibiotics to treat fire blight, but, except in extreme cases, this is not advised for home gardeners.

Making a Chlorine Bleach Disinfectant

Mix 1 part chlorine bleach to 9 parts of water. Dip tools in it, and dry immediately. Don't mix more than you will need at a time, because the solution loses the chlorine gas fairly quickly.

Peach leaf curl overwinters on tree twigs and spreads rapidly in the spring, and the infected leaves curl, crinkle, and thicken. To prevent, apply a fungicide before the buds begin to open in the spring.

Peach scab attacks both peaches and plums, causing velvety blotches to appear over the mature fruits. Fungicides give good control.

Powdery mildew shows up as a white, velvety substance covering leaves, twigs, and fruits of grapes, currants, and tree fruits. To prevent, plant mildew-resistant cultivars, provide sanitary conditions, don't allow the plants to become crowded, and prune rather heavily to permit good air circulation and allow more sunshine into the plants. Bordeaux or wettable sulfur have long been the standard treatments, but several fungicides now on the market give better control.

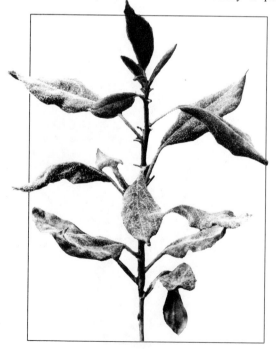

Root (crown) gall is a bacterial disease that causes large swellings on roots of fruit trees and bramble fruits. Some cultivars and rootstocks appear to be more susceptible than others, and in some cases the gall doesn't greatly affect the plant or the crop. Since there is no known cure, plant only certified healthy trees and plants.

◄ **Powdery mildew affecting the top of a young apple tree** *(Gertrude Catlin)*

▶ Verticillium wilt on a strawberry plant *(Gertrude Catlin)*

▼ Peach leaf curl *(Gertrude Catlin)*

Wilt in plants can occur for a variety of reasons including a lack of moisture, but it is also caused by several viruses, fungi, and bacteria. The term "wilt" usually refers to a disease that causes a sudden shutting off of moisture to a limb or portion of a plant, and different wilts trouble an assortment of tree fruits and berries.

Verticillium is one of the most common wilts, attacking vegetables and shade trees as well as fruits. Control of wilt is especially difficult, so plant your fruit trees and berries away from vegetables, such as potatoes, that may have the disease. Cut out any infected limb and burn it at once, or in the case of berry plants, dig out and destroy the entire plant. Sterilize any pruning tools and shovels used on infected plants with chlorine bleach solution immediately after using.

Insects and Their Larvae

One day in high school biology class, our teacher confided in a hushed voice that a single insect could produce 100,000 or more descendants in a few weeks. While all of us were showing the expected proper degree of amazement, the boy sitting behind me whispered loudly, "Imagine what would happen if she ever got married!"

That little remark stayed with me, and I think of it each spring as cocoons burst and larvae proliferate. No longer do I pretend to be amazed at the procreative ability of bugs. I truly *am* amazed. Early control of orchard pests prevents a great deal of trouble later on.

The many different types of insects attack fruit plants and trees in different ways. Some chew the leaves or burrow into the trunk or cane. Others suck nutrients from the leaves or through the bark. Here are some that may show up in your orchard or berry patch:

Aphids of various kinds attack the bark, leaves, or fruit of almost every tree and plant, and although no visible damage shows at first, they suck out the juices and greatly weaken the plant; they can also transmit viruses. A tight curling of new leaves at the ends of branches on young fruit trees is a good indication that aphid colonies are at work. Ambitious ants often spread them because they collect the sweet substance they secrete.

You can often knock out small infestations with a few light squirts of an aerosol insecticide or a sprinkling of rotenone dust. Both methods are easier than mixing up a tank of orchard spray. Repeat the treatment in one week to catch any that appear later.

Apple maggots are, in my opinion, among the meanest villains in the fruit world, and many a beautiful crop of apples has been wrecked by these persistent pests. They are sometimes known as "railroad worms" and can reduce a good-looking apple to a pulpy brown mess. An insect closely resembling a housefly but slightly smaller, pierces the skin of the growing fruit and lays its eggs in the fruit flesh. Then the larvae, often in large numbers, hatch and "railroad" through the fruit. Larvae live in apples that are left on the ground during the fall, then burrow underground for the winter, ready to emerge as flies the following

▲ Aphids on new growth of an apple tree *(Gertrude Catlin)*

summer. You can often see swarms of these flies buzzing under fruit trees in late summer in unsprayed orchards. Cleaning up all the old fruit and using maggot traps are the best deterrents. But once-a-week spraying during the early and middle part of the summer may be necessary if the maggot becomes a problem.

Borers are small larvae that burrow into the trunks of trees, often near or just above ground level. A pile of sawdust and excrement, together with the weakened condition of a tree, indicate the presence of this fat, alien invader. Even one borer can weaken a tree enough to cause it to break off at ground level. The most effective means of disposing of it is to brutally punch the fat grub with a wire inserted into the hole in the trunk, since sprays are not likely to reach it. Tree wraps help discourage this creature, but, unfortunately, trees from nurseries sometimes contain young larvae when you buy them. Inspect your trees frequently and look closely at the trunks of all new purchases. We have imported them twice to our area in the young trees we bought.

Codling moths. "What is worse than finding a fat worm in your apple?" The answer is, of course, "half a worm." The larvae of codling moths are the culprits

▲ The adult apple maggot sits beside some of his handiwork. Top photo shows external injury to an apple; the bottom, internal injury. *(all photos, Gertrude Catlin)*

that cause those wormy apples. The plump, white or grayish grub and its excrements around a hole in the fruit are solid indicators that this insect has been active. The codling moth lays its eggs in the flower at blooming time, so the best way to control it is to spray after the bees leave — directly after the petals have fallen — but before the new fruit has formed enough to protect the hatching eggs. Sometimes a second and third generation may appear later the same year. Codling moths overwinter in sheltered spots, and a favorite one is under the loose bark on older fruit trees.

Curculios are small insects that puncture the fruit just as it is forming and lay eggs, often causing the fruit to drop prematurely. You'll find dark blotches around the punctures on the fruits that remain on the tree. Spray regularly with an orchard spray.

Mites are small sucking insects that attack leaves and fruit. Although they seldom become a nuisance in home gardens, they occasionally increase in numbers during dry summers. Ordinary orchard sprays control them.

Oriental fruit moth larvae occasionally strike peaches and nectarines, attacking twigs and fruits, and may have four or five generations in a summer in warm climates. Early and repeated spraying is the best control.

Pear psylla is the most common pear insect pest. A gang of these small creatures can soon strip the leaves off a tree and ruin a crop with black, sooty secretions unless it is controlled. It can also beget several generations each summer, so early spraying is important.

San José scale, despite the name, is not a skin disorder or musical term but an insect so tiny you need a magnifying glass to see it. It works under a hard film or scale it has built for protection and, along with its numerous relatives, sucks nutrients from the twigs in such quantities that the branches often die. Few fruit trees are immune from this pest, but the standard orchard spray program controls it very well.

Sawflies, especially the European sawfly, attack the fruit in summer causing a circular raised ridge on the skin. The same controls suggested for apple maggot are effective.

Tent caterpillars, cankerworms, and **webworms** create cobweb masses that are a familiar sight. The webs protect the worms from birds as they consume large quantities of leaves during the summer months. Cut off and burn the webs to get rid of them, or use the standard spray program to control them and prevent future generations.

Spraying: How, When, and What

We have friends who search for wormy fruit each fall, because they believe it has never been sprayed, and, consequently, is more healthy to eat. However, with all the safer methods of pest control now available, anyone should be able to grow fruit that is free of disease and insect damage, but is still safe to eat. In some localities, in fact, the laws require that if you raise certain fruits, you must spray to control such insects as fruit flies.

▶ **Peach tree borer in a tree trunk** *(Gertrude Catlin)*

◀ Adult codling moth and injury (Gertrude Catlin)

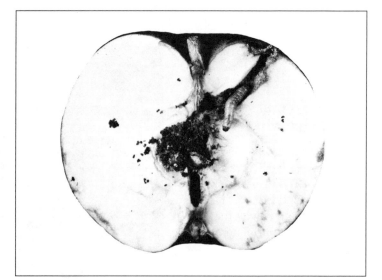

▲ Codling moth larvae at work in an apple (Gertrude Catlin)

◀ Plum curculio on an immature cherry (Gertrude Catlin)

MAJOR INSECTS AND DISEASES

Disease	Enemy of	Attacks
Apple scab	Apple	Leaves, twigs, fruit
Black knot	Plum, cherry, other stone fruits	Branches
Brown rot	Peach, plum, nectarine, apricot	Fruits
Canker	All trees, some bush fruits	Trunk, limbs
Cherry leaf spot	Cherry	Leaves
Fire blight	Apple, pear, quince	Branches, twigs
Peach leaf curl	Peach, nectarine	Leaves
Peach scab	Peach, plum, nectarine	Leaves, fruit
Powdery mildew	Many fruits, berries	Leaves, twigs
Root gall	Tree fruits, berries	Roots
Rust	Apple, currant, quince, berries	Leaves, twigs
Wilt	Tree fruits, berries	Leaves, branches

Insect	Enemy of	Attacks
Aphid	Fruit trees, berries	Leaves, fruits
Apple maggot	Apple	Fruits
Borer	Fruit trees	Trunks
Cherry fruit fly	Cherry	Fruits
Codling moth	Apple, pear	Fruits, leaves
Curculio	Most fruits	Fruits
Mites	Most fruits	Fruits, leaves
Oriental fruit moth	Peach, apricot, plum	Fruits, leaves
Pear psylla	Pear	Leaves
San José scale	All fruits	Fruits, leaves, trunk, twigs
Tent caterpillar	All fruits	Leaves
Weevil	Strawberries	Stems of developing fruit clusters

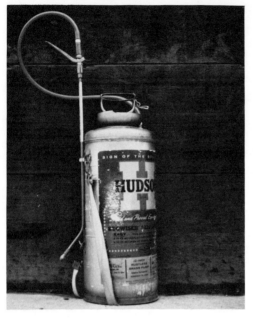

◄ An inexpensive sprayer, suitable for the home orchardist *(University of Illinois)*

Orchardists who insist on perfect fruit usually decide to expect the worst and carry out an annual spray program rather than guess what pests are going to be prevalent any one year. Whether you use chemical or organic sprays, timing is very important. All diseases and insects have times when they are most vulnerable, and since both can spread at an alarming rate, knocking out the first wave saves much work, money, and grief later on.

The amount of spray you use is also an important factor in success. Most home orchardists tend to cover only a small part of the tree, but for good pest control, you must get thorough coverage at the top of the tree and also the inner branches. Choose a day with no wind for the job. We prefer to do any spraying in the early morning when the air is usually quiet, and it is not too warm for the protective clothing we all should wear. I choose a nice day, too, because rain within a few hours is likely to undo everything. Cold, rainy seasons are difficult ones for the orchardist.

Use care. Even with the safest sprays, it's best not to breathe the spray or get it on skin, or in your eyes or hair. Wear a raincoat, goggles, rubber or plastic boots, and a cap. Always stand well behind the spray. If you accidentally get any chemical on you, wash it off immediately and thoroughly. No matter how harmless a pesticide is supposed to be, you can be sure it's not going to do your lungs, skin, or eyes any good.

Common Orchard Chemicals

The common chemicals used in fruit and berry growing are insecticides, fungicides, and herbicides. Insecticides are used to control insects, and these can include miticides for mites. Some insecticides are systemic, which means the plant absorbs the chemical, and the bugs avoid it all summer. Most of these are not recommended for food-producing plants. Fungicides, both chemical and organic, are now available for treating a wide variety of fungi. A variety of herbicides for eliminating unwanted weeds, grasses, and woody brush are also on the market.

Ask at your Extension Service or Agriculture Canada office, or your local garden center or farm store which pesticides are currently being recommended for home gardeners in your area.

Buy Only What is Needed

New pesticides are introduced every year that are safer and more effective than the existing ones, so don't buy more than you can use within a year or two. Shelf life for many of them is limited, too, and their potency may increase or decrease over time. Always store them in a dry, cool place, secure from children and pets, and away from all foodstuffs.

Spraying Equipment

Spraying equipment available to the home orchardist ranges from small, trombone sprayers that spray from a pail and cost only a few dollars, to large, power-driven machines. Avoid buying a cheap model of whatever sprayer you choose. The trombone type is easy to clean, has few parts to wear out, is convenient to store, and is ideal for someone who has only a few trees. Trombone sprayers are not handy to use, however, so an easier-to-carry sprayer is better if you have more than a dozen trees. The compressed-air tank type works well and is perfectly satisfactory if you have low-growing trees, but the spray may not reach the tops of full-size trees. For larger orchardists there are backpack sprayers, both power- and hand-operated, electrically powered mist blowers that can cover a tree with only a small amount of spray, and large sprayers that can be pulled behind tractors. Personally, I avoid those powered by a gasoline engine, for they always seem to need a lot of tinkering because I use them so little.

Always clean your sprayer after use. Leftover spray will corrode the tank and plug the small orifices. Replace worn gaskets immediately, so that the spray doesn't squirt out on you, and, for the same reason, never open a tank sprayer before the pressure is relieved.

Pesticides for Organic Gardeners

Many of us use a dormant oil for the first spray of the season. We apply the oil just as the first bit of green shows in the swelling buds. This helps control the rosy aphids and hatching insects, as well as the proliferation of disease spores, such as scab, that overwinter under tree bark or on leaves on the ground. This one spray is sometimes all that is necessary if you have planted disease-resistant cultivars and follow sanitation practices. Dormant oil spray is available at many garden stores, or you can make your own by mixing 2 quarts of light motor oil (not kerosene or fuel oil) with 1 pound fish oil soap or ½ cup of liquid detergent. Mix 1 part of this solution with 20 parts water, as needed. Use it immediately after adding the water, because the oil and water will separate if you store it for any length of time. For the best control, completely cover the trunks and branches of the dormant trees with the dormant oil. Allow it to spread over the ground below the trees, too. Never spray oil after the leaves have begun to develop.

The following organic sprays, and others, are available at many garden stores or can be purchased by mail from the firms listed in the Appendix. Although organic sprays vary in toxicity, like synthetics, they must be handled with care, since they may be harmful to humans, fish, pets, and beneficial insects. Follow the directions on the package carefully. The residual life of organic pesticides is much shorter than most chemical ones and thus may have to be applied more frequently.

Insecticidal soap controls aphids, mites, mealybugs, scale, whiteflies, and other insects.

Rotenone and pyrethrum are insecticides made from plants. Both wash off easily and have low toxicity. They kill a large range of insects, but their effective life is short so they need to be applied frequently to be useful.

Ryania, another plant-derived insecticide, gives good control over codling moths and certain other insects.

Tri-excel, a mixture of several organic insecticides, is a good all-around spray for organic gardeners.

Sabadilla is a potent insect killer derived from a Latin American plant of the Lily Family.

Tobacco dust kills many insects and is widely used to control aphids.

Biotrol and Thuricide are both trade names for *Bacillus thuringiensis,* a biological control that kills the larvae of certain harmful insects.

Although it is still difficult to find effective all-purpose fungicides that meet the qualifications demanded by organic gardeners, new ones that use fungi to fight specific fungi are showing great promise. In the past, orchardists used bordeaux mixture, sulfur, copper sulfate, and lime-sulfur, and sometimes tossed wood ashes through their trees early on spring mornings when they were wet with dew. They felt it helped control both diseases and insects, added potassium and calcium to the soil, and increased the pH.

Chemical Orchard Sprays

For those who prefer to use an all-purpose chemical orchard spray, they are available in most hardware or garden stores. Most consist of a mixture of one or more insecticides and a fungicide that enables you to control both insects and disease with one shot. Large orchardists usually make their own spray mixture using whatever pesticide is necessary to control the problem present at that time. Chemicals are more tricky to use than organic sprays so be sure to follow the instructions on the package to avoid serious damage to yourself and your trees.

Spray Schedule for Most Home Orchards

If all goes well, and your sanitation methods take care of your orchard pests, you may not need this section at all. Even if you do need to spray, there are times when you definitely should *not,* even if you use organic pesticides. First, *never* spray when the trees are blooming, because you are likely to kill off the pollinating bees. Second, do not spray within two weeks of picking — humans are an important part of the life chain, too.

Spray Schedule for Tree Fruit

(Use an all-purpose mixture of fungicide and insecticide)

1. **Dormant spray.** When tips of buds are swelling and turning green. (Use dormant oil for this one, if you like; see page 79.)

2. **Bud spray.** When leaf buds are just beginning to open.

3. **Pink spray.** When blossom buds show pink and are nearly ready to burst open.

4. **Petal-fall spray.** When nearly all petals are off tree. This is the most important spray of all.

5. **Summer sprays.** Two or more additional sprays may be necessary in some areas, and in some years. Space these seven to twelve days apart after Spray 4 to control mites, sawflies, apple maggot, and summer diseases such as brown rot and scab. Discontinue all spraying at least two weeks before harvest.

Since trees bloom at different times, the second, third, and fourth spray will have to be done according to the flowering period of each species. After that fourth spraying, the whole orchard may be sprayed at one time if additional sprays are needed.

Sprays for Grapes

(Use an all-purpose mixture of fungicide and insecticide)

1. Shortly before blossoms open.
2. Just after fruit has begun to form.
3. Two weeks later.
4. Two weeks later, if necessary.

This spray program should control flea beetles, curculios, berry moths, root worms, and fruit rot.

Sprays for Small Fruits

(Be sure the product you use is labeled for the crop you are treating.)

1. **Fungicide.** In spring, when canes are dormant, to control spur blight.

2. **Orchard spray.** When new canes are 4 to 6 feet tall, for control of anthracnose, tree crickets, and cane borers.

3. **Orchard spray.** Directly after berries are harvested.

4. **Fungicide.** After leaves have begun to come off and canes are dormant, if necessary.

Sprays for Strawberries

Leaf spot control. Orchard spray at ten-day intervals the first summer following planting.

Cyclamen mite control. A miticide, following directions on package.

Weevils and tarnished plant bug control. Use orchard spray just as bud clusters start to form.

Although the control of orchard problems may seem somewhat overwhelming to read about, don't be discouraged by the long list of possible troubles. As I have already pointed out, you can safely control most fruit pests by orchard sanitation, a simple spray program, and ordinary care. The beautiful blemish-and-worm-free fruit you harvest will be worth the trouble.

CHAPTER 10

Animals and Other Hazards

Over the years my attitude toward wildlife has changed quite a bit. When we had a flock of chickens, I thought of coyotes, bobcats, and fishers as villains. Since we have been raising trees and plants, I look at these former so-called varmints, along with owls, hawks, and weasels, in a different way. Those predators consume rabbits, mice, and woodchucks, which, along with porcupines and deer, have become the bad guys in my book.

Gardeners and orchardists in many parts of the country have found that all wildlife is not vanishing, and in fact, the numbers of some animals are increasing. Abandoned farms and ungrazed pastures in rural areas have encouraged wildlife, as has the fact that there are fewer hunters and trappers. Whatever the reasons for the current proliferation of wild animals, some of them can be among the fruit grower's most serious problems. In a few months under favorable conditions, mice and rabbits can multiply astronomically.

If you live in the back country and are surrounded by woods, you rather expect and probably welcome some visitations by wildlife. But nature has adjusted to today's changing world, and city and suburban gardeners often find woodchucks, skunks, raccoons, and rabbits in their gardens. Deer and moose occasionally stroll down the streets of good-size cities. So wherever you live, you may face the problem of these unexpected, uninvited guests. Of course, some people plant fruit trees and bushes because they want to attract animals and birds. Most of us, who toil over our trees, however, hope to keep at least a small part of the fruits of our labors for ourselves.

As one who has tried to garden and grow fruit for four decades on the edge of a wilderness, I sympathize with any gardener who must battle the wildlife. Besieged by everything from mice to moose, I've found that the one plant we grow that some form of animal life doesn't relish is rhubarb, and that escapes, I'm sure, only because of its poisonous leaves.

Mice Control

Mice and voles are among the worst problems facing orchardists, simply because of their sheer numbers. Particularly upsetting is their habit of chewing

82

the bark off the trunks of trees beneath winter's snow, so that you don't see what is happening until spring. Even though a girdled tree may leaf out, it will soon die, and there is usually no practical way to save it.

Mice not only girdle fruit trees that have been newly planted, but often debark those up to 8 inches or more in diameter. Some years the damage is worse than others, and since you cannot predict when they'll strike in full force, it is best to be on guard at all times.

A good hunting cat is fine control in a small orchard, but in case she misses a mouse or two, it is more reliable to wrap your young tree trunks in hardware cloth or heavy metal screening. These can be left on the tree all year, but remove them before they constrict tree growth. You can also wrap the trunks carefully each fall with two or three thicknesses of aluminum foil, or use the plastic tree guards available at most garden supply firms. Remove these in the spring, however, because insects like to work in the dampness there. Guards should extend at least 2 feet above ground and be sunk at least 2 inches into the ground to offer adequate protection.

It is more difficult to keep mice away from large trees, but

▶

Top: Mouse damage that will kill the tree because the bark is completely girdled

Bottom: Plastic guards or similar material protect young trees from rodent damage.

various paints and repellents are used with some success. Commercial orchardists spread poison corn or oats around their trees. The poison used — zinc phosphide — is effective against mice and is apparently harmless to most larger animals and pets. They place the grain under mulches or in small cans so birds won't eat it; or else scatter it just before the first snow comes. This orchard bait, as it is called, is available in many farm stores, or contact the state horticulturist at your state Extension Service office (addresses are given in the Appendix) or Agriculture Canada.

Rabbits, Porcupines, Raccoons, and Squirrels

These small animals were seldom a problem when hunting was more intensive and when dogs ran more freely, but now they cause a lot of grief in some places. Rabbits eat the branches and bark off trees. Porcupines chew the bark and sometimes cut off entire limbs, dropping them to the ground for easier nibbling. Several times these prickly creatures have invaded our garden, cutting down and completely consuming a whole long row of raspberry canes in a single night.

Raccoons and squirrels are more likely to eat mature fruit, and they often invade our barns to steal nuts and fruit we have already picked. The raccoon doesn't wear his bandit mask for nothing! Gray squirrels often run merrily all over a tree taking one bite from each apple, ruining the whole crop.

Some dogs chase away these animals very effectively. Fencing them out is practically impossible, although electric fences sometimes keep away porcupines and raccoons. Hunting and trapping, where it is allowed, may be the only solution. Catching the animals in box traps for release several miles away is a more humane way of handling the situation, but transferring the problem to another neighborhood may not be a morally sound solution, either.

Deer Control

Although bear, moose, and elk occasionally damage fruit trees, deer are usually the only large wild animals that bother orchards. In fact, in comparison with fighting bugs and mice, the deer seem like monsters. They love both apple twigs and fruit, and also seem to get a kick out of scrubbing the bark off any valuable tree with their antlers. In many areas it is impossible to grow even one fruit tree without a high fence surrounding it.

Control of the super-smart deer is difficult. They are well protected by both game laws and public opinion, so off-season harvesting is not at all wise, although sometimes a local game warden will give his blessing if your orchard is beginning to look like a disaster area. Mothballs, hair from a barber shop or beauty parlor, dried blood, small cakes of smelly soap, rotten eggs, lion or tiger manure (if you live near a zoo), sweaty underclothes, and human urine have all been used as repellents with some success. Unfortunately, in cold areas, they freeze up and stop working in early winter just as browse becomes scarce, which is when most orchard damage occurs.

▲ **A high, strong fence may be necessary to keep out larger animals.**

A free-running dog can help, if you are smart enough to train him to chase out the invaders and return home. Game wardens shoot deer-chasing dogs in some areas. We have used noisemakers, radio music, and flashing lights, and all seem to work for a short time, but then the deer become accustomed to them. Most gardeners have found that a high, tight fence is the only answer to a serious deer problem. In our experience, they will give up on an orchard only when it is made completely impossible and not merely difficult for them. A deer fence must be extremely well built, since deer can and will squeeze through the most unlikely places. The larger your orchard, the higher the fence needs to be, and although a 4- or 5-foot fence seems adequate for a few trees, a large orchard needs a fence at least 9 feet high.

To Hunt or Not to Hunt

Much as I enjoy wildlife in the woods, I have always found it hard to understand why the hungry hordes will walk past acres of wild berries, apples, and tasty plants of all kinds and come a quarter of a mile farther to chew up those I have slaved over. Yet every time I suggest violence, there are those who view me as some sort of Genghis Khan. Many people who move into our area from the city believe that everything in nature is good, and they find any control of wildlife difficult to accept. "I always plant extra for my friends, the birds and animals," one lady gardener told me proudly. The next week her friends cleaned out her garden, leaving her nothing, and she quickly changed her tune.

I've noticed that many of our new anti-hunting neighbors often have a change of heart once they've tried to garden in animal country and have seen years of work wiped out in a single night. Folks around here speak in awed tones of a woman who, in the midst of an elegant dinner party, heard a noise in her garden. Graciously excusing herself, and still in her dinner gown, she grabbed a .22 rifle, left her shocked guests, and rushed out to dispense with a porcupine who was busy with his own dinner party.

Other Hazards

Besides animals, we fruit growers have learned to expect other problems. In snow country, snowmobilers don't always bother to go around young orchards, especially at night. Trail bikers and horseback riders sometimes view a new planting as only a bit of brush. But probably the biggest mechanical threat to your trees is your own lawn mower, so impress whoever mows the lawn or uses a tiller or any other machinery to use care around your trees.

If you live in agricultural country, you can expect farm animals to break loose occasionally, and if they do, they are almost certain to head for your orchard or garden. In only a few minutes, a herd of cows or a few horses can devastate the best planting, as can wandering goats, sheep, or pigs. Children may thoughtlessly bend over and snap off a limb or even a small tree to use as a whip or cane. Puppies tend to try out their growing teeth on new trees, and cats like playing games in them. If any of these hazards are likely in your backyard, maybe the best answer is a strong fence with a sturdy gate.

Fences can't keep out bird intruders, though. We welcome birds for their cheery songs and colorful ways, and since they are great insect eaters, we don't want to lose them. Still, some species, such as jays, waxwings, and blackbirds, can be problems at harvest time. Not only do birds love cherries and nearly all kinds of berries, but they often ruin large amounts of apples and other large fruits. Fruit isn't all they may bother, either. Sapsuckers often bore hundreds of orderly holes in the bark of the trunks of our crab apples during the winter and spring.

We have used all the ploys in defense of our crop — strips of fluttering aluminum foil, noisemakers, radios, scarecrows, cats, netting, and plastic snakes, and they all help. We have learned, also, to install bird-scaring devices just before the fruit is mature. If we put them out too early, the birds get used to them; if too late, the feathery gourmets have already developed a craving for the delicacies and have no intention of giving up.

Young fruit trees lead hazardous lives, all things considered, and need your constant vigilance to guard them through their formative years and into production.

CHAPTER 11

Pruning

Years ago, when I was in the nursery and landscaping business, I often pruned fruit trees, shrubbery, and hedges. I soon learned that the job went best when the owners were away. Everyone seemed to like the finished results, but to many people watching, the procedure seemed a bit like slaughtering a steer. "You'll kill that tree!" or "How can you be so ruthless?" were frequent comments along with frantic hand-wringing. Pruning can be puzzling to many orchardists, too. A few people seem happy as larks when they are snipping away at their trees and dreaming of harvests to come, but many others prune far too cautiously or not at all.

Should We Prune?

One of the reasons Europeans and Japanese are considered such good gardeners is because they are not afraid to prune severely when necessary. Americans are learning, but there are still avid gardeners who are not convinced it is important. They stoutly maintain that pruning is contrary to nature.

This argument doesn't really make much sense, because nature does prune, and sometimes far more heavily than I would. She gets rid of dead or surplus limbs by high winds, ice, and snow, and sometimes with a little help from porcupines and beavers. Humans simply do it more neatly and with an eye to producing better fruit — something that doesn't greatly concern nature. No gardener should feel it is wrong to prune, even if you are one of the folks who suspect trees and plants have feelings. If trees could talk, they would probably say, "Please give me a haircut and a manicure." There is no doubt that proper pruning improves a tree's appearance and, even more important, it conserves its strength for a longer, healthier life. It also helps it to produce better fruit.

My wife is one of those gardeners who believes in pruning but is so afraid of doing it wrong that she can't bring herself to cut a branch. She feels that if she were to err even slightly the tree would never forgive her. People like her often read many books on pruning, and the more they read the more confused they become. So, their tools stay sharp and their trees grow bushy and thick, producing lots of small fruit every other year, most of which never gets very well colored and goes unused. Gardeners who are too permissive with their trees for whatever reason are likely to regret it. Actually, pruning is not at all difficult when you understand the reasons and procedures.

As you approach your orchard, saw and clippers in hand, keep in mind the reasons for pruning:

1. To train the tree to grow into a good shape and be strong enough to hold up its fruit load.

2. To keep it at a size that is convenient to spray, prune, and harvest. Our standard fruit trees would grow to 25 feet tall, but we keep them cut back so that we can reach nearly all the fruit from the ground.

3. To remove broken branches, or any suffering from winter injury, as well as any infected by disease or insects.

4. To decrease the amount of bearing surface of the tree. By thinning out the limbs, a smaller number of fruits will result, but they will be larger, the total yield greater, and the tree will be more likely to bear every year.

5. To remove any crossed limbs. Limbs that rub against each other in the wind open wounds where disease can start.

6. To remove any extra tops that can form bad crotches that will split when the tree is loaded with fruit or ice.

7. To open up the tree so that more sunlight can reach into the inner branches. An open tree allows fruit to ripen even in the interior and helps control diseases.

8. To renew bearing wood. You can completely renew most of the bearing surface of the tree every few years by removing a few of the older limbs that have lost vigor. New healthy limbs will replace them.

When to Prune

If you planted a bare-rooted tree you probably pruned it severely at that time (see page 44). As your tree grows, about all you'll need to do is correct any bad crotches; keep a strong central trunk (leader) and prevent it from getting too wide or too leggy; and remove extra tops, branches growing in the wrong

directions, and any suckers or sprouts coming from the roots or below the graft. Until fruit trees begin to bear, they should have very little pruning; over-pruning at this stage is likely to cause excessive growth, which can delay bearing. After the tree begins to bear fruit, however, you should get more serious, and prune more heavily and every year.

◀ **Fifteen-year-old semi-dwarf apple tree after pruning** *(University of Illinois)*

▲ Top: Five-year-old sour cherry tree (left) before pruning and (right) after pruning to a modified leader *(both from University of Illinois)*

Bottom: Six-year-old peach tree (left) before pruning and (right) after pruning. Peaches of this age and older need moderate to heavy pruning to keep them in good production. Note that most of the pruning was done on small branches. *(both from University of Illinois)*

Pruning a fruit tree for maximum production is different from pruning it for beauty. A properly pruned orchard tree is not beautiful, especially in winter when the leaves are off and it looks slaughtered. A tree that is important in the landscape should have less pruning. We have an apple tree in our backyard and enjoy both beauty and good crops of fruit by pruning it only moderately every year.

Long-time orchardists love to argue about the best time to prune. A few maintain that they prune whenever their tools are sharp or whenever it fits their schedule. In the northern states, most orchardists prune on warm days in early spring before any growth begins. In warmer climates, you can prune safely all winter, as long as the trees are dormant. In all areas it is best not to prune in late spring or early summer because the trees "bleed" badly, or whenever the

temperature is below freezing, because it damages the wood cells. A few fruit growers prune their trees in late summer while the leaves are still on but after all growth has stopped. They feel that much less regrowth takes place the following year when they prune at that time.

We prune our orchard in early spring, because it is much more pleasant to work on the bright spring days, and I find it easier to see where to cut when there are no leaves or fruits on the branches. At that time, I can also nip off any boughs that have been chewed by the deer and those broken by snow and ice. I find, too, it's easier to check for fire blight, black knot, and sunscald then.

Methods of Pruning

Just as orchardists disagree about the best time to prune, each has his or her own method of pruning. If you turned a dozen loose on your trees, no two would trim them quite alike, yet each might do a good job.

The three different methods of pruning are the *leader, modified leader,* and the *open vase.* Pruning to a leader means simply keeping a strong, central trunk in the middle of the tree, and letting the other branches come from it. A modified leader means keeping a central stem partway up the trunk, then allowing it to branch more freely into several tops. Pruning to an open vase shape means that you keep the center of the tree open and allow limbs to grow around this open

▲
Top: Spur-type apple, which requires less pruning than the regular kinds *(University of Illinois)*

Middle: A regular apple tree, which produces most of its fruit on the limbs *(University of Illinois)*

Bottom: Sweet cherry tree after pruning to a modified leader system. Usually, sweet cherries require less pruning than most other fruit trees. *(University of Illinois)*

space. This arrangement allows a maximum amount of sunlight into the tree's interior.

Generally speaking, trees that produce heavier fruits, such as apples, nectarines, pears, and peaches, grow best when the tree has a strong central or modified leader. Apricot, cherry, and plum trees, which are less likely to split from heavy fruit loads, are more suitable for the open vase treatment.

Before pruning, notice the fruiting habits of each tree. Some produce their fruits along the branches, and you should prune these normally. Others tend to bear mostly on short, stubby spurs. Stone fruits are especially likely to bear on spurs, as are certain cultivars of other fruits. Some popular spur-bearing apples include Crimson Spur, Goldspur, and Starkspur. Spur-type trees make less limb growth than regular trees, so they tend to grow more slowly, but still often bear at an earlier age. A big plus is that they require less pruning than a regular tree, and they are more productive than dwarf trees. All these factors make them popular with commercial growers, but they are equally good for the home gardener. Whenever the tree produces too many of these spurs, snip off part of them to prevent a lot of extra fruits that will need heavy thinning later. After you have grown trees for a few years, you will be able to judge the right amount to leave, according to your tree's strength.

Pruning Tools

Although the old pruning hooks sound romantic, I don't know of anyone who uses them today. Hand clippers, long-handled pruners, and a fine-toothed saw for large cuts are all the tools necessary for a small orchardist. If you have large trees, pole pruners that reach up into trees will also be useful.

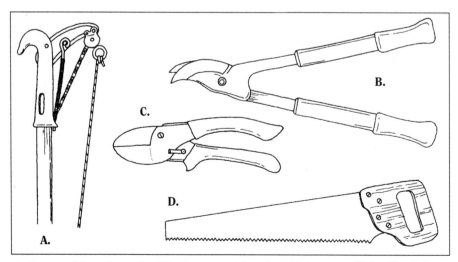

▲ Some useful pruning tools: (A) pole pruners for cutting high branches, (B) long-handled pruners for medium-heavy pruning, (C) hand clippers or pruners for light pruning, (D) saw for making large cuts

I like the snap-cut, hand-held clippers best, but others prefer the ones with blades that cut past each other like scissors. Snap clippers make a smooth cut, can be sharpened easily, and some have blades that can be replaced if necessary.

Avoid buying bargain tools, because they get dull quickly and break easily. Even with good tools you may want to keep a spare handy. It is a nuisance to stop in the middle of a pruning job to find a new pair of clippers.

Whenever I prune, I carry along a can of tree paint to seal any cuts over an inch in diameter, and to fill breaks or holes in the tree. This point is somewhat controversial; some expert orchardists say that tree paint does no good whatsoever. Many of us believe, however, that keeping weather and bacterial infection out of cuts until they heal over is an important part of orchard care, especially on mature, less vigorous trees.

Making the Cuts

In pruning, how you make the cut is as important as when. Always cut small limbs back to another branch, bud, or the trunk (see page 93, bottom right) without leaving a lifeless stub. Such a stub will rot, and often develop into a canker, or invite other diseases that can kill the tree. When cutting off the top or end of a branch, cut on a slant about a quarter inch above the bud (see page 93, top). Also, always cut above a bud that is on the outside of a branch so a spreading tree (see page 93, middle) will result. Branches growing from inside buds will turn inward, and form a pyramid-shaped tree.

Make all large cuts in three stages. Fruit tree limbs are heavy and when partially sawed off are likely to split into the main trunk with a large, ragged

▲ **Pruning cuts should be made with sharp tools and close to the trunk or branch.**

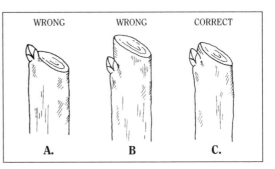

► All cuts should be made to a bud. (A) The cut on the left was made too close to the bud and may kill it. (B) The cut in the middle is too far from the bud, leaving a dead stub. (C) The cut on the right is correct.

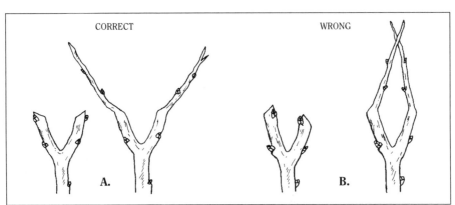

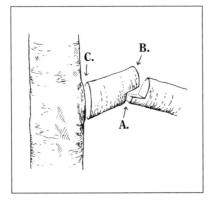

▲ Make all large cuts in three steps. First, make an undercut at A, so the limb won't split. Then, cut the limb completely off at B. Make a final smooth cut at C.

▲ Prune all branches to outside buds, as shown at A; this type pruning encourages spreading of branches and a more open tree. Pruning to inside buds causes ingrown limbs and crossed branches, as shown at B.

▼ Be sure not to leave stubs when pruning. (A) shows a good cut, ready to heal; (B) shows a stub that will soon die and possibly spread rot into the tree.

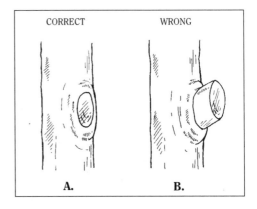

wound. Lighten the load by cutting off the main part of the limb first (see page 93, bottom left). Make undercut A first, then B. Finally, make cut C, and cover it with tree paint to keep out the weather. Use a fine-toothed saw so the cuts will be smooth for faster healing. If necessary, smooth over any rough spots with a rasp.

Keep your tools clean and sharp, so that you can make smooth cuts. Be careful when working in tall trees.

Pruning Tips

When you prune, don't butcher the tree, but don't be stingy, either. Just as in thinning the fruit, my Scottish blood kept me from doing a good job at first. I would prune and prune, yet my trees didn't look like the pictures. Now I have a very effective method. I go out one day, cut off all I dare to, and haul off the prunings. I then return the next day and cut off more — about as much as I cut the first day — and that appears to be about right.

Old-timers said that you should open up the tree enough so you can "grab a cat by the tail, twirl it around your head three times, and fling it through the tree in July and never hit a branch." I have never heard of anyone actually flinging the cat, but while I'm snipping away I try to keep it in mind. It adds drama to the pruning job.

Prune each tree according to its growth habit. Every fruit tree grows differently. For example, Stayman apples are spreading trees, but Yellow Delicious tend to grow upward, as do most pear trees. Adjust your pruning to these natural habits. On spreading trees, you may occasionally need to prune the ends of branches so the tree won't get too wide. On upright-growing trees, correct bad crotches and prune to force the limbs to spread out more.

Don't allow trees to branch too close to the ground in heavy snow country. Settling snow can break the lower branches. As trees grow and begin to bear heavy loads of fruit, branches that formerly grew upright tend to move downward. Since these are likely to be in the way, eventually they will have to be removed. By cutting off such growth when it is still small, you can avoid much heavy pruning later on.

Remove the wood and trimmings. After you've finished pruning, always remove the branches you've cut off and burn them or take them to a landfill, so you aren't providing a place for insects and diseases to spend future winters.

Prune every year. A tree suffers far less stress if you prune it moderately every year instead of cutting off a large amount of wood every few years.

Avoid chain saws for pruning. Tempting as it is, I would never use a chain saw, even to make large cuts. Even small power saws are hard to control when you're doing precision work, and it is too easy to cut into a nearby branch that you don't want to harm.

Be careful not to prune neglected trees too heavily. It is a shock for an old tree to be pruned heavily if it hasn't been touched for many years. Before restoring a neglected tree or orchard, read Chapter 14.

Prune with confidence. As you prune, keep telling yourself it is for the good of the tree — if you're a convincing speaker it may help. If you still have doubts about the advantages of severe pruning, drive past a commercial orchard after it has been pruned and you'll probably be surprised at how much wood they cut out.

Keeping Tall-Growing Trees Low

Occasionally people ask me if they can keep their standard-size fruit trees low by pruning. The answer is yes, if you begin early enough and if you're persistent. If you have old trees that have grown very tall, perhaps from being planted too close together, cutting back the tops can be tricky, and probably not a good idea.

If you prefer to grow standard trees, or if you garden where dwarfs or semi-dwarfs are not hardy, you can keep a standard-size tree at a manageable size for an indefinite period. As soon as the tree is about 7 to 8 feet tall, cut the tops back to about 6 feet. The tree will grow back during the summer, so repeat the cutting back each spring.

It takes awhile to develop the right mental attitude toward pruning, but when you have spent some time around trees and watched how they grow and how they react to various cuts, you will soon become a master pruner. It doesn't take great skill and knowledge, only a normal concern for your tree and your larder.

CHAPTER 12

The Harvest

A surprisingly large number of gardeners plant their fruits and berries properly, tend them with great care, and then woefully neglect to harvest them correctly. Every year bushels of fruit spoil just because people are careless or don't know for sure when and how to gather their crop.

"To everything there is a season," and each fruit is best harvested at a particular time. Picking and using your fruit at its peak is what home fruit growing is all about. Not only does homegrown, tree-ripened fruit taste better and need less sweetening, but it also contains more vitamins. Prime-time harvesting is the big advantage we have over commercial growers, who must harvest their perishable fruits before they are completely ripe and while they are still firm enough to ship. Often, too, commercial growers have no choice but to pick all the fruit on a tree at once, because it is inefficient in a large operation to select only the fruits that are really ready for picking.

How can you tell when a fruit is ripe? It isn't always easy, until you have had some experience. Squeezing and poking is our natural impulse, but it leaves bruises and isn't always a reliable method. Most varieties of tree fruits fall from the tree soon after ripening, so as soon as the fruit will separate from the branch with an easy twist it is ready. Most change color as they ripen. Plums, blueberries, and grapes become covered with a powdery bloom. Cherries, apples, peaches, and pears each develop a characteristic color and blush, so you should be certain what that color is. Some of the best-flavored apples are yellow, green, or russet brown, not necessarily red, for example. If you are in doubt about the ripeness of an apple or pear, cut one open. If the seeds are dark brown, the fruit is ripe and ready to pick.

Only pears, a few varieties of peaches, and winter apples that finish ripening in storage should be picked before they are tree ripened. If you leave pears on the tree until they are soft enough to eat, they will quickly rot, as we have learned from experience. Instead, pick them just before they are ripe and store them in a cool place. They will be perfect for eating within a few days or weeks, depending on the variety.

The taste test is very reliable when it comes to judging berries. Strawberries become red all over and begin to soften. They and raspberries stay at their prime

96

for only a short time and then deteriorate rapidly, so you should pick them every day during their season. A raspberry slips off its core freely when it is ripe. Blueberries, blackberries, currants, and gooseberries are ready for picking when they have developed their full color and flavor.

Many of the best apple, peach, and plum cultivars ripen their fruits over a long season, and these are usually good choices for home orchardists, although obviously not for commercial growers.

The Picking

Except for eating the fruit, I feel that picking is the most enjoyable part of fruit growing. Often the two activities can come very close together. When we were kids picking raspberries, we were usually given a couple of sticks of chewing gum before we went to the patch, the theory being that if the mouth was full and busy, at least a few of the berries would get to the pail. It was only moderately successful, because I loved raspberries, and it was easy to park the gum temporarily on a bush.

▲ Grapes should not be picked before they are completely ripe. They are one of the few fruits that will not continue to ripen after picking. *(USDA)*

How you pick the fruit and handle it afterwards is as important as picking it at the prime time. Pick on a dry day, if possible. If the fruit or berries are wet, they begin to spoil much faster than when they're dry. For the same reason, if you need to wash berries, don't do it until you are ready to eat or process them.

Put the fruit in a cool place as soon as possible after you pick it. We move our berries into the shade as soon as we have picked a few containers full, then move them into a cool room or refrigerator as soon as possible. Baskets or kettles are fine for picking most berries, but raspberries should be picked into small containers. They crush so easily that unless they will be used within a few hours, only a small amount should be heaped together. Pint baskets work best for transporting them.

For picking bush and bramble fruits, I like to use a small kettle or pail that can be easily attached to a belt. This leaves one hand free for picking and the other to hold up canes and branches, because as any berry picker knows, the biggest and best ones invariably hide under the leaves.

Ordinary plastic pails are satisfactory for picking cherries and plums. You can also use them for apricots, peaches, nectarines, pears, and apples, but for these fruits we prefer the bags used by commercial growers. They hang like knapsacks on

▲ These Yellow Transparent apples are developing nicely and will ripen in a few weeks.

the front and are easy to use, even when you are working from a ladder. You can dump the fruit into baskets without bruising it or removing the bag.

All fruit growers warn their pickers to treat all fruit like eggs. Pick each one by hand, and never club or shake it from the tree. Bend the fruit upward, twist it gently, and if it is ripe, the stem will separate easily from the tree and stay on the fruit. Never pull out the stem, or it will leave a hole where rot will quickly develop. Be careful, too, not to damage next year's crop by breaking limbs or fruit spurs as you pick.

Beware of long fingernails that can easily pierce the skin of a fruit. And don't dump fruits from one box to another or handle the containers in a rough manner. Bruised fruit starts to rot quickly, and any rot will spread rapidly to all the fruit it touches. The old proverb that one rotten apple can spoil a whole barrel is all too true. Use all windfalls and any fruit that has been accidentally damaged immediately.

Look after yourself as well as your fruits. Picking from large trees can be especially hazardous. Ladders have a nasty way of tipping when they are leaning against a high branch and supporting a heavy load of picker and pickings. It is always tempting to climb a trifle too high for a luscious-looking plum that's just out of reach. Lifting heavy boxes of fruit can be hard on your back if you aren't used to it, so unless you work regularly as a stevedore, use containers you can safely handle, and move them with a wheelbarrow or garden cart.

After the Picking

Once your kitchen shelf is laden with beautiful fruits, you'll find that any number of wonderful things can be done with them. My favorite way to eat most fruit is fresh off the tree, with no middleman — direct from tree to me. But that doesn't mean I don't enjoy applesauce or strawberry shortcake with whipped cream, raspberry ice cream, blueberry pie, apple pandowdy, peach sherbet, or cherry tarts. They are all fit for serving on Mount Olympus on a sunny Tuesday.

We use a lot of fruit and berry juices, and credit them with health-giving properties. Elderberry juice, crab apple juice, and raspberry juice are some of our favorites. We stew the fresh fruits as if preparing them for jelly, then strain. We either bottle and seal the juice while still hot, or cool it for freezing.

We also use a Finnish Mehu-Maija steam-process juice extractor for juice making. It is sold by many nurseries and garden centers and by Osmo Heila (for address, see Appendix). In the winter we often mix our homemade juices with orange juice or cider and add no other sweetening.

Apple cider-making with our old Sears & Roebuck press is a fall ceremony we wouldn't want to miss. Most years we freeze large quantities for winter drinking and put aside a gallon or two to turn into vinegar.

Some of our friends make a variety of fruit wines, including apple, currant, elderberry, grape, cherry, and raspberry; others prefer the rugged hard cider, as brewed in the old days.

We freeze most berry and tree fruits raw in plastic bags or sealed containers, with the exception of applesauce, and they come out of the freezer tasting almost like fresh. We enjoy strawberries blended into milk shakes, blueberries that are thawed enough to bake into muffins, and raspberries in pies. Just-thawed, spiced, whole crab apples on their stems have become our traditional garnish for Thanksgiving turkey. Freezer jams of all kinds make winter fruits taste harvest fresh, and cooked berries make excellent jams, jellies, conserves, marmalades, and "butters" that brighten up the breakfast table when the snow-storms swirl outside. They are also welcome homemade gifts.

Fruits are easy to preserve in glass canning jars, using the water-bath method. Apples, peaches, pears, cherries, and plums are satisfactory as canned fruits; in fact, in my opinion, pears taste better when canned than when frozen.

One of our favorite uses for the big, early-ripening fall apples, like the Duchess and Gravenstein, is to make them into apple pickles. We use an old family recipe that should never go out of style (see page 231).

Drying is an old-fashioned, but still good, way to preserve fruits. Our cold, damp autumns are not conducive to good outdoor drying, but we sometimes use our oven. Others use solar- or electric-powered food dryers, or microwave ovens. Apricots, apples, and peaches cut into thin slices dry well; blueberries, elderberries, and black currants can be dried whole. Dried fruits will keep for months on a pantry shelf if stored tightly in an ordinary paper bag that is insect proof.

While we're on the subject of eating, you should be aware that some tree fruit seeds are toxic. The pit of the nectarine and peach may look and smell like an almond, but it contains small amounts of hydrocyanic (prussic) acid, a deadly poison. Consuming a few apple seeds is not likely to be at all dangerous, but they also contain small amounts of poison, so don't include them in your diet.

For some of our own favorite fruit and berry recipes, see Chapter 30, pages 226-41.

Storage

Many tree fruits keep well for months in controlled storage. Commercial growers are able to store Delicious, Cortland, and other winter apples in good condition until summer, and home growers can keep them all winter in a simple, inexpensive, and easily built root cellar.

Although home root cellars cannot duplicate the scientifically controlled conditions that large growers maintain, they make it possible for home growers to eat good fruits and vegetables throughout the winter. We have a small one partitioned off in a corner of our basement. It is insulated, has an outside window for ventilation when necessary, and a dirt floor to increase humidity. Cortland apples will keep there until April, if we don't eat them all first. We can't always maintain the ideal climate of 34°F and 85 percent humidity, but our fruits stay remarkably firm. Some of our friends use a small air conditioner in their basement, which has a concrete floor.

Better store your apples and vegetables in separate areas, or keep one or the other tightly sealed in plastic. Apples give off ethylene gas, which causes pota-toes to sprout if the temperature is much above freezing.

Some fruits will keep well for a short time when stored in an unheated room in the cool areas of the country. An old refrigerator in good running condition makes a good storage unit, too.

Many good books are now available on processing and storing home fruits. Here are some of our favorites:

Putting Food By, by Janet Greene, Ruth Hertzberg, and Beatrice Vaughan (1988, Stephen Greene Press).

Keeping the Harvest, by Nancy Chioffi and Gretchen Mead (1991, Storey Communications).

Root Cellaring: Natural Cold Storage of Fruits & Vegetables, by Mike and Nancy Bubel (2nd edition, 1991, Storey Communications).

See the Appendix for a list of companies that sell harvesting supplies, home cider mills, and orchard equipment. Hardware, farm, and garden stores can also supply many of the items you'll need for harvesting and preserving.

CHAPTER 13

Little Trees from Big Trees

I once saw a classified ad in the newspaper asking if anyone had a Yellow Transparent apple tree. Someone wanted permission to dig up a sprout from it to start her own tree. I've often wondered if she found one and, if so, what the results were.

Beginning growers are sometimes puzzled about how fruit trees get their start. Some plant seeds from their favorite apples, expecting they will grow into trees that will bear fruit exactly like the original apples. Others, like the woman in the ad, believe they can dig up the suckers that grow around the trunks of larger trees in the orchard, and eventually these will grow into trees that produce the same kind of fruit. Both are likely to be disappointed.

Over the centuries fruit trees, like humans, have accumulated a great many ancestors, all of whom have influenced their genes. An apple seed can take on any combination of all their good and bad characteristics. Seedlings are most likely to resemble their "wild" ancestors, and their fruits are apt to be small in size and inferior in flavor.

This genetic inheritance doesn't mean that all fruit trees grown from seeds are worthless. Some produce fruit suitable for cooking, jelly-making, or cider. Occasionally, a chance seedling is very good, and even more rarely, one produces fruit equal or superior to other existing kinds. This lucky chance on nature's roulette wheel is the primary way that we get new fruit varieties. Still, these are exceptions.

A fruit tree's seedlings are used mostly as rootstocks upon which good varieties are grafted. The suckers growing from the roots of grafted cultivars are not going to bear the same kind of fruit as the cultivar.

Trees from Seeds

You can easily grow trees from seeds. The seeds from any locally grown, vigorous fruit trees will usually grow into small trees that make good rootstocks for grafting. They will be acclimated and hardy, but you should be aware they will produce full-size trees even if you got the seeds from a dwarf tree. If you like to gamble, you may want to plant a few seeds from a choice fruit, and try for the long shot that it might result in that one-in-a-million super cultivar.

Plant the seeds or pits as soon as the fruit ripens in the fall. Plant three or four in a pot, and place it in a sunny window. If you want a lot of seedlings, plant them in a flat indoors or in beds outdoors. Use a sterile starting mix (available in most farm and garden stores) instead of soil, so plant diseases are less likely to be a problem. If you plant the seeds in an outdoor bed, scatter a few mothballs throughout the bed to protect the seeds from mice and squirrel pilferage. Cover the bed with a mulch to prevent frost from heaving the seeds out of the ground over the winter.

The seeds planted indoors should begin to grow within a few weeks and the outdoors ones by early summer. Allow them to grow a year where they are, whether in pots or in the ground. Then, the following year in early spring, transplant them to a suitable spot where they will have room to grow. In another year or two they should be large enough for budding or grafting, or to grow into your own "mystery" trees.

Layering

One way to start a plant that is "true to name," or the same as its parent, is by layering. This simple process is especially successful with most small fruits, but it can also be used for propagating trees. All you need is a tree or bush with branches close to the ground.

Bend down one of the branches after you have loosened up the soil beneath it, and bury a section of the middle part of the limb. If necessary, place a rock over it so it won't pop back out. Stake the end of the branch so it is pointed straight up (see below). Roots will eventually form on the section of the limb that was buried. When enough roots have developed to support the plant, cut it from its parent, but leave it to grow in the same spot so it can develop a strong root system. The following spring before growth starts, dig up the new plant and transplant it to where you want it to grow.

You can hasten the rooting process by scraping a bit of bark from the bottom part of the limb that is to be buried in the soil, and dusting the wound with a rooting compound such as RooTone or Hormodin before burying it.

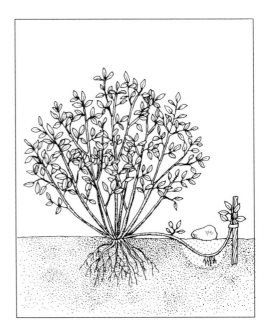

▶ **Layering is a simple way to start new plants.**

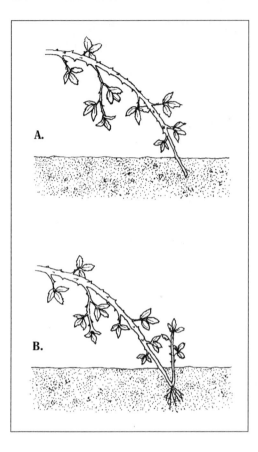

A.

B.

◀ **Black raspberries and trailing blackberries (dewberries) are started by tip layering the new plants. When the tip of a branch is buried in the soil (A), it will take root and develop into a new plant (B).**

Layering works well with gooseberries, currants, grapes, filberts, quince, black raspberries, elderberries, and certain other fruits, all of which often root within a few months. It is likely to take at least a year before plums, peaches, apples, blueberries, and cherries form good roots, and pears may take several years.

Be sure to let your spouse and other members of the family know what you are doing. Soon after we were married, my wife "rescued" all the layered limbs of a currant bush by carefully pulling them up, thinking something drastic had happened to them.

Division

Dividing the parent plant is one of the easiest ways to propagate many small fruits. By the time a berry bush is several years old, new plants usually have started to form around the original one. If you want to start as many new little bushes as possible, the best way is to dig up the entire plant and split it with your axe, knife, or pruning shears. Just make sure, before you cut, that each division will have a good clump of roots on it. If you want only two or three new plants, you can sometimes sever them from their parent with a quick thrust of a sharp shovel without greatly disturbing the main plant. The best time to make divisions is in early spring before any growth starts. The brambles (raspberries and blackberries) are especially easy to divide.

Some bush fruits — currants, elderberries, and gooseberries, for instance — can be started by dividing the large plants. Blueberries can also be divided, but, except for the lowbush kinds, they do not form offsets as easily. You can get the bush fruits to produce large numbers of new plants by cutting back the top of the bush to about 6 inches in height, and piling rich soil or compost over it, completely covering it. New shoots will grow through the soil, and roots will form on their stems. Replace any soil that may wash away in rains, and, the

▶ Gooseberries may be started by a form of division called *stooling*. Soil is heaped over plant to encourage roots to form on the branches, which are later severed from the main plant.

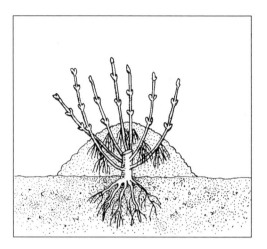

following spring, dig up the entire plant, cut the new plants apart, and transplant them. This process is called *stooling* the plant.

Cuttings

When I was a child, I overheard someone say that if you took a small branch off an apple tree, stuck it into a potato in the early spring, and planted it, it would grow. Even then I was anxious to start replacements for our diminishing old orchard, so I stuck twigs into potatoes left and right. Then I planted them in a long row and waited.

The "expert" was right. But he had carefully not said *what* would grow. We had a beautiful crop of potatoes that year, with a dead apple branch in each hill.

Cuttings are one of the fastest ways to increase many plants. Nearly everyone is familiar with the practice of taking slips from geraniums or chrysanthemums and using the small tips to start new plants. Most of us also know of people who started weeping willow trees by sticking branches into moist ground. Over the years I have tried many methods to start fruit trees from cuttings. Most have not been very successful, but I have had great luck using this method with some small fruits.

Types of Cuttings

Three types of cuttings are commonly used: hardwood stem cuttings, softwood stem cuttings, and root cuttings. Currants, grapes, elderberries, and quinces start well from either hardwood or softwood cuttings. Gooseberries, saskatoons, and blueberries are more easily started from softwood cuttings.

Hardwood cuttings. Take hardwood cuttings from the tips of branches when the plant is dormant in the winter or early spring. Make them 6 to 15 inches long, and store them for three or four weeks in slightly moist sawdust or vermiculite in a cool root cellar or refrigerator. By planting time, a fleshy callus should have formed over the cut ends. Dust the calloused ends with rooting powder (available in most garden stores), then stick the treated ends of the cuttings about 2 inches deep into fertile, well-tilled light soil, and keep the soil moist. Mulch the cuttings with a thin layer of lawn clippings to help hold moisture between regular waterings. In a few weeks, both leaf and root growth should start, and this is a good time to give them weekly light applications of liquid fertilizer or manure water for several weeks. Allow the cuttings to stay in

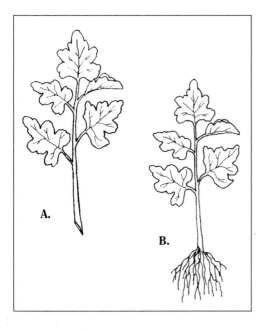

A.

B.

◀ Currants and grapes may be started by softwood cuttings. (A) A freshly cut branch with the cut made on a slant to encourage heavier rooting. (B) A well-rooted cutting.

the bed for a full year, and transplant them the following spring.

Softwood cuttings. Take these in early summer when the plant is growing vigorously. Make each cutting 4 to 10 inches long from the new, soft sprouts, and root it in moist sand, perlite, or sphagnum moss in a small pot. Provide the high humidity the cuttings need by enclosing them in a plastic bag and by sprinkling them frequently. Rooting should take place within a few weeks. Commercial propagators use a system that intermittently sprays mist over the cuttings, and smaller versions of these are available for hobby gardeners who want to start lots of plants.

After the cuttings have formed good root systems, move them gradually from their humid mini-climate into an ordinary environment. Shade them at first on sunny days, and water them frequently to prevent wilting. After each cutting is well established in its pot, transplant it into a larger pot to grow into a husky plant that can later be transplanted to a permanent location.

Root cuttings. These are a fast way to grow large numbers of blackberry and raspberry plants, and can also be used for starting blueberry, elderberry, currant, and gooseberry plants. They are also useful for propagating dwarf rootstocks, such as the Mallings, for grafting purposes.

To make root cuttings, either dig up the whole plant, or, if you want only a few and don't want to greatly disturb the parent plant, cut down close to the main stems of the plant with a sharp shovel and dig up a mass of roots. With a knife or pruning shears, cut them into pieces about 2 inches long. Plant these about 4 inches apart in a well-prepared bed, and cover them with about ½ inch of a mixture of compost, sand, and soil. Water them frequently.

It will be tempting, I know, to dig them up from time to time to see if they are sprouting, but resist. They never will grow if you disturb them too much. After a few weeks, sprouts should appear and a new bush will start to take shape. After the plants have grown for at least a year in the bed, transplant them to their permanent location.

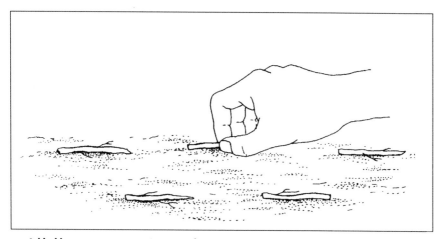

▲ **A blackberry root cutting. Sections of root cut into short pieces and planted in early spring will sprout and grow into good-size plants by fall.**

Tissue Culture

Plant tissue culture is no longer a laboratory experiment but has become a standard method of propagation, and the cloning of plants in huge numbers has become routine. Some plants frequently propagated in this manner are blueberry, raspberry, strawberry, and dwarf fruit tree rootstocks used for grafting. Kits are available for hobby gardeners to use on houseplants and perennials, but the tissue culture of woody plants is very demanding and requires expensive equipment.

Simply stated, technicians place a small piece of a plant, usually a growing bud, in a special solution in a test tube where it begins to grow. Then, they divide it and put the divisions into larger jars with a different solution where the divisions develop stems and roots. Workers must maintain a hospital-like sterility throughout the entire operation, and everything — the cuttings, containers, tools, water, and even the air entering the area — is carefully sterilized. Temperature, pH, and humidity also must be carefully controlled.

The advantages of tissue culture are many. Huge numbers of plants can be started without having large amounts of stock plants on hand, since the culture can be stored and plants started as needed. Each is completely free from all diseases, including the viruses that are so difficult to control, so everything produced can be certified as disease-free.

Grafting

Grafting, the method most often used in propagating fruit trees, hybrid nut trees, and certain grapevines, is simply the joining of two different plants by surgery. Some people still consider grafting a mysterious and somewhat magical process that a few gifted individuals perform on inferior fruit trees to make

Glossary of Grafting Terms

Budding. A method of uniting two plants by attaching only a single bud, instead of a scion or branch, to the rootstock.

Cambium. The thin layer of tissue, often green or greenish yellow, between the bark and the wood on a tree.

Graft. The surgical union of two different plants or trees by attaching a branch (scion) to a rootstock.

Grafting tape. Moisture-proof tape that can be used instead of wax in grafting.

Grafting wax. Material used to seal grafts so they don't dry out.

Rootstock. The root upon which the scion is grafted.

Scion (pronounced *Sī on*). The part of the tree that is grafted or budded to the rootstock.

---

them produce bushels of good fruit. For some reason, they suspect that the grafting ability is a borderline science somewhat like faith healing, water dowsing, and the ability to bend spoons by telekinetic energy. The truth is, grafting is merely the transplanting of one plant upon another, and anyone can do it. All it takes is a little patience.

Over the years, so many wild stories have been told about grafting that it's no wonder people have a fuzzy idea of what it is all about. Old-timers used to tell me with complete honesty about seeing, in their youth, large trees that were completely loaded not only with different kinds of apples but with peaches, plums, pears, cherries, and even tomatoes and squashes. Since all scientific knowledge points to the impossibility of such a spectacular event, I suspect someone was either pulling a fast one with some wire, or time had dimmed the memory of the storytellers.

Contrary to the wild stories, only plants that are closely related can be grafted together. Most, but not all, kinds of apples can be grafted upon each other. Most stone fruits — cherries, plums, peaches, nectarines, and apricots — can be grafted on each other and on wild stone fruits. Pears can be grafted on quinces, and vice versa. Pears can also be grafted on apples, but the resulting tree is likely to be short-lived. Tomatoes can even be grafted on potatoes since they are closely related members of the Nightshade Family (Solanaceae).

Grafting is the best way to propagate most tree fruits, for several reasons. It is a fast method to start large numbers of trees of the same cultivar. It also allows the orchardist to choose from a variety of rootstocks that will determine whether the tree will be dwarf, semi-dwarf, or full-size. Grafting can also determine the age that a tree will begin to bear and how well it will adapt to your soil and climate.

Rootstocks sometimes affect a tree in other ways, in addition to changing its growing habits. They can also alter the quality of the fruit. I once grafted a branch from a Yellow Transparent apple tree onto a seedling grown from a wild, hard green apple. When the new tree began to bear fruit, instead of the soft, mild Yellow Transparents, the apples were firm, kept longer, and had a zippy flavor. When I grafted a McIntosh on a similar wild seedling, the apples it produced ripened late and were rather sour.

Another time I grafted a branch from a Waneta plum onto a wild chokecherry. The graft was successful, but the roots suckered so badly and were so determined to grow into a cherry bush that the union was completely impractical. Certain apple rootstocks also tend to sucker very badly, as do many wild plums.

Now and then someone tells me they have an apple tree 20 or 30 feet high and they wonder if I can graft it so it will produce good fruit. They are discouraged when I tell them that in order to do this, one would have to cut back and graft a few different limbs each year until they were all done, which would take many years. Even though it is possible, it is far more practical to start with a new tree.

Cleft Grafting

For a home gardener, cleft grafting is the most practical and easiest of the many types of grafting. (For illustration, see page 110.) You can use it to graft small trees or to graft new cultivars on the limbs of large trees, a process known as "top working."

The best time to cleft graft is in early spring, just as the leaf buds are swelling and beginning to turn green. Sap is flowing at that time, so scions are not as likely to dry out before they begin to grow, as they would if grafted earlier or later. For cleft grafting you'll need a high-quality, sharp knife, some grafting tape, wax, or tree compound to cover the wounds, and, of course, the scion and the tree to be grafted. Choose a tree or limb ½ inch to 2 inches in diameter for best results.

First, cut off the tree that you're using for the rootstock a few inches above the ground, or, if you are doing a branch on a larger tree, cut the branch off wherever you want to put the graft. Make the cut as smooth as possible. Next, with a sharp knife or grafting tool, split this cut end in the middle about ¾ to 1½ inches deep, depending on the size of the branch. Don't let the knife get away from you, though, and cut too deep.

Now prepare the scion. Cut a piece from the branch of the fruit tree you want to propagate. A scion from 2 to 5 inches long with not more than two or three buds is about the right size. It should be about the same diameter or slightly smaller than the limb or stem it is to be grafted upon; it should never be any larger.

Never let your scions dry out before the operation. I like to gather them the day before and put the cut ends into a pail of water so they will be turgid. As insurance against the scions' drying out after being grafted, some gardeners dip the entire scion except for the bottom cut end into melted grafting wax before it is attached to the rootstock.

After splitting the rootstock, sharpen the cut base end of the scion into a wedge (not a point), using a sharp knife so the edges will be smooth. Don't drop

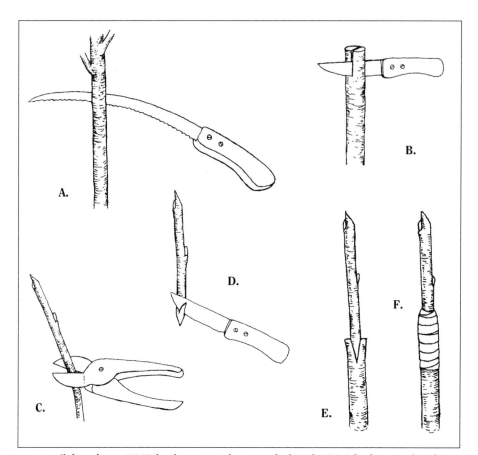

▲ **Cleft grafting. (A) Make the cut straight across the branch. (B) Split the cut end, making a vertical cut 1½ inches deep. (C) To prepare the section, cut a piece 2–5 inches long that has one or two buds. (D) Sharpen the bottom of the scion to make a thin wedge. (E) Slide the wedge into the split end, with the cambium layers lined up on one side. (F) Cover the wound with grafting wax, tree dressing, or rubber tape.**

the scion or allow the cut edges to touch anything that could infect it, not even your fingers.

Next, pry open the split part of the rootstock with your knife and slide the wedge-shape scion down into it. Since your scion and rootstock are not likely to be exactly the same diameter, carefully align the cambiums (green layers under the bark) of both on one side. Exact alignment is necessary so the sap can flow from the rootstock to the scion. You'll need a steady hand, so don't be nervous. The tree won't scream during the operation.

When the scion is solidly in place, cover the wound to keep the air from reaching it and drying it out. Regular grafting wax is the conventional way of sealing the wound, but it is a bit messy to melt and brush on. There are various imported waxes that are soft enough to ply in the fingers, but many of us prefer to use one of the tree compounds such as TREEKOTE, or to wrap the juncture with strips of rubber electrical tape, available in most hardware stores. The plastic electrical tape is not as good, because, unlike rubber electrical tape, it doesn't expand, and thus constricts growth.

Grafting Tips

Some people gather the scions one to three weeks before they plan to graft, and keep them sealed in a plastic bag in the refrigerator. The advantage of this technique is that the scions are still dormant but the rootstock is coming alive, and the sap can immediately flow into the dormant scions. This makes them less likely to dry out before growth starts. If you do this, don't keep the scions in cold storage for more than a few weeks, or they may have trouble breaking dormancy.

After growth starts, keep the sprouts that emerge on the tree trunk below the graft rubbed or cut off so all the plant's energy will be directed into the scion. Stake the new tree as it grows, because the graft union will be fragile at first and can easily break off in the wind. Label all grafts and keep a written record in a safe place. It will be several years before your new trees begin to bear, and you'll want to know what they are.

Be patient. A new graft is likely to begin to grow a week or more after other buds. Not all grafts start at once, either. Give them all several weeks before giving up on them, and don't let failure discourage you. Even experienced grafters always start more than they need, knowing that there is no guarantee of 100 percent success.

If grafting fascinates you, you may want to read more about it and try some of the other kinds, such as bark, whip, splice, side-tongue, and side veneer (see pages 244–45 in the Appendix).

Budding or Bud Grafting

Cleft grafting is a precision operation and requires considerable care in lining up the cambium layers perfectly. Bud grafting is less exacting, however, and therefore easier for a beginner. I prefer it, too, because it requires no wax and can be done over a longer season. (For illustration, see page 112.)

To bud graft, you insert only a single, tiny bud, rather than a scion, into the tree to be grafted. Since budding is a mid- to late-summer operation, the bud you use is actually the start of the next season's leaf. You'll find this little bud under the current year's leaf, at the spot where the leaf stem comes out of the branch.

The budding season varies year by year and may be as early as June in the southern states, and as late as August in the North. You must wait until the bud you want to use has grown large and fat, but it is essential to insert it into the rootstock before the sap flow ends. Begin bud grafting as early as possible in your location, so that if the first bud you insert doesn't "take," there will still be time to put in another. Like cleft grafting, budding can also be done on limbs of larger trees if you want to change the limbs to new varieties.

The day before you plan to use them, cut your budwood sticks from the cultivars you plan to use. The branches should be 8 inches or more in length,

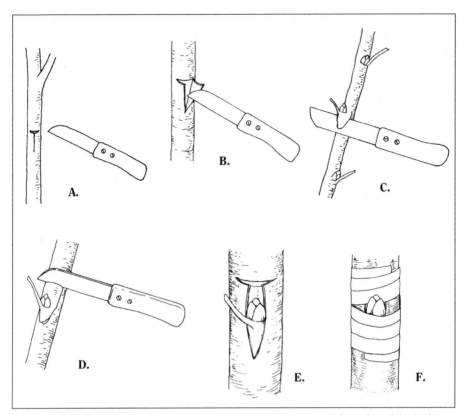

▲ Budding is a fast, easy way to propagate fruit trees. (A) Cut a T shape through bark of tree. (B) Open bark flaps at side of T. (C) Insert knife below base of bud, and carefully cut out the bud and with it, a small sliver of wood. (D) Make a horizontal cut above the bud, so that you can cut it from the budstick. (E) Slip the bud, top-side up, into the opening, and secure it against the sap-covered surface of the wood. (F) Tie the bud securely within the bark by wrapping a rubber budding strip above and below the bud; note that the bud itself is not covered.

cut from growth that has been made during the current season. Pinch off the leaves on the bud stick leaving about ½ inch of the leaf stem on each one. These stems will make convenient handles when you insert the bud. Put them in a cool place with the cut ends in a pail of water to allow the buds to fill with moisture.

To bud graft, first cut a T-shaped incision in the bark of the tree to be budded. Do this as close to the ground as you can conveniently work, so there will be less trunk space for suckers to grow. Remove the bud from the bud stick by cutting a small shield-shape piece that includes the new bud, the leaf stem handle, and a thin sliver of bark and wood underneath the bud. The fat buds in the middle of the branches are the best ones to use. Make the cut with a sharp knife, and use a sliding motion so the cut will be smooth with no rough edges. Don't touch the cut edge. As in cleft grafting, all operations should be sanitary

Sports or Mutations

For reasons that remain a mystery, a limb may suddenly begin to produce a different kind of fruit from that on the rest of the tree. For instance, a tree that formerly produced all yellow apples with red stripes may "sport" a branch that has solid red fruit.

Such a mutation may also produce fruit that is noticeably different in size or quality as well as color. The fruit may be better or worse than the fruit of the rest of the tree. Sports are not common, although they happen more often in some varieties of trees than in others. I mention them here only so you'll be aware of them if they occur, and so that when you are gathering grafting scions you'll be sure to get them from limbs that haven't changed for the worse.

Not only limbs, but occasionally whole trees may change. Some nurseries advertise "pedigree" trees, claiming that their grafts are selected from trees that produce better fruit than is usual with that particular cultivar. Some horticulturists feel, however, that "superior" characteristics are more likely to be due to soil nutrients. Sports are rare, and most of us have never encountered one.

---

to avoid possible infection. Next, pull open the flaps of the T-mark on the bark, and use the stem handle to insert the shield-shape bud, making sure it is right side up, the way it was growing originally. Line the top of the bud tightly against the top of the T. Let the flaps close back around it, and tie the bud in place. Tying used to be done with raffia or ordinary wool yarn, but rubber strips made especially for the purpose are much better and don't need to be removed, because the rubber will rot away as the tree grows. Wrap the rubber budding strip bandage-style around the new bud, completely covering the entire incision but not the bud itself. The flaps must hold the bud tightly so the sap will stay in and the air out. In order to shade the graft from the sun, some propagators insert the buds on the north side of the tree, or cover them with a small piece of cloth or loose-fitting black plastic.

If the bud still looks fat and green after a week or two, it has "taken" and all is well. If the bud shows no sign of life after this length of time, put another bud in the same tree, but in a different place.

Allow the tree to grow naturally the rest of the season while the bud just sits there doing nothing. The following spring, cut off the top of the tree with a slanting cut about ¼ inch above the new bud. The bud should then grow into a completely new tree, the cultivar of your choice. As in grafting, rub or pinch off all the sprouts that grow below the new bud to prevent competitive growth from the rootstock.

With the top gone and the root system intact, the new sprout should grow fast. Stake it to prevent undue strain on the new union, and within a few months the rootstock and top should become firmly attached. Leave the stake in place for a year or more to encourage a straight-growing tree.

It is certainly not necessary to know how to graft in order to raise good fruit. You can probably find the cultivars you want by studying nursery catalogs. Still, it is nice to know how trees are started, and grafting can be a fascinating, practical hobby.

Sources of Grafting Supplies

Grafting tape, waxes, tree-dressing compounds, knives, and other tools are available at most garden stores and in many nursery catalogs. See the Appendix for a list of firms selling these items.

CHAPTER 14

Reviving an Old Orchard

If you buy property in the country, it is likely that there may be a few fruit trees already growing there. The orchard may even have been a strong point in favor of buying the property. Old fruit trees are beautiful, and everyone knows that the perfect country home always has a big, spreading apple tree in the backyard. The salesman probably knew this too: "And here is your orchard. Can't you visualize those big crops of delicious plums, pears, apples, and peaches right on your own trees!" So it may have been a surprise to find, when fall arrived, that those beautiful old trees produced little but a few small, wormy fruits.

But now you own an orchard. Some of your friends are congratulating you on your good luck, and others are recommending a weekend with a chain saw. You have to make a decision. Are those old trees worth saving?

If your trees are old and in really decrepit condition — badly broken, hollow inside, and falling apart — or if the fruit is small, hard, and unusually sour or bitter even when ripe, well, let's face it: The most practical thing to do is to turn the old trees into firewood and start over with young, healthy trees of good varieties. Fruit tree wood burns beautifully in a variety of flame colors.

On the other hand, if many of the trees appear to be in sound condition and the fruit is of good quality even though small, the orchard may well be worth the considerable work of reviving it. Since it takes many years for a newly planted orchard to get into full production, there is a definite advantage in renewing an old one, if it's at all practical. Also, old orchards often contain some fine antique cultivars that are hard to come by.

Before you decide, examine your orchard thoroughly to see what is happening there. In the old days, most home orchards were planted with a dozen or more cultivars in well-spaced rows. Over the years, grazing animals or rough weather may have killed the original trees. When this happened, new sprouts from the wild rootstock grew into relatively worthless specimens that produced inferior fruit. If the trees in your old orchard have more than one trunk or are growing in tight clumps, this is probably what took place.

Seeds from fallen fruit also often sprouted and grew into full-size trees. If your trees are growing much too close together and in a haphazard manner rather than in orderly rows, the trees are probably seedlings. Not all seedling trees are worthless, but unless you're convinced the fruit is good for sauce or cider, better take the saw to these, too.

Both wild and domestic animals often browse the lower branches of trees in abandoned orchards. This forces the growth upward and makes the trees grow very tall. Not only are high trees difficult to prune and spray, but thinning and harvesting the fruit can be difficult and dangerous. If any of your trees are more than 18 feet tall, with few lower branches, you may not want to keep them either.

If it turns out, however, that the trees in your orchard are worth the time and trouble of saving, then you will want to get them to produce quality fruit in the shortest possible time.

The first step is to remove all the worthless trees. This means taking out all the evergreens and hardwoods that definitely do not belong in an orchard, all fruit trees growing in clumps, and those so obviously decrepit that they would be hopeless to revive. Cut out all seedling trees and the sprouts that are growing from the roots of the good trees you want to save. For sanitary reasons, burn or chip all the branches and wood you remove.

Next, if the remaining trees appear crowded, sacrifice enough of them to allow the others plenty of room to grow. In many old orchards, the trees were planted too close together or the filler trees were never removed when they should have been (see pages 10 and 136). Fully grown trees should never touch each other.

Tackle the pruning next — a job you must do carefully. A tree that hasn't been touched in decades is not ready for the severe cutting necessary to bring it back into shape. Although a young vigorous tree can stand having up to one third of its limb area removed, this would be far too much shock for an elderly one. Resist the temptation to remake your trees all at once, and instead, spread the operation over a period of years. The first pruning should be light, and this is especially important in areas where the growing season is short. If heavy pruning doesn't kill a tree outright, it is likely to stimulate an abundance of new growth that will be killed during the winter.

To begin the pruning job, first cut out all the broken limbs, dead and diseased branches, and all sucker growth at the base of the trunks. You can do this kind of pruning at any time of the year, but don't remove any healthy branches until the tree is dormant. When cutting off large limbs, take care so that no splitting back into good healthy wood occurs (see how to cut large limbs, pages 92-94), and cover all large cuts with tree paint to keep out infections and weather. Remove any branches that are growing crosswise or are rubbing against each other. This limited pruning is about all the tree should be forced to withstand the first year.

The second year, begin to thin out the regular tree wood when the tree is dormant but the weather is above freezing. Prune to let sunshine into the tree's interior to improve fruit color. Thinning out some of the bearing wood will cut down on fruit production, but increase its size and quality, and also encourage annual bearing.

By the third year it should be safe to prune more heavily, and in the years that follow, if you have been successful and the trees have survived, you can begin to prune in the usual way (see Chapter 11).

The first year after cleaning out the orchard, feed the remaining trees. It should be quite a treat for them after years without a decent meal. Soils in old orchards are usually worn out and lack the elements necessary for good growth, and for many years the weeds, grass, and brush have competed with the trees for what little fertility was available. Nitrogen is likely to be in short supply, and it is one element that fruit trees especially need. Early spring is a good time to start feeding. If you are an organic gardener, spread around each tree at the outer spread of the branches 100 pounds of dried cow manure or its equivalent in cottonseed meal, soybean meal, or a similar organic fertilizer that is rich in nitrogen. Non-organic gardeners can use a complete chemical fertilizer, 5–10–10 for example, at the rate of 5 to 7 pounds for a large tree. Cut a slit with a shovel, or use a bar to make a hole to insert a cupful of fertilizer every 8 feet in this circle just outside the branch spread.

This is also the time to check the soil's pH. Years of air pollution, acid rain, and other factors may have made soil that was already somewhat acid even more so. Whenever soil is too acid, the fertilizer will be "locked up" and unavailable to the trees. It is not unusual for worn-out soil to test less than 5, and as I said earlier, apple and pear trees do best with a pH of from 6½ to 7; and plums, cherries, and peaches like only a slightly more acidic soil, about 5½ to 6. As soon as you have determined the state of your soil, add the lime necessary to correct it (see pages 30-31).

Unless the area around the trees is to be mowed weekly throughout the growing months, I recommend using a mulch. In addition to all the benefits listed in Chapter 5, a mulch keeps the soil cool in spring and can often delay blooming for a few days, thus protecting the blossoms from a late spring frost.

Although you shouldn't prune off any of the trees' bearing wood the first year of orchard renewal, you can improve the quality of the fruit immediately by thinning it. In early summer when the fruits are about the size of marbles, thin them so that each fruit is at least 6 inches from any other. In a productive year, you may need to pick and throw away about 80 percent of the crop. As I said before, the tree's energy is then diverted to the remaining fruits, allowing the 20 percent that are left to grow larger, often so much so that they will add up to more bushels than if you'd kept them all.

Diseases and Insects

Diseases and insects may be serious problems in old and neglected orchards because both thrive on broken limbs, exposed wood, loose bark, and weakened trees. Many pests also spend the winter in decaying branches, dead leaves, and decaying fruit on the ground.

Orchard sanitation will help you solve many bug and virus problems. As soon as you spot them, clean all tree wounds and seal them with a tree paint to prevent the spreading of insect- and wind-spread diseases such as canker and fire blight. Pick up unused fruits from the ground each fall, or allow animals to clean them up. Remove all tree prunings to a safe area and chip or burn them. Finally, cut down any diseased and insect-infested wild fruit trees that are near the orchard, and use for firewood so they won't infect your good trees. If spraying is necessary, use the safest materials that will do the job.

New Trees among the Old

Should you plant new trees in those bare spots among the older kinds? The presence of fruit trees should indicate that the growing conditions are good and new ones ought to do well in that location. But before you replant, you should be aware that there may be drawbacks.

Years of misuse may have made the soil far less fertile and more acidic than it was in the original orchard. Since there is about as much of a tree below the ground as above, the thin soil of an old orchard may already be full of roots from living or long-gone trees. Rotting roots need nitrogen for the bacterial action that takes place in the decomposition, so adding more fertilizer will speed up the process, but it will be many years before the roots of a large tree completely return to the soil. Furthermore, a little-understood affliction commonly called *replant disease* is often prevalent in new plantings in old orchards.

For all those reasons, I would advise planting in a new spot entirely, if that is possible. If not, and you must plant new trees where old ones once stood, before you order any trees, get the soil in as good condition as possible. A new lawn tree often does poorly when planted near the stump of an old one, because the soil doesn't have enough nitrogen for both the decomposition of the old roots and nourishment of the new young tree. Adding nitrogen to the soil should thus be one of your primary concerns. It is difficult to know how much extra nitrogen is safe to apply without burning the new trees, so it is best to supply part of it with a fast-acting liquid fertilizer and the rest in a slower-acting organic fertilizer or slow-release plant food that can supply the nitrogen and other nutrients gradually as they are needed.

Identifying Trees

If there are trees of merit in your old orchard, you naturally want to know what varieties they are. Some kinds, such as the Yellow Transparent apple or the Green Gage plum, can be readily identified by their fruit, but most are not that easy. An old-timer can often be helpful, but I've found that an honest face and knowledgeable manner don't always mean that the memory is completely reliable. People used to bring us fruit to identify, but usually we were of little help. The list of apples and other cultivated fruits is so huge, and some varieties resemble each other so closely, that identification even by experts is almost impossible. Of course, there is always the exciting chance of discovering a long forgotten old-time fruit, or even a chance seedling of a superior new kind on your lot, but the odds are slim. It makes sense simply to enjoy what you have, without worrying too much about their proper names.

Keep Orchard Size within Reason

In reviving an old orchard, as in starting a new one, a small number of well-cared-for trees will be far more productive and much more satisfying than a large orchard of even partially neglected ones. Limit your orchard to a size that fits in with the time you can spare for it, and save only the trees that are worth the time and effort.

To sum up, bringing an old orchard back into good production requires time and hard work. If the trees are cultivars that produce good fruit, are vigorous, and are not too tall, renewing it can be a rewarding, worthwhile venture. If their life expectancy appears limited, however, or if their fruit seems of doubtful quality, your time and labor will be better spent if you start a brand-new orchard in another location.

There are times, of course, when sentiment alone should rule. There is something majestic, nostalgic, and beautiful about a gnarled old apple tree. It exudes character. It may not matter in the least that its fruit is not the best. The flowers will be just as sweet, it may have a nest of robins in its hair, and the sour apples will furnish food for the deer, raccoons, and birds. Only a practical gardener would destroy a stately old tree. Alas, however, practical we must sometimes be.

CHAPTER 15

The Apple
(Malus spp.*)*

When the wicked old witch selected an apple for poisoning beautiful Snow White, she knew exactly what she was doing. So did the serpent when he made his proposal in the Garden of Eden. There's no doubt that the apple is the most enticing and irresistible of fruits. No other is available in so many varieties and flavors and can be eaten and drunk in so many delicious ways. We grow many different fruits, and I love them all, but every time a new nursery catalog arrives, I automatically turn to the apple section first.

Hardiness

One good reason for the apple's popularity among home fruit gardeners is its ability to adapt so well to different soils and climates. One cultivar or another will grow in all fifty states and home gardeners everywhere have a good selection from which to choose. Many apple cultivars are among the hardiest of tree fruits and will grow where peaches, apricots, and pears haven't a chance of survival. Apples have been developed that will grow in the northern windswept prairies of Saskatchewan and Alberta, and the Russian apples brought to North America by early settlers are nearly as hardy. Alexanders, Astrachans, Duchesses, Transparents, and many of their more recent hybrids are still being grown and enjoyed in the mountains of the northeastern and north-central states, and the Canadian provinces.

During the big freeze in the winter of 1917, when temperatures stayed below -40°F for days, many tender apple varieties in northern United States and Canada were knocked out. This event paved the way for increased planting of the hardy, Canadian-originated, high-quality McIntosh and other members of its huge family. Today the McIntosh is the most popular commercial apple in the East.

Further south and in the Pacific Northwest, where growing seasons are longer and winters milder, the Baldwin, Delicious, Granny Smith, Grimes Golden, Jonathan, Spy, Winesap, Yellow Delicious, and all their hybrids are widely grown in commercial orchards.

Rootstocks

As you study various fruit catalogs, you may be surprised that sometimes the same apple cultivar is available as a full-size standard tree, a medium-size tree (semi-dwarf), or small (dwarf) tree.

Most dwarf apple trees for sale in North America are grafted on one of the Malling (pronounced "Mauling") or East Malling crab apple roots developed in England. There are many varieties of these rootstocks available, and the tree that each produces varies in size, shape, and vigor. Malling 9 (M9) produces the smallest trees, seldom over 6 or 7 feet high. Other Malling and East Malling (EM) rootstocks produce trees from 8 to 12 feet high, and these are sold as dwarf or semi-dwarf. Although the different Malling rootstocks are suitable for most parts of the country, they vary in hardiness, and nearly all are a bit tender for zone 3. A list of the most common rootstocks appears in the Appendix on pages 245-46.

Some apples are grafted on Dolgo crab seedlings. These are hardy and vigorous and are widely used in the north and north-central states. They grow into fairly large, long-lived trees, but the rootstock suckers badly. Nurseries also sometimes offer trees grafted on a Russian stock called Antanovka, which produces a nearly full-size tree.

Canadian nurseries often supply trees grafted on Robusta No. 5 crab apple rootstocks. These produce fast-growing, hardy trees about 16 feet high. They sucker badly, and they are not recommended for warmer climates, however.

Standard trees — growing from 15 to 25 feet high — are usually grafted on apple seedling rootstocks raised from seeds collected at processing plants, such as cider mills. Cultivars grown on these seedlings vary in hardiness depending on the hardiness of the apple cultivar from which the seeds came and where they were grown. Thus, as you might expect, a tree grafted on a seedling grown from a Duchess apple in Minnesota would be hardier than one grafted on a Delicious apple raised in Alabama. If possible, find out the point of origin of your rootstock.

Although full-size trees require more pruning and other care than their dwarf and semi-dwarf relatives, they produce much more fruit and, as a rule, live longer. If you have space enough for large trees, don't mind working on a ladder, and want a huge, old-fashioned, spreading tree for the kids to climb, then standard rootstocks are good choices for you. If you don't want them to grow tall, you can do as we do and prune to keep them low.

To sum up: when choosing a rootstock, if you live in zone 3 or the colder parts of 4, avoid trees on Malling or East Malling rootstocks and standard trees on nonhardy seedlings. Instead, choose some of the hardier kinds listed above. Most catalogs indicate their rootstocks, or will furnish the information if you ask.

You who live in the warmer zones have a wider choice of rootstocks, and nearly all the dwarf and seedling ones will flourish wherever apples grow well. The rootstock you choose depends on the tree size you want.

Culture

If you follow carefully the general directions for planting and growing fruit trees, you should be picking your apples within a few years. Generally, apples that ripen early in the season start to bear at a younger than average age, so a newly planted crab apple or Yellow Transparent may reward you with fruit within one or two years. A Delicious or Winesap, on the other hand, may take four or five years, and some, such as the Baldwin and Northern Spy, often wait up to ten years before bearing their first apple. Luckily, though, unlike the earlier bearers their first crop is usually a big one. Dwarfs tend to bear earlier than full-size trees.

Since you must wait a few years for your trees to produce, keep good records of your plantings. We've heard of gardeners who lost their whole crop of luscious yellow apples because they were patiently waiting for them to turn red. Other friends picked their Delicious crop too early because they didn't realize that "winter" (late-ripening) apples need to stay on the trees for a few weeks after they begin to show color in order to develop their flavor. A few light frosts don't hurt the hard-fleshed apples a bit.

This brings up an important question. When is an apple ripe enough for picking? If it separates easily from the tree, it should be ready. If you're uncertain, cut open an apple. If the seeds are still white, it is not yet ripe, so wait until they turn brown. The catalog descriptions indicate whether the fruit ripens in summer, fall, or winter. Summer apples usually ripen in July or August, and most remain in good condition for only a few days after picking. Fall apples are ready for use in late August or September and, if stored in a cool place, will keep in good condition for a month or two. Pick winter apples in late fall and store them in a cool place where they can continue to develop their flavor. Depending on the variety, they will last from a few months to all winter in a well-made root cellar or similar storage place.

Some cultivars ripen their fruits more or less all at once, but others need several pickings. Among those that have a short harvest season are Baldwin, Black Twig, Cortland, McIntosh, York Imperial, and Northern Spy. Those that ripen over a longer season are especially good home varieties, since all the fruit doesn't need to be used at once. Among these are Ben Davis, Gravenstein, Jonathan, Wealthy, Winesap, and most summer-ripening apples.

You can use apples for cooking before the fruit is fully ripe. We often find we can't wait for that first pie or dish of applesauce, and we've found that raccoons, birds, deer, and small boys don't wait either.

Crab Apples

Crab apples are often neglected children in the *Malus* genus, which is too bad. I feel that one or two crab apples are important additions to any home orchard, not only for their fruit and beauty, but because they are excellent pollinators for the large-fruited apples, as long as they blossom at the same time. There are many good varieties from which to choose, and some of the ornamental crabs

▲ To most people, fruit means apple. Off the tree, as cider, or in any of the countless ways they can be consumed, apples mean good eating, good health, good living. *(USDA)*

have usable fruit.

Our favorite crab apple, however, is the Dolgo — often described as the perfect fruit tree. Not only is it beautifully shaped, vigorous, pest-resistant, regular bearing, and likely to bear early in life, but it is also very hardy. The flowers are more frost-resistant than those of most fruits, and it is a prolific producer. Like the other crab apples, it is a good pollinator, even though it may start blooming a few days ahead of some of the large apples. Our Dolgo's large white blooms are so abundant that they hide the leaves, making the tree a mass of white beauty in the spring. In early fall it is red with ripening fruit. The fresh fruit is a bit sour for most people's taste, but can be made into the most beautiful jelly, spiced apples, and juice. My wife, suspicious of food colorings, also uses it to color frostings and other foods.

Insects and Diseases

Apple trees, like any other living thing, have their share of life's ills. As you read the list of possible problems, it may seem overwhelming, but as I said before, if you practice good sanitation, many will never bother your trees.

Probably most of the established apple trees in North America are infected with numerous viral diseases, and, until recently, most young trees being sold were also infected. Viruses are difficult to control. They weaken the tree and shorten its life by many years. Thanks to new propagation methods, such as tissue culture, many trees now available are virus-free, but if you buy these, always plant them several hundred feet from other fruit trees to avoid infection.

The three pests your apple trees are most likely to encounter are the apple maggot, codling moth, and apple scab. The aphid, mite, sawfly, and San José

DISEASE RESISTANCE OF SOME APPLE VARIETIES

Apple Scab

Most Resistant	*Fairly Resistant*	*Least Resistant*
Dayton	Baldwin	Cortland
Freedom	Beacon	Delicious
Jonafree	Duchess	McIntosh
Liberty	Grimes Golden	Northern Spy
MacFree	Honeygold	Prairie Spy
Nova Easygro	Idared	Quinte
Novamac	Spartan	Red Astrachan
Prima	Starkspur Earliblaze	Rome
Priscilla	Stayman	Winter Banana
Redfree	Sweet Sixteen	
Sir Prize	Yellow Delicious	
William's Pride	Yellow Transparent	

Fire Blight

Most Resistant	*Least Resistant*
Baldwin	Beacon
Crispin	Connell
Delicious	Cortland
Hazen	Greening
Keepsake	Grimes Golden
King David	Haralson
Liberty	Hazen
Macfree	Honeygold
McIntosh	Jonathan
Northern Spy	Keepsake
Spartan	Yellow Transparent
Stayman	
Sweet Sixteen	
Wealthy	
Winter Banana	
Yellow Delicious	

Cedar Apple Rust

Most Resistant
Arkansas Black
Fireside
Jerseymac
Keepsake
Liberty
Macfree
Nova Easygro
Wealthy

scale are other insects that may appear, and other possible diseases are canker, cedar apple rust, mildew, and fire blight. All can be quite troublesome, especially to the cultivars that are most susceptible to them, but the main reason that we spray our trees is to control the codling moth, maggot, and scab. If you do not spray because you are growing the newer scab-resistant trees, you may be bothered by several other fungus diseases. Keep a constant watch on your orchard, and use control measures quickly if any minor outbreaks of insects or diseases threaten to become epidemic. See Chapter 9 for more information about apple pests and how to cope with them.

Choosing Cultivars

A century ago if you wanted to buy apple trees you would have had a tremendous selection from which to choose. There were a great many nurseries selling them, and each listed all the local favorites. Unfortunately, however, the customer didn't always get the variety he or she was promised in those free-for-all days. I've heard tales about one northern nursery where the proprietor wrote out a label for whatever variety was ordered, attached it to any fruit tree he picked out of his large pile, and sold it to the unsuspecting customer.

In the 1920s home fruit growing began to go out of style. In fact, forty years ago when I first went scouting for trees there were almost none available that were suitable for home gardeners. Most catalogs listed only half a dozen commercial varieties that needed a lot of spraying and a long growing season. Delicious, Jonathan, Northern Spy, McIntosh, Baldwin, and Winesap were mentioned most often.

Now, due to increased demand, the selection is much better, and we home gardeners are not only being considered but even courted once again. Nurseries are propagating many old-time fruits, and experiment stations are developing new cultivars especially suited for home culture. So many new kinds have been introduced and old kinds rediscovered, it would be impossible to list each one. Catalog descriptions are so glowing that we almost dread making a choice for fear of missing out on something better. Happily, these days almost every nursery is reputable.

Flavor is an important consideration in choosing fruits, but because flavor is a personal thing, recommending one over the other is unwise. Customers at our nursery often asked which apple was the best. Over the years I became pretty adept at wriggling out of a direct reply. Usually I hemmed and hawed and ended up saying, "That depends." If I attempted to make a list of the best-flavored, best-for-cooking, best-for-freezing, or best-growing varieties, there's no doubt I'd be drummed right out of the apple-growing world. Orchardists are very loyal to their favorites and would get "mighty het up," as we Yankees say, if their choices went unmentioned. So when an old-timer fondly remembers the Wolf River as the greatest fruit of all time, I'm not likely to compare its flavor with that of a wood chip. Likewise, I hope he won't shake his head too violently when I extol the virtues of my favorite Hazen, Northern Spy, or Cortland. Once, many years ago on a trip to Maine, we had lunch in a little seaside restaurant. The menu listed "Apple Pie, 40 cents a slice" and "Duchess Apple Pie, 45 cents." There was no doubt about the favorite apple around those parts.

Some people like soft apples, and some prefer those that are nearly as hard as rocks. Some like a slightly sweet flavor but others claim they eat only very sour kinds. Then there are those who hold out for juicy or dry or mealy or crisp or all sorts of textures, aromas, and other qualities they feel make an apple perfect.

In this age of popular opinion polls, it was inevitable that someone would survey the favorite apples of a large number of people, and in one such study, these are the ten choices for best flavor in descending order: Jonagold, Gala, Golden Delicious, Cox's Orange Pippin, Fuji, Elstar, Empire, Red Delicious, Braeburn, and Granny Smith.

Kenneth Parr, an apple aficionado who raises nearly two hundred different apple cultivars in East Burke, Vermont, rates his favorites, in order, as Jonagold, Hawaii, Sweet Sixteen, Macoun, Braeburn, Granny Smith, Golden Delicious, Fuji, Empire, and Northern Spy. Since most of his favorites don't ripen well in zones 3 and 4, he rates the best-flavored appples for those locations in this order: Sweet Sixteen, Macoun, Cortland, Burgundy, Mantet, Summer Red, Dudley, Prima, Bethel, and Prairie Spy. I would include Crispin, Connell Red, Hazen, and Viking in a list of my favorites, and it is likely that your choices would be quite different. I'd suggest you don't pay much attention to other people's favorites when you select your apple trees. If they will do well in your climate, grow the kinds you like best.

If you would like to sample an apple before buying a tree, many cultivars are available at country roadside stands and farmers' markets in the fall. A large number of different apples are also available for tasting and evaluating from Applesource (see Appendix for address).

I am listing some of the better-known, widely available cultivars with brief descriptions, hoping that it may help you make a better selection than if you throw darts at catalogs. See the list of nurseries in the Appendix for sources.

OLDER CULTIVARS

This listing is alphabetical, with point of origin when known, as well as color, ripening season, and recommended planting zones. See the planting zone map on pages 26-27.

ALEXANDER. Russia, red, fall. Used mostly for cooking. Zones 3–6.

AMERICAN BEAUTY STERLING. New England, dark red, winter. High-quality eating. Zones 4–6.

BALDWIN. New England, bright red, winter. Dessert and cooking. Zones 5–7.

BEN DAVIS. Upper South, red or striped, winter. Fragrant and good keeper, but poor-quality. Zones 5–8.

BLUE PEARMAIN. Probably New England, red with blue blush, fall. Mildly aromatic and highly flavored. Zones 5–8.

CHENANGO STRAWBERRY. Northeast, yellowish with red stripes, summer. Very aromatic, high-quality cooking and dessert. Zones 5–8.

COX'S ORANGE PIPPIN. Europe, red and yellow, fall. Dessert, rich flavor, aromatic. Zones 5–8.

DUCHESS OF OLDENBURG. Russia, red striped, late summer. Excellent for cooking, pies, sauces, pickles; long-lived. Zones 3–6 and milder parts of zone 2.

DUDLEY. Duchess seedling originating in Maine. Good cooking apple, crisp, juicy, keeps for a few weeks. Zones 3–5.

EARLY HARVEST. Unknown origin, yellow, winter. Excellent dessert and cooking. Zones 5–8.

FALL PIPPIN. Unknown origin, yellow, winter. Excellent cooking or dessert. Zones 5–8.

FAMEUSE (SNOW APPLE). Probably from France, red with blue blush, winter. Quality dessert fruit; aromatic. Zones 3–6.

GOLDEN RUSSET. Unknown origin, yellowish bronze, winter. Dessert and cooking; aromatic. Zones 5–8.

GRAVENSTEIN. Probably Germany, orange-yellow with red stripes, fall. Good cooking apple; aromatic. Zones 5–8.

GRIMES GOLDEN. West Virginia, yellow, early winter. Cooking and dessert; aromatic. Zones 6–8.

HUBBARDSTON. New England, yellow-green with red, early winter. Dessert quality. Zones 5–7.

JONATHAN. New York, red, winter. Dessert or cooking; aromatic. Zones 5–7.

LADY. France, red and yellow, winter. Beautiful apple formerly prized for dessert, especially at Christmas. Zones 5–7.

MAIDEN BLUSH. Unknown origin, light yellow with red blush, fall. Primarily for cooking. Zones 5–7.

MCINTOSH. Canada, red, fall-winter. Dessert and cooking; aromatic. Zones 4–7 and milder parts of zone 3.

NORTHERN SPY. New York, red, winter. Aromatic; high-quality dessert, cooking; excellent keeper; hardy but too late for zone 3. Zones 4–8.

PEACH APPLE. Russia, yellow, red blush, early fall. Dessert. Zones 3–6.

POUND SWEET (PUMPKIN SWEET). New England, greenish-white, early winter. Used for baking and canning; sweetish. Zones 4–8.

RED ASTRACHAN. Russia, red, summer. Cooking and dessert; aromatic. Zones 3–6.

RHODE ISLAND GREENING. New England, greenish yellow, early winter. Dessert and cooking; unusual flavor; good keeper. Zones 4–6.

ROXBURY RUSSET. New England, greenish-yellowish brown, winter. Very good home-type apple; one of the oldest American varieties. Zones 4–8.

ST. LAWRENCE. Canada, red, fall. Large and high-quality. Zones 3–6.

SHEEPNOSE. New England, dark red, early winter. Baking and dessert. Zones 4–8.

SMOKEHOUSE. Pennsylvania, reddish yellow, fall. Dessert; aromatic. Zones 5–8.

SPITZENBURG. New York, orange-red, winter. Dessert; supposedly Thomas Jefferson's favorite apple. Zones 4–8.

Summer Rambo. France, red striped, summer. Dessert and cooking; very disease-resistant; one of the oldest varieties. Zones 4–8.

Tompkins County King. New Jersey, red with yellow, fall. Considered by some as the finest apple for dessert and cooking. Zones 5–8.

Tolman Sweet. New England, yellow, winter. Baking and cooking; sweet. Zones 3–6.

Twenty Ounce. New England, greenish yellow, fall. Cooking; large and coarse. Zones 4–8.

Wealthy. Minnesota, red, fall. High-quality cooking and dessert; aromatic. Zones 3–6.

Westfield (Seek-No-Further). Massachusetts. Yellow with red stripes, early winter. A favorite old-time eating apple; one of the best flavored. Zones 4–6.

Winter Banana. Indiana, yellow with red blush, winter. Superb dessert quality; aromatic; regular bearer; excellent keeper. Zones 4–6.

Wolf River. Wisconsin, red, fall. Cooking; very large but not of high quality. Zones 3–6.

Yellow Transparent. Russia, yellow, summer. Excellent eating and cooking; juicy, soft; very early; poor keeper. Zones 3–6.

Twentieth-Century Apples

This list does not describe the fine differences among the many kinds. Check with catalogs for more complete descriptions.

Zones 2–3

These apples have been tested in Alberta and Saskatchewan and are among the hardiest apples grown. They should be hardy in zone 3 and all but the most severe sections of zone 2.

Dolgo Crab. Beautiful red fruit and one of the best-growing trees. Very hardy and a regular bearer.

Heyer No. 12. Green, fair-to-good quality, regular bearer.

Miami. Good flavor, green with red blotches, may not be hardy in the far North.

Osman. Very hardy, prolific bearer. Small, red fruit. Can be eaten out of hand.

Red Siberian Crab. Probably the hardiest of the group. Nearly frostproof and a regular bearer.

Reid. One of the hardiest of the group. Excellent for cooking.

Zones 3–4

These apples are hardy in zone 3 except the very high elevations and worst frost pockets.

Beacon. Large red fruit, early fall or late summer. Excellent cooking apple, similar to Duchess in flavor. Vigorous grower, heavy bearer.

Braeburn. Late-ripening apple from New Zealand. Excellent flavor. Yellow with red-orange blush.

BURGUNDY. Dark red, fall-ripening apple with excellent flavor.

CONNELL. Hardy red winter apple with flavor somewhat like Delicious. Good quality. Bears young.

CORTLAND. Red with blue blush, winter. Excellent flavor, large size. Ripens late but keeps well. White flesh of fruit doesn't brown quickly after cutting.

DUCHESS RED. The old Duchess in a redder color. Late summer. Excellent sauce and pies. Very hardy.

EARLY MCINTOSH. Red. McIntosh flavor in an early fall apple. Good bearing habits. Poor keeper.

ELSTAR. Yellow with red stripes. From Holland. Excellent for eating and cooking. Late ripening.

FIRESIDE. Greenish red, winter. Another hardy Delicious type from Minnesota. Good flavor.

HARALSON. Red. Popular hardy winter apple in the colder parts of north-central states. Good flavor and keeper.

HAWAII. Sweet apple with a pineapple-like flavor. Inclined to bear biennially.

HONEYGOLD. Yellow, winter. A Yellow Delicious and Haralson cross that gives northerners a chance to grow Delicious-type apples. Ripens too late for zone 3 in some years.

JERSEY MAC. Red, winter. Good color. Flavor similar to McIntosh.

LOBO. Red, fall-winter. Good-flavored McIntosh type.

LODI. Yellow, summer. An early apple of the Transparent type, but firmer.

MACOUN. Red with blue blush, winter. Good-flavored apple of the McIntosh type. Tends to be a biennial bearer.

MANTET. High-quality, good-flavored early apple. Yellowish color with red blush. Tree is very hardy, and best in cooler climates.

MELBA. Red, early fall. Excellent flavor, good for eating, cooking, cider.

MILTON. Pinkish red, fall. Large, early, nice fragrance. Regular bearer.

NORTHWESTERN GREENING. Hardy yellow-green, winter. Good cooking, fair eating. Good keeper.

NOVA EASYGRO. Red, scab-resistant. From Nova Scotia.

ORIOLE. Early-ripening, large, red summer apple. Needs sheltered spot in zone 3.

PARKLAND. From Alberta, good for short seasons, good keeper.

PRAIRIE SPY. Green with red blush, winter. Late-ripening. Fine flavor, large size. Good keeper.

QUINTE. Red, early fall. Attractive Canadian apple. Good eating.

RED BARON. Red, fall. A Yellow Delicious-Duchess hybrid. Hardy, high quality. Keeps until December.

REDWELL. One of the reddest hardy apples, winter. Keeps well.

REGENT. Red. High-quality winter apple. Cross between Duchess and Red Delicious. Hardy, but may not ripen fully in areas with early fall frosts. Good keeper.

STATE FAIR. Summer apple, but keeps well. Yellow with red-orange cast. Hardy, and high quality.

SUMMER RED. High-quality, early apple. Hardy, but does well in warmer zones, too.

Sweet McIntosh. Red, fall. Sweet apple with typical McIntosh tree characteristics. Good eating and baking.

Sweet Sixteen. High-quality, good-flavored, hardy apple. Good keeper, vigorous tree. Scab- and blight-resistant.

Zones 5–8

Most of the apples in this list are suitable for the major part of the continental United States. Only the western mountains, north-central plains, upper New England, and the Adirondacks of New York State, plus the warmest areas of the southern states and California, are off limits to this important apple group. Many will succeed in sheltered sections of zone 4.

Arkansas Black. Dark color, winter. Older variety. Popular in the southern states. Improved variety is Starkspur Arkansas Black.

Black Twig. Dark red, winter. Formerly widely grown but now pretty much replaced by the Delicious and Winesap.

Crispin. See Mutsu.

Criterion. A Miller introduction, good keeper, and a good all-round apple. Shaped like Yellow Delicious but with bright red blush.

Delicious family. A chance seedling in an Iowa orchard began to change apple history about a century ago. Not only is the Delicious the most widely grown apple by far in the United States, but it probably has produced more sports and hybrids than any other. This red apple with its distinctive five bumps on the blossom end is easily recognized, and the distinctive flavor universally liked, although it can become "mealy" in improper storage.

The Delicious family consists of so many different varieties that it is impossible to describe even a small part of them. Each section of the country has developed favorites that are liked best in that region — from the Vermont Spur Delicious to the Oregon Red. Study catalogs and check Extension Service recommendations for your area. When in doubt, stick with the old reliable Red Delicious, still considered the best flavored.

Here are some other members of this large group: Double Red, Early Red One, Improved Ryan, Molly's Delicious, Red Bouquet, Red Gold, Red King, Red Spur, Richared, Sharp Red, Skylene Supreme, Skyspur, Star Crimson, Starking, Starkrimson, Starkspur, Sweet Delicious, Topred, and Vance Double. When planting any of these apples, be sure to plant another variety that is not in the Delicious family, for cross pollination.

Empire. McIntosh-Delicious cross, considered one of the better new introductions. Ripens late and tends to color before it is fully ripe. Excellent red, winter apple for eating. Not large.

Freedom. Disease-resistant, good-quality fruit. Keeps until mid-winter. Hardy, but ripens in October, so may get damaged by hard frosts.

Fuji. Highly flavored Japanese apple. Yellowish green, late-ripening.

Gala. Golden color with red stripes. From New Zealand, but hardy in zones 5 and warmer. Fall-ripening, and of excellent quality.

Granny Smith. Green-yellow, high-quality, tart, winter apple from New Zealand that has become very popular. Best in warm zones with long growing seasons.

Jonathan Family. Red, winter apple. Once regarded as one of the best eating apples, it lost favor because of poor keeping qualities, small size of the fruit, and susceptibility to disease. Certain hybrids have been developed that overcome many of these drawbacks, so are a worthwhile addition to the home orchard. Some are sports and some, as the names suggest, are crosses between Jonathan and other popular apples. Varieties most often for sale now include Idared, Jonadel, Jonagold, Jonalicious, Jonathan King Red, and Minjon.

Liberty. One of the most disease-resistant apples. Good quality, good keeper. Vigorous tree, needs no thinning.

Mutsu (Crispin). A Yellow Delicious hybrid developed in Japan. High quality, good keeper. Ripens late.

Novamac. Green with red stripes, good quality.

Paulared. New, early, red apple, late summer. High-quality dessert apple.

Priscilla. Red, fall-ripening. Slight resemblance to its Red Delicious parent. Excellent quality. Very disease-resistant.

Rome Beauty. Originated in Ohio from a grafted tree planted in 1816. The graft died, but a tree growing from the roots produced such good fruit it was named and soon widely planted. Popularity faded as it became apparent the trees were very susceptible to most apple diseases. New hybrids have been developed to improve pest resistance and fruit size. The following are available and are suitable for home plantings: Gallia Beauty, Monroe, Red Rome Beauty, and Ruby.

Rubinette. Golden Delicious and Cox Orange hybrid, medium-size, orange-red with yellow stripes, from Europe. Sweet flavor with a bit of tartness. Ripens late. Zones 5 and 6.

Spigold. Yellow-red winter apple, cross between Northern Spy and Yellow Delicious. Good eating and good keeper. Very late ripening.

Winesap Family. Dates back to the early days of the Republic, probably starting in New Jersey before 1800. Best suited for the milder climates and longer seasons of Virginia, Washington State, and similar areas. Many hybrids and sports have developed from it, including the famous Stayman. Regarded as an excellent cider apple — no small deal in the old days — and an exceptional keeper. Also enjoyed for its pink blossoms. Other members of this family include: Double Red Stayman Winesap, Red Stayman Winesap, Stayman Winesap, and Turley Winesap.

Yellow Delicious. The Yellow (or Golden) Delicious is another of Stark Brothers' famous apples. They paid West Virginia farmer Anderson Mullins $5,000 for the original tree in 1914 — another chance seedling that made good. With Stark's tremendous capacity and know-how, the variety was an instant success and soon proved the public would buy an apple that wasn't red if it was of high quality. Like the Red Delicious, many hybrids and sports soon were developed from it. One, Honeygold, is now being planted in zone 4, where Yellow Delicious usually can't be grown. Some others are Blushing Golden, Gold Spur, Prime Gold, Gala, Starkspur Golden, Virginia Gold.

Zone 9

For very warm climates, such as Florida and Southern California, these apples are worth trying: Adina (Stark), Anna, Beverly Hills, Dorsett Golden, Ein Shemer, Fuji, Granny Smith, Tropical Beauty, Valmore, and Wiregrass. Fuji is a high-quality Asian apple.

CHAPTER 16

The Plum

(Prunus spp.*)*

If you've never picked a fat, sweet plum off a tree in late summer and eaten it on the spot, you've missed one of the great adventures of gastronomy. One year I got impatient for ours to ripen and in a weak moment went out and bought a package of plastic-wrapped, commercially grown plums. They were much larger than ours and a beautiful deep burgundy color, but the taste was disappointingly flat. Plums picked before they are ripe and shipped hundreds of miles can never compare with those sun-ripened on the tree.

Only a few parts of the country are considered perfect plum-growing regions, and these are the only places where they should be grown as a commercial crop. The rest of us have to settle for less than perfection and expect a year now and then when there will be light crop or none at all.

Nevertheless, I feel that every home fruit grower should include plum trees, because the fruit is so delicious. When I was growing up, there were none in our family orchard, unfortunately, but our neighbors always had them. We children were always ready to help out at plum-picking time, although I doubt if we were ever actually invited. We identified them by their colors — red, yellow, and blue — and because I never heard their real names, I have no idea now what kinds they were. The old trees got no care whatsoever, but they bore fruit nearly every year. And how we missed them when they didn't! Several native species of plums grow wild in different sections of the country, often in hedge-rows or along the seashore. They produce vast amounts of small fruits that birds and animals devour and people collect to make into tasty jams and jellies. These include

Prunus americana, the native wild plum that grows from 20 to 50 feet tall, and bears small red or yellow fruits varying considerably in quality.

P. besseyi, the dwarf growing Sand Cherry of the Midwest.

P. hortulana, the wild plum of the Midwest.

P. maritima, the Beach Plum that thrives along the sandy shores of the North Atlantic Coast.

P. munsoniana, the wild plum that grows freely in the South.

P. nigra, the northeast species that grows far north in Canada.

These days, plum trees rarely live to a ripe old age because, like many other fruits, they have picked up a variety of virus diseases that shorten their lives. Try to buy trees that are certified disease free, and plant them several hundred feet from any other plum or cherry trees that might be infected.

Possibly because plums originated in so many different places, few fruits vary as widely in size, shape, color, and flavor. The range is even more varied than that of apples — from small, native American types to large European prunes and giant Japanese cultivars. Yet, despite their differences, each type is recognizable as a plum, both by taste and appearance. Each cultivar is either a "freestone" with a pit that separates easily from the flesh, or a "clingstone" with a pit that does not. The dried prunes we buy are made from European prune-plums that contain less moisture and more sugar than most plums. If you have lots of time and patience, you might want to try drying them, but it is a rather involved process and better left to commercial growers.

If you intend to grow a few plum trees in your orchard, you should know about the four different species. Although the trees and fruits of each species look similar, they are different enough that they usually won't pollinate each other. This, of course, causes trouble for growers who plant two unrelated plum trees.

1. The European *(Prunus domestica)* is the most widely planted species. These plums got their start in the southern regions of Europe and include many superior hybrids, among which are prunes.

2. The Damsons *(P. institia)* are closely related to the European species and probably originated in the region that is now Syria. They might even have been one of the fruits that escaped from the Garden of Eden! Only a few Damson cultivars have been introduced in this country, and many nurseries don't carry them.

3. The Japanese *(P. salicina)* very likely actually originated in China and were introduced into this country from Japan more than a century ago. Although some cultivars are fairly hardy, most are best suited for warmer regions, and some can be grown as far south as Florida.

4. Hybrids of the American plums *(P. americana)* comprise the fourth group. Most are hybrids of native wild plums and the other three species, mainly the hardiest Japanese. They produce good-flavored fruits of various sizes, and are the best choices for growing in the colder zones and on soils that are too moist and heavy for other plums, provided they are also grafted on American plum rootstocks.

Hardiness

American hybrids are the hardiest of the plums, so these are the trees to select if you garden in the cold parts of the U.S. or Canada (zones 3 and 4). European and Damson cultivars are less hardy than the American, and most of the Japanese are the least hardy of all, although there are cultivars in each group that can stand sub-zero temperatures.

Frost Protection

If you're lucky to have enough land so that you can shop around for places to plant your plum trees, choose the high spot of a slope where spring frosts aren't as likely to strike the flowers. Plums bloom early, usually a week or two ahead of apples, which makes them a special target in the frost belt.

Once the trees are in bloom, if the temperature drops down into the mid-twenties (°F), there is little you can do to save the blossoms. We've tried everything from wrapping blankets and plastic sheets around limbs on cold spring nights to running sprinklers, but with little success.

Heavy mulches help keep the roots cool, which may delay blooming for a few days. But in climates like ours, this precaution doesn't always help, because frost patterns are unpredictable and sometimes early blooming is good. Some years our trees have bloomed during a warm spell and set little fruits. A few days later the temperature dropped to the low twenties, but no damage was done to the crop, since the forming fruits are apparently more cold-resistant than the flowers. All in all, it's pretty much Mother Nature's whims that determine whether or not people in frost pockets get their annual crop of plums.

Rootstocks

Full-size plum trees never get very large, and most orchardists prefer them, so dwarf plums are not as readily available as are dwarf apple trees. However, you may want to grow dwarfs if you have a limited space, or if you like the novelty of growing miniatures, or trees in large tubs. Dwarf plum trees are usually grafted on *Prunus besseyi,* the Midwest sand cherry. These rootstocks are hardy, so if you choose hardy cultivars as well, this is one dwarf fruit tree that you can grow in zone 3.

Almost all European and Japanese plum trees are grafted on either peach seedlings or on the roots of the Myrobalan plum, a hardy Asian tree. Unfortunately, this rootstock has become infected with a virus, so many of the trees sold until recently had their life-span greatly shortened by this disease.

Pollination

Lots of gardeners plant a few plum trees without considering the pollination factor at all, and they have wonderful crops every year. Others have a terrible time, and we continually hear a lot of grumbling from people whose plums bloom heavily and set lots of tiny fruits, most of which then fall off.

There are numerous reasons for crop failure, including poor soil, shortage of bees, and frost damage, but lack of pollination is the most likely cause. To get fruit, two different cultivars of the *same* plum family are necessary. For example, if a gardener has only one tree, or one Japanese, one European, and one American, fruit will probably be missing because of improper family planning. Only a few plums, including Stanley and Yellow Egg, produce without cross-pollination, and even these do better with a partner.

A further confusing thing about defining the rules for plum pollination is that the viability of the pollen of certain plums varies considerably, depending upon where they are grown. In some areas the cultivars of different families interpollinate with no problems. In other spots, however, two kinds that *should* mate perfectly will not, either because of weak pollen or because the trees do not bloom at the same time.

Don't be discouraged by the complexity of plum pollination. We always advised our customers to plant three different cultivars of the same plum family for pollination insurance. If they didn't have room for that many, we suggested that they talk their nearby neighbors into the advantages of diversified fruit growing. If your garden center or nursery catalog recommends a plum cultivar that is an especially good pollinizer for your area, include one of those in your orchard. Compass, a small cherry plum, produces so much vigorous pollen that you may want to use it as a pollinizer for American hybrids.

Culture

If you start with the kinds best suited for your region, you will find plum trees are easy to grow. Their small size makes them easy to prune, spray, if necessary, and harvest. They start producing early in life and seldom are subject to blights or other epidemics that sometimes wipe out large numbers of other fruit trees. Aphids, mice, and deer don't bother them nearly as much as they do apple and pear trees.

Since plums produce a large amount of fruit on a relatively small tree, adequate amounts of fertilizer and moisture must be available throughout the growing season. A thick mulch and a generous amount of organic fertilizer around each tree every year help to provide this.

Because plums bear big crops early in life, some orchardists plant them as fillers between full-size apple or pear trees in new orchards in order to make use of land that would otherwise be wasted for many years. Of course, they have to remove these fillers after eight or ten years when the other trees begin to reach full size. If you are reluctant to cut down a tree that is bearing well, this may not be the technique for you.

Pruning

Several years ago I found two articles related to plum growing in the same issue in a garden magazine. One expert stated that plums needed little if any pruning. The other said that they were one fruit that should be pruned severely every year. Probably the writers had two different types of plums in mind, because the fast-growing American hybrids certainly need more pruning than the slower-growing Europeans.

There's no doubt that certain small-fruited plums produce well with no pruning at all, but I have found that most varieties greatly benefit from pruning. As with the other tree fruits, you should prune to decrease the bearing wood (and thus cut down production), to let in more sunshine (for healthy and better-colored fruit), and to shape the tree into a stronger and more attractive unit.

Proper pruning results in fewer but larger fruits, encourages annual bearing, and helps prevent breakage by eliminating bad crotches and weak limbs. Since plum trees bear their fruit on short, stubby spurs, be careful not to cut off too many of these. Light pruning to shape the young plum tree when it is still small will save you a great deal of corrective surgery later on and be less of a shock for the tree.

Plums have a bushy habit of growth, so it is hard to grow a plum tree that has a central trunk with branches coming from it. Rather, try to adjust your pruning to their irregular style. Like apples, all plum trees don't grow in the same fashion. Certain kinds, such as La Crescent and Santa Rosa, tend to grow skyward — even the outside branches turn up. Other varieties spread so wide that the outer branches become weepy and hang on the ground.

Prune both kinds so that the tree becomes nicely shaped, easy to work with, and productive. Cut back the tops of upright trees occasionally to encourage a more spreading, lower-growing tree, and prune back all branches that are spreading too wide before they begin to trail on the ground.

Plum Diseases and Insect Pests

Although the list of plum annoyances is not as great as for many fruits, be on the lookout for the following. Chapter 9 gives further descriptions and suggests control measures.

Black knot is a common disease of plum and cherry trees, and the black excrescences on the limbs are most noticeable during the winter when the leaves are off. The European cultivars are most susceptible, but the Japanese are fairly immune to it. Even though native plums often have the disease, many American hybrids appear quite resistant.

Brown rot, another common disease, strikes just before the plums begin to ripen and almost every fruit becomes a mushy rot, covered with evil-looking white flakes. The Japanese and native hybrid plums are most susceptible; the European and Damson, somewhat less.

Plum curculio is a tiny little insect from Europe that attacks the growing fruit much as the maggot does the apple. It can be controlled by any of several low-toxicity sprays, which are also effective against scale and other insects. If you want to avoid spraying, put several bed sheets under your trees on summer mornings when the air is quiet. Shake the tree so the insects fall onto them; then collect and destroy them.

In various parts of the country, the **fruit fly** and **fruit moth** may bother plum trees, and in some sections the **flathead borer,** which bores into the tree trunk near ground level, may even kill the tree. Inspect all new trees before planting to be sure that there are no holes in them, and if you find evidence of their presence, follow the directions in Chapter 9.

Harvesting

Plum trees are extremely productive, and if all goes well the large-fruiting kinds should bear two to three bushels per tree. The fruit is ripe when it is well colored and has a powdery "bloom." At this time it should separate from the branch easily and be sweet and juicy to eat. Only Japanese plums may benefit from picking a short time before they are tree-ripe; allow them to ripen in a cool but not cold room for a few days before eating. Since many plum cultivars ripen over a fairly long season, they are an excellent home fruit. They will keep for a few weeks in a refrigerator or cool place, but check them occasionally and use them before they get mushy.

Besides eating them right off the tree, we enjoy our delicious plums in lots of other ways. They make excellent dessert sauce, pie, and coffee cake. Nancy preserves plum conserve for winter treats, and freezes them both raw and cooked. Sometimes we freeze the tangy juice for a punch base — in fact, chilled and mixed with ginger ale, it is our traditional Christmas cocktail. For recipes, see Chapter 30.

Plum Cultivars

It would be a hopeless task to try to list all the many hundreds of plums grown in North America, and new ones appear each year. Here are a few that are widely available:

European Plums
Zones 5–9, unless otherwise noted

Fellemburg. Large, oval, purple, prune-type plum with red flesh of excellent quality. Tree is productive, and moderately hardy.

Green Gage. Old-time plum, still considered one of the best. Sweet, juicy, and early.

Italian Prune. Large, purple-black fruit with yellow flesh. Tree is fairly hardy. Self-pollinating, but bears better with a mate.

Mount Royal. Prune-type, blue, excellent flavor. Moderately hardy.

President. One of the latest European plums, with large, blue-black fruit. Heavy bearer.

Reine Claude. Green Gage type but ripens later. Yellow, medium-size, fine quality. Not very hardy.

Stanley Prune. Sweet, large plum with blue skin and yellow flesh. Can be used fresh, preserved, or dried. Tree is productive, self-fertile, and a good pollinizer for other European plums. Worth a trial in zone 4.

Valor. Large, purple, high-quality plum. Tree is vigorous and productive.

Yellow Egg. Yellow skin and flesh. Large, sweet, and juicy.

Japanese Plums
Zones 6–9 and warmer parts of zone 5

Abundance. Medium size, red with yellow flesh, productive. Thin fruit for best results.

Burbank. Old-time favorite, red with yellow flesh. Good for home use where hardy. Ripens over a long season.

FORMOSA. One of the finest of the Japanese cultivars. Yellow with red blush, juicy.

RED HEART. Large, high-quality, dark red with red flesh. Bears early, and needs thinning. Resistant to brown rot and canker.

SANTA ROSA. Reddish purple with red flesh. High quality.

SHIRO. Yellow, round, early, excellent quality. One of the hardier Japanese plums.

STARKING DELICIOUS. Moderately hardy, disease-resistant tree is a heavy bearer. Red with blue blush.

WICKSON. Large, sweet, greenish-yellow fruit ripens in mid-season.

DAMSON PLUMS
ZONES 5–9

DAMSON. Heavy bearing, moderately hardy tree. Small to medium-size fruit. Heavy bearer.

SHROPSHIRE. Improved Blue Damson. Tree blooms late, but bears early in life and regularly.

AMERICAN HYBRIDS
ZONES 4-8 AND MOST OF ZONE 3

EMBER. Hardy, productive plum from Minnesota. Fruits are red and are early.

LA CRESCENT. Small, sugary-sweet, yellow plum with small stone. Tree is fast-growing and vigorous.

PIPESTONE. Fairly large, juicy, high-quality, red fruits that ripen early.

REDCOAT. Red, good-size fruits in midseason. High quality.

SUPERIOR. Large, pink, high-quality fruit. Vigorous tree.

UNDERWOOD. Large, red fruit with yellow flesh. Good quality, but tree is not too productive.

WANETA. Small, red plum, very productive tree. Midseason. Fine for eating fresh.

AMERICAN CHERRY PLUM HYBRIDS
ZONES 3–6

COMPASS. Dark-color fruit. Trees are productive, and good pollinizers.

OKA. Black with purple flesh. Tree is very hardy and productive.

Sapalta. Purplish fruit, sweeter than Oka; productive, extremely hardy tree.

CHAPTER 17

The Pear
(Pyrus spp.*)*

Two days after Christmas one year, I found a partridge in the pear tree in our backyard. Even though three French hens and two turtledoves never did appear, it seemed like a special holiday happening, and another of the many unexpected delights of growing your own fruit.

A soft, juicy, ripe pear is one of the finest fruits, and at a picnic or in a box lunch it makes the whole meal something special. In my opinion, it is the perfect dessert fruit, and a fruit salad or fruit bowl without it always seems to be missing something. Not only is it delicious raw, but it is also one of the few fruits that tastes nearly as good canned as it does fresh. In fact, unlike most other fruits, it tastes better canned than frozen.

Most pears grown in this country today originated in southwestern Europe. They came to America with the earliest settlers and were grown in Salem, Massachusetts, as early as 1635. One variety or another now grows in most temperate areas of the world, but they do their very best only in a few spots, where climatic conditions are ideal for them. I always used to warn prospective pear growers that our northern region is not one of the great pear-producing areas of North America, but the fruit is so beloved that gardeners here keep planting pear trees, even though they know a good crop every year is rare.

In addition to their being fussy about climates, they are also selective about soils and, unfortunately, susceptible to fire blight. New disease-resistant cultivars keep appearing, however, and these will improve the pear's popularity as a home-type fruit.

Hardiness

Although a few pears will grow in zones 3 and 4, most of the best-known kinds are a bit hardier than peaches but less hardy than most apples. Almost all pear cultivars need a period of low temperature during the winter, so only a few are suitable for the nearly frost-free areas of Florida and California. Most pear cultivars sold in nursery catalogs are suitable for zones 5 through 8.

▲ **Pears, a choice fruit for the home orchard** *(USDA)*

The delicious and versatile Bartlett is the most popular pear in this country as well as in Europe, where it is known as the Williams. Kieffer is also widely planted, because it grows well and is a bit hardier than the Bartlett, or about as hardy as the Baldwin apple. It is also less fussy about soils and does well farther south than many of the common kinds. Its quality leaves a lot to be desired, but it is productive and reliable.

In many sections of North America, pear growing should be treated as experimental, and most orchardists should not expect a big crop every year. If they grow well in your location, though, you'd be missing a good bet if you fail to plant them.

Rootstocks

When you go shopping for pear trees you are likely to find that not only are there several different kinds available, but also, some are available on either standard or dwarf roots. Standard trees produce much more fruit per tree than dwarfs, but dwarfs begin to bear earlier, take less room, and are easier to care for. Usually, dwarfs are grafted on quince roots, and standard pear trees are grafted on pear seedlings.

Hardiness is generally about the same for standard and dwarf trees, and the seedlings grown from the hardiest pears produce the hardiest rootstocks.

Pollination

It is usually safest to consider that all pears need cross-pollination for maximum yield, although some, such as Comice and Flemish Beauty, are somewhat self-fertile.

Even pears that are self-pollinating bear better when they are growing near a different cultivar. Usually, if two different cultivars bloom at the same time, they will cross effectively. An exception to this rule is the Bartlett and Seckel, which apparently are socially incompatible and need a third kind to pollinate them both if they are planted together. Oriental pears appear to mate best with other Oriental kinds, too.

Because pears bloom early, poor pollination is not uncommon, especially during cold, wet springs. Some years I have had to resort to hand-pollination in order to save our crop when the bees failed to appear during bloom time. In addition to weather interference, bees sometimes neglect pear blooms because they are less fragrant than plums or cherries, and this is particularly critical because the blossoms stay on the tree for only a very short time. Orchardists who keep bees often place a few pear blooms inside a hive to encourage the bees to visit their trees. A strong hive of bees in the neighborhood during the spring is an invaluable asset to any orchard and is especially beneficial for pear growers.

Culture and Soils

Pear trees are usually regarded as delicate, but strangely they can tolerate more moisture in the soil than either apple or peach trees. They thrive in cool, moist, cloudy weather, which is why they do so well in the Pacific Northwest. They also love a heavy organic mulch, and, except for Bartlett and Seckel, they do not care for sandy, light soils.

Pruning is similar to apple pruning, and after the trees have begun to bear, a moderate amount should be done each year. Thin out the fruits of the large-fruiting kinds when they are small if too many have set. Allow only one fruit in a cluster to remain. Seckel and other small-fruited pears seldom need thinning.

Some pear cultivars take a long time — sometimes six or eight years — to bear their first crop, but others, such as Golden Spice, Lincoln, and Duchess, tend to bear when quite young.

Diseases and Insects

By far the most serious trouble encountered by pear trees is fire blight, which can strike the flowers, limbs, and fruit, all of which turn black as though they had been burned. Other common pear diseases are anthracnose, canker, crown gall, leaf spot, powdery mildew, and scab.

The insects that attack the pear are similar to those that bother other fruits. Codling moth and San José scale are the most common, but pear slugs, psylla, and **pear mite** may all pay visits to your trees. See Chapter 9 for disease and insect control.

Harvesting

Beginning pear growers are often unsure of when to harvest their fruit, because, unlike other fruits, pears must be picked early and never allowed to ripen on the tree. If you leave pears until they are perfectly ripe, they develop hard, gritty cells in the flesh and begin to rot inside. Many homegrown pears are lost because people wait too long before picking them.

Begin to harvest as soon as the fruit is well developed, separates easily from the tree, yet is not quite ready to eat. Pick your pears with extreme care, because if you even slightly damage the delicate skin, the fruit will spoil quickly. A sharp fingernail can be devastating.

Pears keep best in home storage if you wrap each one in tissue paper and store them in a cool place free from odors. They will be ready to eat anytime from a week to a couple of months later, depending on the kind. For the best, full, mellow flavor allow them to ripen at room temperature for a few days after you remove them from cold storage.

In addition to canning, the buttery pear can be processed in a great many delicious ways. A typically southern use is pear "honey," which combines them with lemons, limes, ginger, or coconut. Then there are tasty pear conserves, chutneys, pickles, butters, and nectars. In Europe, large amounts are pressed into a cider called . . . what else? Perry.

Pear Cultivars

The following list includes some standard, old-time pears as well as some of the newer cultivars that are available in different sections of the country. All are suitable for growing in zones 5–8.

ANJOU. Yellow-green, late, good for winter eating and for preserving. Must be picked quite green. Trees sometimes bear irregularly.

AYERS. Suitable also for many areas of zones 8 and 9 where other pears are difficult to grow. Grows rapidly but takes quite a while to bear.

BARTLETT. Popular, large, beautiful pear for cooking or dessert. Productive tree but subject to blight.

BEURRE BOSC. Winter ripening, dark brown, dessert quality, aromatic fruits. Trees are subject to blight.

CLAPP'S FAVORITE. Large, beautiful, late-summer pear with excellent flavor, but it doesn't keep long. Tree is subject to blight.

COLETTE. Large, excellent new pear that ripens over a long season and is well suited for home use. Good for preserves.

COMICE. Attractive pear of fine quality from France. Ripens midseason, and keeps well in storage. Tree not particularly rugged.

DUCHESS. Very large, good-quality dessert pear, and good for preserves. Ripens late, and is quite reliable.

Early Seckel. Early-ripening Seckel (about three weeks earlier than its parent). Vigorous and healthy tree.

Kieffer. Blight-resistant, fair quality, late ripening. Good in North and South. A long-lived tree.

Moonglow. Blight-resistant early pear, regular bearer. Yellow with pink blush. Good for canning.

Orient. Round, yellow fruit with red blush. Good canning pear. Vigorous, blight-resistant, productive tree.

Seckel. Small, sweet, high-quality, yellowish brown fruits in midseason that are good for canning. Vigorous, healthy tree. Worth a trial in zone 4.

Starkcrimson. New, all-red pear. Early, colorful, high quality.

Starking Delicious. Stark Brothers calls this the best pear for home growers. Tree is blight and scab resistant.

Tyson. Early-ripening, sweet, juicy dessert pear. Good for canning. Tree is a heavy bearer, long lived, and fairly blight resistant.

Pears for Zone 9

For nearly frost-free areas Flordahome, Hood, Magness, and Pineapple are good choices.

Hardiest Cultivars

These are worth trying in zones 3 and 4.

Andrew. Very hardy but only fair quality. From the University of Saskatchewan.

David. Firm, thin-skinned pear that is best grown for cooking and preserving.

Golden Spice. Small, juicy, attractive fruit. Good for sauce, pickling, and canning.

Jubilee. Very hardy Canadian pear suitable only for cooking.

Manning-Miller. Strong, vigorous tree produces good-quality fruits with no cross-pollination.

Nova. High-quality, large, round fruits. Tree is hardy and fairly disease resistant.

Parker. Good-size, yellow, sweet, juicy, fine-grained fruits. Developed at University of Minnesota.

Patten. Yellow, good-quality, medium-size fruit that resembles Bartlett. Also from the University of Minnesota.

Others worth a try in these zones are Clark and Mendell.

Oriental Pears

Asian fruits have become increasingly popular in recent years as people have discovered their high quality. Most have a round shape, but the trees are likely to be susceptible to fire blight. Some of these are self-fruitful, but better crops result if you plant at least two different kinds of Asians. Some of the most readily available cultivars are Chojuro, Hosui, Korean Giant, Seigyoku, Shinseiki, and 20th Century. Most are suitable for zone 9.

CHAPTER 18

The Peach and
the Nectarine
(Prunus persica)

When I was young, I loved to eat fruit even more than maple sugar and ice cream, which certainly took second and third place. My love for fruits included all of them except peaches, which I thought didn't quite measure up to the rest. Then one day I ate my first peach that had been ripened right on the tree. Wow! From then on I liked *all* fruits.

What a different taste that tree-ripened peach had, compared to the small, hard, sour ones that had come from the store. That difference is why most home fruit gardeners want very much to include some peach trees in their orchards. The peach is a challenge to grow, though, and it brings out the competitive spirit in gardeners, like growing the biggest and best tomatoes or the finest roses. Just as those plants are a step harder to grow than radishes and marigolds, so the peach is slightly more difficult than apples and plums, unless your soil and climate are right.

The peach and the nectarine, like their close relative the apricot, are among the most "foreign" of the temperate zone fruits. They are thought to have originated in China and were taken to Europe by early traders. The Spaniards planted peach trees in Florida soon after their first settlement there, and from then on they were well established in the New World.

Although selection of outstanding seedlings and cross-breeding have developed peaches that are hardier and of higher quality than the original imports, the growing range is still much smaller than that of pears, plums, apples, and cherries. Peaches grow well in the Niagara peninsula of Ontario and even along coastal regions of British Columbia, but most of the rest of Canada and the northern United States still remain off limits to them. Each year, probably more little peach trees die in the northern parts of Minnesota, North Dakota, Wisconsin, Maine, Vermont, and New Hampshire than all the apple trees Johnny Chapman ever planted. Even in these areas where a peach cannot grow, gardeners just won't give up. If it is at all possible, everyone wants his own peach tree.

▲ Peaches, where they can be grown, are an excellent choice for the home gardener. *(USDA)*

One of our neighbors wanted one so badly that he built a greenhouse especially so he could grow his own tree-ripened peaches.

In addition to its aversion to cold temperatures, the peach tree also needs a long growing season to harden its new growth and develop the fruit buds for the following year. For this reason, peaches can sometimes withstand low temperatures for a short time, but are unable to survive where the frost-free season is less than five months. The flower buds and blooms are also very susceptible to spring frosts.

Even though they prefer a warm climate, like all temperate-zone fruits, peaches need a chilling period — a certain amount of cold weather — in order to survive. Gardeners in zones 8 and 9 must be careful to plant only those varieties that require very little winter chilling. (See list on page 149.)

The fussy peach tree is not only particular about temperature but also about soils. It is never happy in the cool, heavy soils that pears and plums enjoy. Commercial peach growers like to plant the trees on a well-drained slope with sandy soil just above a fairly large lake or river, so the temperature will remain more uniform. Most home gardeners are not likely to have such an ideal location, but, fortunately, peaches will grow well in ordinary garden soil if it is fairly light.

Rootstocks

Throughout most of the country, peaches are budded or grafted on seedling peach tree roots. Peaches have been grafted on plums, almonds, and cherry stocks, too, in an attempt to get them to adapt to heavier soils, but the seedling peach is still the most commonly used rootstock.

Peach seedlings grow rapidly and vary widely in their growth habit. If possible, when you buy peach trees, select them personally at a nursery and choose only the largest, one-year-old, most vigorous-looking trees. Smaller trees, according to the West Virginia Experiment Station, may have been stunted either by a virus disease, an incompatibility between rootstock and top, or some other difficulty that will later get worse.

Dwarf Trees

Because of the strong demand for small trees, many nurseries supply dwarf trees that grow only to about 6 feet tall and 6 feet wide. Because they are easy to care for and bear at an early age, they are ideal for pot culture or for home gardeners with small lots. As with all dwarfs, the trees are less vigorous than full-size trees grafted on seedlings and, since they are shallow-rooted, they often need staking to prevent leaning when loaded with fruit. Their crops are smaller than those of full-size trees, of course, but you can fit more trees in the same space.

Pollination

Most peach trees do not need a partner to produce fruit. A few cultivars do, however, so follow the instructions given for the ones you purchase. The J. H. Hale, for example, should always be planted near a peach tree of a different variety. Most catalogs spell out the pollination needs of each cultivar, but when in doubt, it's always best to plant two different kinds, unless your neighbor has a peach orchard just over the fence.

Culture

Dry, sandy soils that warm up thoroughly are the best possible home for your peach trees. Peaches tend to be in a hurry to grow up. In fact, they are often in too much of a hurry, so fast growth should be discouraged. It usually results in a weak tree that breaks easily, gets winter injury, and is short lived. Fertilize a peach tree only if it needs it, and then only early in the spring. Leave the area around it in sod, and keep the grass mowed rather than mulching or cultivating it, if it appears to be growing too fast.

Because of its vigorous growth habit, a peach tree requires severe pruning, and the forming fruit needs thinning. Leave a space of 5 or 6 inches between fruits to help them develop to their ideal size and best quality. Annual pruning and thinning not only help the tree to produce better fruit but also aid in keeping it healthy.

A word of caution: Plant only the number of peach trees that you can care for easily. Of all the orchard fruits they are perhaps the most demanding because of their pruning needs and pest problems, and even a partly neglected tree will be a great disappointment.

Harvesting

If you grow your own peaches, you can especially revel in your harvest, because not only can you get better-flavored peaches than commercial growers, but you can also pick them at the best possible time. Although peaches are often picked slightly green for cooking, like the plum they are best when fully ripe, as I found out when I ate my first perfect peach.

When the fruit comes off the limb with a slight, gentle twist, the peaches are ready, and after a little experience you'll pick each one like a connoisseur. Always handle them carefully and never yank them from the tree, because tree-ripened peaches bruise extremely easily and damaged fruit rots quickly.

If you plan to store your peaches, keep them in a cool place, such as a refrigerator, cool basement, or root cellar. In a warm room they continue to ripen and soon spoil. Each of us has a favorite peach dish. Shortcake, pie, cobbler, and salads abound when peaches are in season, and I don't know of anyone who would refuse a fresh peach pie, sundae, milkshake, or ice cream. Since nobody wants to be without peaches for long, we preserve them in jams, conserves, butters, chutneys, and pickles. Some people even dry them. Though most cultivars can be frozen, the flavor and consistency are usually better when they are canned.

Diseases and Insects

The preventative measures and spray program in Chapter 9 will effectively control the diseases that afflict peaches. They are susceptible to brown rot and many of the other diseases that affect plums, plus a few of their own, such as the following:

Powdery mildew. A gray-white, velvety, powderlike substance that covers the leaves and twigs. Prune away the infected parts as soon as you spot the mildew, and apply a fungicide immediately, before it gets worse.

Leaf curl. Early in the season the leaves curl up, turn yellow, and finally fall off. A lime-sulfur spray has long been used to control this ailment, but the newer fungicides are more effective. Apply them in early spring.

Most insects are not a great threat, luckily, because the delicate peach is less able to resist insects and disease than most other fruits. Here are some of the most likely:

San José scale and **Plum curculio.** Control these insects by using the spray program in Chapter 9.

Tree borer. Check now and then to make sure that this creature isn't a tenant in your orchard. These large, fat grubs have such a hearty appetite that even one can bore into the trunk at near-ground level or just below, eat out the wood, and cause the tree to tip over. If you see a pile of jelly-like excretion and sawdust at the base of the tree, cut out the grub with a knife or kill it by ramming it with a stiff wire. After you're sure of its demise, seal the wound with a tree compound or dressing to prevent weather and rot from entering and further deteriorating the tree.

Cultivars

Compared to pears and apples, peaches are not long-lived trees, so you must make new plantings more frequently than you need to with other tree fruits. On the positive side, newer and better cultivars are constantly being developed and introduced, so your new plantings may be even better than the old. Check catalogs from nurseries that grow trees suitable for your area. Also study the bulletins supplied by your local Extension Service (see Appendix). The following lists may help you choose trees for specific purposes:

For canning: GOLDEN JUBILEE, HALE HAVEN, JUNE ELBERTA, RED HAVEN

For freezing: ELBERTA, FAIRHAVEN, GOLDEN JUBILEE, HALE HAVEN, REDHAVEN

Trees with somewhat frost-resistant fruit buds: CANADIAN HARMONY, CANDOR, HARBELLE, HARBINGER, HARBRITE, HARKEN, MADISON, RED HAVEN, and also a series of Virginia developments called the Presidential Series, including HARRISON, MONROE, TYLER, ZACHARY TAYLOR, and others

For areas with warm winters (zones 8–9): DESERT GOLD, EARLIGRAND, FLORDAHOME, FLORDAPRINCE, JEWELL, KEYSTONE, RED GLOBE, REDSKIN, RIO GRANDE, SAM HOUSTON, SOUTHLAND, and SUWANEE

The following are listed according to their season of ripening.

CULTIVARS FOR ZONES 5–8

VERY EARLY

EARLIGLO. Yellow flesh, one of the best-quality early peaches. Vigorous and fairly hardy tree.

FINGERLAKES S.H. High quality, fairly hardy red.

GOLDEN JUBILEE. Yellow with red blush. Freestone. Productive and vigorous tree.

MIKADO. Yellow, clingstone, fair quality. Good tree vigor, productive, needs cross-pollination.

RED HAVEN. High quality, red with yellow flesh. Fairly hardy.

RELIANCE. Medium size, yellow flesh, good quality, early ripening. One of the hardiest peaches. Developed at the University of New Hampshire.

ROCHESTER. Old favorite, long ripening season, vigorous.

STARK'S EARLY WHITE GIANT. White flesh. Disease-resistant tree.

VALIANT. Yellow with red blush. Freestone, round, good quality, productive.

MIDSEASON

CRESTHAVEN. High quality, yellow with red blush, nearly fuzzless. Vigorous tree, self-pollinating.

EARLY CRAWFORD. Yellow, medium size, freestone. Tree not very hardy, needs pollinator.

ELBERTA. Yellow, freestone, fair quality. Vigorous and productive tree but lacks hardiness.

HALE HAVEN. Yellow with blush, fine quality, freestone. Attractive, vigorous, fairly hardy tree.

J.H. HALE. Good size and fine quality, nearly fuzzless, clingstone. Good for all peach uses. Needs pollinator.

LATE

AFTERGLOW. Large fruit, good quality. Tree is vigorous and productive.

Nectarines

If you've noticed that the scientific name for the nectarine is the same as that of the peach, you might conclude there was a mistake. Actually, botanists can't find any real differences between the two trees. Only the fruit is different — the nectarine is simply a peach without the fuzz. It is also somewhat juicier and has a sweeter taste. Like the peach, it may have either white or yellow flesh. Nectarine pits will often grow into peach trees and peach pits into nectarine trees. The two are so alike that culture and insect and disease control, as well as pruning and harvesting, are the same for both.

Most nurseries don't offer many kinds of nectarines, and the ones they list are hardy only where the more tender peaches do well. Formerly, nectarines were seldom recommended for the home garden, but many new cultivars are easier to grow than the older kinds.

CULTIVARS FOR PLANTING IN THE EAST, ZONES 5–8

FLAMING GOLD, HUNTER, MERICREST, NECTACREST, STARK DELICIOUS, STARK RED GOLD, SUNGLO, and SURE CROP. HARDIRED is considered one of the hardiest.

MOST OFTEN GROWN ON THE WEST COAST IN ZONES 7 AND 8

DIXIE, GOLDMINE, JOHN RIVERS, MABEL PIONEER, and SILVER LODE. (Some of these are worth trying in zone 6.)

FOR ZONE 9 AND OTHER FROST-FREE AREAS

COLUMBIA, SUNGEM, and SUN RED

CHAPTER 19

The Apricot
(Prunus armeniaca)

As a young boy on a Vermont farm, the only apricots I ever saw were dried and came from white paper boxes. They were one of the few foods we bought at the store and, like raisins, salmon, and cornflakes, were treats and a change from our homegrown diet.

Not everyone likes the taste of the apricot. Many people, in fact, have never eaten one that is fresh and tree-ripened, so they may not be sure whether they like them or not. Most of the commercially grown apricots are raised on the West Coast and canned or dried before they are shipped to the rest of the country.

The apricot got its start in China many centuries ago. It apparently reached Rome by the first century, and by the early 1700s was growing and thriving in Virginia. Presently, the Soviet Union is the world's leading producer, and several hardy varieties that have originated there have extended apricot growing into the northern parts of North America where it had never before been possible to grow them. Because apricots bloom very early, the flowers are often hurt by late frost, however.

Only in recent years has the apricot become popular as a homegrown fruit. The noted horticulturist U. P. Hedrick, in his well-known book *Fruits for the Home Garden* (1944), scarcely mentions them. Now that their growing range is so greatly enlarged, many amateur orchardists are discovering and enjoying their own tree-ripened apricots. Much about this fruit, including its flavor, resembles the peach. The trees are ornamental and well shaped, and tend to bloom early in the spring. Soil requirements, pruning, and spraying are the same for both fruits. Culture and harvesting are also similar.

Apricots grow easily from seed, and many of the seedlings produce very good fruit. Moorpark, one of the most popular varieties, has spawned so many seedlings that closely resemble it that nowadays it's difficult to be certain what is a true Moorpark. You'll have to be patient, though, if you plan to grow the fruit from seed. A small, grafted tree may produce a few fruits in only a couple of years, but a seedling quite likely will take many years and be quite large before it produces a single fruit.

Apricots are usually grafted on peach, nectarine, or apricot seedlings, but sometimes plum seedlings are used to make them more suited for growing in cool, northern soils. Like the peach, they tend to grow very fast and usually live only a few decades. Most nurseries offer only standard-size varieties, although a few sell dwarf varieties grafted on *Prunus besseyi,* the same dwarfing stock used for plums and peaches.

Because apricot trees, like peaches, grow fast, be careful not to overfeed them. Excessive growth results in a weak tree that can be easily damaged by disease, insects, and sudden temperature changes.

Harvesting

Allow apricots to ripen on the tree, because once they are picked, their sugar content does not increase. When they are ripe, they have a beautiful blush but are still firm to the touch. Although they are not quite as tender as their peach cousins, they bruise rather easily, so be careful not to poke them or throw them around.

Ripe apricots are delicious to eat right off the tree and cooked in any number of ways — from marmalade to mousse. They are sometimes frozen raw, but freezing toughens the skin so you should peel them first. More often they are canned in syrup or dried. They are one of the best fruits for drying and are good for winter snacks or to use in granola, breads, or the paper-thin confections called leathers. Last but not least, they make wonderful preserves. One of the best spreads we've ever had on toast is homemade apricot jam.

Diseases and Insects

The problems that beset apricot trees are very much like those that affect the peach, and the controls listed in Chapter 9 are usually adequate. Ordinarily, apricots are slightly more resistant than peaches to insects and diseases, and if you practice good sanitation methods they may need little or no spraying. Some of the hardier cultivars are also less troubled by late winter frost damage to the fruit buds.

Cultivars

Apricot cultivars do not vary tremendously except in their hardiness. Most are suitable for planting only where summer seasons are long and winters are relatively mild — zones 6–8. Many cultivars are at least somewhat self-fertile, but nurseries usually advise planting two or more kinds for better crops.

Popular apricots for the Southwest and West Coast in zones 6–8

Blenheim, Hungarian Rose, Moorpark, Perfection, Tilton, and Wenatchee

Frequently planted in the East in zones 5–8

Goldcot, Henderson, Hungarian Rose, South Haven, and Stark Earli-Orange

Hardiest cultivars of all

Moongold and Sungold from Minnesota, Andy's Delight and Scout from Canada, and Manchu from South Dakota are all being grown in zone 5 and sheltered parts of zone 4. Sungold and Moongold should be planted near each other for best pollination. Seedlings from hardy fruits often produce worthwhile trees for the colder zones, too.

CHAPTER 20

The Quince
(Cydonia oblonga)

When the word quince is mentioned, it usually doesn't create much enthusiasm among home gardeners. Few claim it for their favorite fruit or describe it in the superlatives used for the apple, plum, peach, pear, or cherry. Some even maintain it shouldn't be dignified by calling it a fruit. Yet it is widely grown in the warmer areas of North America, and it has admirers who praise it highly. If you want to have a complete orchard and add variety to your fruit diet, and if quince will grow in your climate, you'll probably want to plant a tree. Greeks and Romans regarded the quince as a health food and gave it much more respect than it generally gets nowadays.

The fruit is shaped like a small pear, the flesh is firm, and the skin is covered with a slight fuzz. It has both an unusual flavor and scent. The odor is so pronounced, in fact, that it is never wise to put it in the refrigerator or leave it near other fruits, because they will soon take on the same smell. Perhaps that is why it is little grown commercially and rarely found in stores or fruit markets.

Some people plant the tree for its attractive appearance rather than for its fruit. The well-behaved trees are small — usually not over 15 feet tall — and have a rather twisted habit of growth. They bloom late in the season, after the apples, so there's not much danger of frost damage.

Culture

Usually quince trees are budded or grafted on quince seedlings or on special Angus-Quince rootstocks. If you are patient, it is also possible to start them from cuttings or by layering them.

Grow them much the same as you would pears, but keep in mind that they are suitable only for zones 6–8. They thrive in similar soils and, unfortunately, have the same susceptibility to fire blight. Although they are slow-growing trees, do not over-fertilize them since this makes them even more vulnerable to fire blight.

Unlike most other fruit trees, quince can grow and produce well year after year with little pruning, although you should remove crossed limbs and any dead or diseased wood. Quinces are bothered by the same diseases and insects that strike pear trees, so if they have problems, follow the suggestions in Chapter 9 for pest control.

It is not necessary to plant two different cultivars, since quinces are one of the few tree fruits that are truly self-pollinating. Also, the trees are so productive that one tree can easily supply all the fruit that an average family needs.

Harvesting

Even if the trees were hardy everywhere, quinces ripen so late that most northern gardeners could never get them to ripen. The fruits should stay on the tree until they have turned deep yellow, developed their strong odor, and can be easily snapped off. Ripening takes place as early as mid-October in some areas, but it is more often well into November.

Handle the fruits with great care because they bruise easily. They will keep in a cool place for a month or more, and it is best to store them in shallow trays where there will be no weight resting on them.

The fruit is seldom eaten raw, even though the cultivar Pineapple was especially developed for that purpose. Most are cooked into jellies, preserves, marmalades, or a sauce that is mixed with applesauce. Some people are devotees of the quince custard pie they remember from childhood. Others enjoy quince ginger, quince honey, or quinces baked and served with whipped cream. The fruits are also delicious canned or spiced. Because of their high pectin content, they are often combined in jellies with berries or grapes that are low in pectin.

Cultivars

ORANGE is the cultivar most likely to be listed in nursery catalogs. PINEAPPLE has the most agreeable flavor when eaten raw but is seldom available, except on the West Coast. Both are best suited for zones 6–8.

CHAMPION, JUMBO, SMYRNA, and VAN DEMAN are all offered by various nurseries and are also suitable for zones 6–8, although they might also be worth a trial in those sections of zone 5 that have a long growing season.

Flowering Quinces

Some gardeners confuse the flowering quince *(Chaenomeles japonica* or *Chaenomeles speciosa)* with the eating quinces *(Cydonia oblonga)*. Flowering quinces are small trees or shrubs used as ornamentals and hedges. They grow up to 6 feet tall and have beautiful flowers ranging from white to bright red.

Because orchard and ornamental quinces are closely related, the fruits of both can be used for preserves, although those of the flowering kinds are small, ripen poorly, and are of inferior quality.

Flowering quinces are more hardy than their orchard-type cousins, although in zone 3 they may grow only 1 or 2 feet high and the fruits seldom ripen.

CHAPTER 21

The Cherry —
Sweet *(Prunus avium)*
and Sour *(Prunus cerasus)*

In school one year we read a book about some English children who had a great many adventures, most of which, I'm sure, were exciting. But the only thing I remember about their exploits was how, on summer mornings, the boys climbed out the upstairs window of their big house into a monstrous cherry tree and ate the giant sweet cherries. That made a big impression on me, and I decided that someday I would have a tree just like that.

Over the years I've planted lots of cherry trees, but most never got over 8 feet tall and only a few reached 10 feet. Even a small child couldn't climb to the second floor in one of them, and we picked most of our cherries while standing on the ground.

The cherry trees in which the English children climbed to such great heights were sweet cherries, probably grafted on Mazzard roots. Because we couldn't grow those in our climate, I was raising sour cherries, which are naturally smaller trees anyway, and they were grafted on an even more dwarfing rootstock, the Mahaleb.

Although I never did climb in a cherry tree — and now I've quite lost interest in doing so anyway — I do love the taste of ripe cherries, sweet or sour. Not only are they one of the most beautiful fruits, but when fully ripe they are scrumptious. Now, thanks to experiment station research, there are cultivars that can grow in almost every fruit garden.

Most of us are familiar with some sort of cherry since wild cherries grow in nearly every region of North America. The black cherry, chokecherry, sand cherry, and bird cherry are all used for jelly and they are also devoured raw by birds and kids. They are valued, too, for their blossoms, because in many areas they are the first trees to bloom in the spring. Most cherry cultivars that are grown in orchards and gardens today originated in Europe. Thousands have been developed and named, although only a few of these are presently being propagated commercially.

▲ There are so many kinds of cherries that one variety or another can be grown almost anywhere. *(USDA)*

When you shop for cherry trees, you'll find two main groups of cultivated cherries — the sweet and the sour — and one lesser group, the Dukes. The sour or tart cherries, often called pie cherries because that's where so many of them are destined, have the widest growing range. Most are about as hardy as the Baldwin and Delicious apples. Sour cherries are the most widely grown types in home orchards in the eastern U.S. and Canada, and even commercially they have a slight edge over the sweet cherries in total production. Although called "sour," most varieties are delicious raw when they are fully ripe. Only the English Morellos are used almost entirely for cooking.

The sweet cherry group includes many more cultivars than the sour and has about the same growing range as the peach. They are either firm-fleshed or soft-fleshed, and delicious when eaten directly from the tree. The Dukes, thought to be crosses between the two, are somewhat more hardy than the sweets, but not as hardy as the sour cherries.

Still another group, the bush cherries, are quite different from orchard cherries, even though the fruit somewhat resembles them. These are very hardy and can be grown even in the coldest parts of the country. NANKING, OKA, SAPA, and SAPALTA are some of these.

Rootstocks

Cherries, like the other stone fruits, can be grafted interchangeably upon other cherry roots or on those of plum, peach, or apricot trees. Nursery-grown trees are usually budded on a semi-dwarf, native European, wild sour cherry called Mahaleb. Although inferior to the Mazzard, a wild, European sweet cherry, nurseries prefer to bud graft on the Mahaleb because they like the uniform, saleable-size trees that result. Other rootstocks sometimes used are the Damil, from Belgium, which produces a semi-dwarf tree that does well on wet soils; Colt, a semi-dwarf from England; and the Western sand cherry, *Prunus besseyi,* the same rootstock used for dwarf plums and peaches. These compact trees are perfect for small lots and ideal for planting in pots or tubs.

Pollination

Sour cherries are self-fruitful, and one alone can produce fruit. Sweet cherries always require two different kinds, and sometimes three, for good pollination. For example, Napoleon and Emperor Francis cannot pollinate each other (probably royal rivalry), so a third kind is needed. Sweet and sour cherries cannot be counted on to pollinate each other, partly because they bloom at slightly different times. Nor can the other stone fruits, such as cherry plums, satisfactorily pollinate cherries. The Dukes, however, are able to pollinate other Dukes and any of the sweet cherries.

Culture

Sweet cherry trees do best when planted in light, sandy soils similar to those preferred by peach trees. Sour cherries can withstand heavier, cooler soils, and more extremes in weather. Because none of the cherries are deep-rooted, droughts are hard on them, particularly when the trees are planted in light soil. All fruit trees need careful planting, but cherries require special care because their roots dry out so easily. *Never* let the roots get dry when you are planting them, and keep the trees adequately watered until they begin to grow well. They thrive under thick, cool mulches.

Cherries need less pruning than most other fruit trees. Removing the broken, crossed, and dead limbs may be all that's necessary for the first seven or eight years. Later on, thin out some of the old bearing wood each year to gradually renew the tree and to permit more sunlight to enter the tree so the fruit will ripen better. Cherries, like plums and apricots, bear their fruit on short, blunt spurs. Don't remove these spurs unless they appear old or are too numerous.

Cherry trees need very little fertilizer, and, if the soil is in good condition, you may not need to add any. Overfeeding will produce a tree that grows too fast, bears poorly, and is more susceptible to disease.

Unlike plums, never use cherry trees as "fillers" between the permanent trees in an apple or peach orchard. Cherries ripen during the summer when spraying may be necessary on other fruits.

Birds love cherries more than any other orchard fruits, and are probably the grower's biggest problem. We growers have worked out many ingenious methods to thwart these same feathered flyers that we value so highly when they're eating bugs. It may discourage some thievery to plant the trees near your home where you can better keep watch over them. Noisemakers are sometimes helpful, too, if your family and neighbors can stand the explosions. Gardeners also use scarecrows, stuffed owls, plastic snakes, and other contraptions. Some desperate growers use netting; others have even built large chicken-wire cages around their cherry trees. I have heard that it helps to plant mulberry trees nearby, because some birds seem to prefer them, but I have never tried it. Some orchardists try to outwit the birds by planting yellow cherries, thinking the birds will wait for them to ripen and turn red. But birds are no fools, at least not for long.

Diseases

Although cherries are subject to most of the diseases that bother the plum, including black knot and brown rot, many home orchardists never spray their cherry trees and have no problems at all. Brown rot is more common during wet years, and the treatment for both diseases is the same as for plums. (See Chapter 9.)

Just as many plum trees are infected with a variety of deadly virus diseases, many cherry trees are grafted on roots that are contaminated. The virus spreads throughout the tree and by the time it has produced for a dozen years or so a few limbs have begun to wilt and die. Often, within two or three years the tree is dead. This problem has been particularly devastating in the Northeast in recent years. Buy virus-resistant or virus-free trees if at all possible, and isolate them from infected trees.

Insects

Tent caterpillars, which are apt to appear on almost anything, are about the only insect that has ever attacked our sour cherry trees. We simply cut off the huge, webbed clusters and burn them as soon as they appear. We have been lucky, though, because the same insects that bother the plum can also strike the cherry, and a few additional pests favor the cherry. One, the cherry maggot, operates in much the same way as the apple maggot, laying eggs inside the fruit which hatch and cause wormy cherries.

Since in your home orchard you will probably have only a few cherry trees, you can thwart most insects by following the sanitary methods described in Chapter 9. When necessary, use the suggested spray program in the same chapter, but be sure to follow all the directions on the package and stop all spraying the specified number of days before harvest.

Frost Damage

Even if you choose cherry cultivars that are suitable for your climate, winter damage may still occur, and it is often mistaken for disease. Although the damage may have occurred during the winter, the splitting and loosening of the bark may not be noticeable until spring. To prevent winter damage, avoid any unnecessary pruning and fertilizing that might overstimulate growth. If injury occurs, repair it immediately. Tack loose bark back on the tree, and seal all wounds with tree paint to protect them from weather and bacterial infection.

Like other Temperate Zone fruits, cherries need a chilling period of several weeks in the winter in order to grow satisfactorily. If you garden in the frost-free or nearly frost-free parts of the country, you are likely to have trouble growing either the sweet or sour kinds.

Harvesting

There's no question the birds that steal cherries have good taste, so don't let the pirates get them all. Cherries are delicious, and among human aficionados there are few leftovers when they are ripe. Their size, color, taste, and ease of "pull" from the branch will tell you when they are ready to pick. The longer you leave sour cherries on the tree, the sweeter they'll become, but be sure to pick them before their skins crack, and leave the stems on the fruits.

Picking cherries is easy and fun. You can pile them in a container without harming fruit, but use them soon after picking because they keep only a short time. (In a refrigerator the firm sweet cherries should keep from two to three weeks, but the soft sweet kinds and the sour ones last only about a week.) If you have a surplus, there are 101 different ways to use them. There are few people whose mouths don't water at the mention of fresh-baked, homemade cherry pie, and cherries can also be frozen, canned, dried, or made into relish, juice, and preserves. At your favorite ice cream parlor you're likely to find a beautiful red maraschino cherry resting on top of your ice cream sundae. The maraschino is simply a sour cherry that has been processed in brine, with a dose of artificial color and preservatives added. At home we prefer to use a less colorful, but equally tasty frozen one for our desserts.

Cultivars

Although new cherry cultivars do not appear as frequently as new apples and peaches, there is a wide choice. Here are a few that are readily available:

Sweet Cherries
Zones 5–8

Bing. Dark red, firm, aromatic. Ripens midseason. Needs a pollinator.

Black Tartarian. Good home cherry. Medium-size, high-quality fruit. Productive tree.

Emperor Francis. Good home cherry. Red, firm, superior flavor. Ripens late. Tree is disease-resistant, productive, less fussy about soils than most sweet cherries.

Kristin. More hardy than most other sweet cherry trees; black fruits, about 1 inch in diameter.

Napoleon (Royal Ann). Yellow with red blush, large, high-quality fruit. Tree productive, but not very hardy.

Schmidt's Bigarreau. Fancy, firm-fleshed, crack-resistant. Good, productive tree.

Stark Gold. Rot-resistant fruit. Vigorous tree. Among the hardiest sweet cherries.

Stark Lambert. An improved Lambert. Huge size fruit, but cracks in wet weather. One of the hardier varieties.

Venus. Excellent home cherry. Red inside and out. Crack-resistant. Tree very productive.

Vista. Early, high-quality, home-type cherry. Tree not particularly productive.

Windsor. Late, black-fleshed. Needs less spraying and is more hardy than most sweet cherry trees.

Duke Cherries
Zones 5–8

Late Duke and May Duke. Later and earlier versions of the Royal Duke.

Olivet. Dark red. Good tree growth and productivity.

Reine Hortense. Pale red, large, showy, fine-flavored fruit, but tree may not bear every year.

Royal Duke. Large, dark fruit in midseason. Productive tree.

Sour Cherries
Zones 4–7, unless otherwise noted

Early Richmond. One of the hardiest old-time pie cherries. Fair quality. Not good in warm climates.

English Morello. Very dark red, late, good quality. Good for cooking and preserving.

Meteor. New, extra-hardy dwarf red. Especially good for northern home gardens. Worth a trial in milder sections of zone 3.

Montmorency. The most commonly planted, best-known red sour cherry. Excellent for home use.

North Star. Very hardy dwarf cherry tree with red fruit. Worth a trial in zone 3.

Suda. Hardy, dark red, Morello-type, late. Good for home use.

CHAPTER 22

The Small Fruits

One wintry evening when we were sitting by the fire making our spring gardening plans, we decided to check over the list of what we had put into the freezer the previous season. We were surprised to find that a large percentage of our frozen food crop consisted of small fruits.

We begin our annual freezing sessions in the springtime with rhubarb, which isn't technically a fruit but tastes like one and has many of the same dessert qualities. In early summer we pick and freeze strawberries, by midsummer the gooseberries, currants, raspberries, and blueberries are ready, and finally, in early fall, the elderberries and tree fruits.

Even if we wanted to, we wouldn't be able to buy all the different kinds of berries we harvest each year. Where could we find yellow and purple raspberries, black currants, elderberries, jostaberries, and red gooseberries for sale? Even fresh red raspberries and strawberries are not easy to find in our area, and when available, they are expensive and in less than perfect condition. As it is, the small fruits cost us very little money and take far less work than our vegetable garden. We feel that the convenience of having them in our own backyard, and their undeniably superior flavors more than offset the work of growing them.

Hopefully, you won't have to make a choice between growing tree fruits and small fruits, but if you do, the latter have certain advantages. They take up little space, need a minimum of care and fertilizer, and the initial cost is small. Once planted, they bear quickly and abundantly, and most go on producing for decades. Many berries are a good cash crop for a bit of extra income, too.

Small fruits are available at most nurseries and garden centers. It is not always a good idea to accept gift plants from a generous neighbor even though strawberries, blackberries, and raspberries are frequently offered, since they create new plants at a fast rate. You might reason that you'd save money and get freshly dug plants as well, which, if they grow well for your neighbor, should do likewise for you. The trouble with gift plants is that you are likely to acquire with them a variety of diseases and insects that will give you a peck of trouble ever after. Nurseries go to a great deal of care to grow disease-free plants, and if you start with a bug-free, disease-free berry patch, your future problems will be far fewer.

▲ Though a fairly new fruit in cultivation, blueberries are becoming more popular with gardeners each year. *(USDA)*

When you select small fruits, just as with fruit trees, it is important to buy plants that are suited for your climate. Berries that have been developed especially for one region are often unsuitable in another, even if climatic differences seem slight. Luckily, experimenters in each section of temperate United States and Canada have been introducing new cultivars for many years, and there are now plants that are suitable for you to grow whether you live on the North Carolina seacoast or on a prairie in Manitoba. Experimenting is fun, but if you are counting on a crop, plant the cultivars you are certain will produce in your corner of the world. Add lots of compost or manure (15 pounds dried or 10 bushels fresh per 100 square feet) to your soil, work it in well, and get rid of all grass and weeds. Prepare the soil as thoroughly for your bed of small fruits as you would for a vegetable or flower garden. It should be rich, loose, and crumbly, so the roots will be able to start growing as soon as you set the plants in.

When you plant small fruits, be careful not to crowd them. Raspberries, blackberries, and elderberries all sucker badly, so don't plant them near a vegetable garden, strawberry patch, or flower bed. The best location is a place where you can mow around the bed or have some other certain way to keep the plants under control. Plant them a good distance apart from shade trees with large roots, too, and away from fruit trees that may need spraying during the summer when the berries are ripening.

Continue to give your small fruits attention every year. Many books say that a raspberry patch can produce berries for ten years, but we are still picking bushels of fruit each year from a patch set thirty years ago, and there is no sign of its retirement. Some of our currant, gooseberry, and elderberry plants are even older. Some people report that theirs have gone on for half a century. It's the care you give them that makes the difference in both productivity and longevity.

How Many?

The number of plants you grow will depend on the size of your family and their preferences, whether you intend to preserve the fruit or not, and how much room you have available for planting. Here is a suggested berry garden for a family of four that plans to freeze or otherwise process some of the fruit. It is only a suggestion, of course, and whatever you choose could be quite different.

Number of Plants	Feet apart in row	Feet between rows	Yield
8 blackberry	3	6–7	16 pints
4 blueberry	5–6	6–8	50 pints
4 currant	5	6–8	10 pints
4 elderberry	5	8–10	10 pints
4 gooseberry	5	6–8	12 pints
10 black or purple raspberry	3	6	50 pints
40 red raspberry	2–3	6	70–80 pints
10 yellow or everbearing raspberry	2–3	6	20–30 pints
25–40 strawberry	2	3–4	25–40 quarts

CHAPTER 23

Bramble Fruits —
The Raspberry
and the Blackberry
(Rubus spp.*)*

We're lucky to have enough land to grow lots of fruits, but I'm sure that if we had room for only one kind, we would choose the red raspberry. The year that porcupines cut off our canes and ate them we were most unhappy, because the loss of that long row of raspberries meant there would be a sharp cut in the amount of fruit in our winter diet. Now we keep a close watch for the prickly pillagers every spring.

One evening we invited some friends for dessert and served raspberry pie á la mode. One gentleman declined saying he didn't like raspberries. We were shocked, because nearly everybody we know loves them, and many people want to know how to grow them. Luckily, raspberries are one of the easiest fruits to grow. The plants usually produce a big crop the third year after planting, and big annual crops after that are almost certain. We expect each foot of row to produce at least a pint of berries during the season, and they seldom fail to live up to our expectations.

Raspberries have lots of other good qualities to recommend them as a home fruit. They blossom late, so spring frosts never ruin the crop. The diseases and insects that trouble them are easy to control if you buy virus-free and virus-resistant plants. They need little care and, last but not least, they are easy to pick without much bending. In my opinion, the raspberry is a near-perfect fruit. Someone else might prefer the rich-tasting blackberry or dewberry, other popular bramble fruits. Equally prolific, reliable, and useful, they, like raspberries, can be counted on to live for many years. You can often find them growing wild in many areas, if you don't have the space to grow them.

You might think that a plant as vigorous as the blackberry would thrive anywhere, but when a friend of ours set in a dozen plants a few years ago, he was surprised and disappointed. The plants barely grew at all on his side of the fence,

▲ Because they bear heavily, they are little trouble, and their fruit is so tasty, red raspberries are a favorite with home fruit growers. *(USDA)*

but the roots slithered over into the adjoining yard and soon his neighbor, with no work or expense whatever, had a blackberry patch that was the envy of the neighborhood. Particularly envious was the man who had bought the plants and done the planting. It was one of those hard-to-explain mysteries in the plant-grower's world.

Unlike almost every other fruit in our diet, blackberries are somewhat constipating, so they are a good complement to the more laxative fruits that ripen at the same time. Even the leaves produce this effect, and a tea made from them is an old-time remedy for dysentery.

Classes of Raspberries

Red raspberries are by far the most familiar bramble, and a few people refuse to eat a raspberry of any other color. The reds come in both one-crop and two-crop varieties. The one-crop type bears fruit that matures in midsummer on canes that have grown the previous season. After bearing, the canes die within a few weeks. Two-crop raspberries are often called "everbearers," which they really aren't. Instead, they bear once during the summer on canes grown the previous year and an additional crop in the fall on canes grown the current year.

Yellow raspberries are closely related to the reds and vary in color from yellow to pale pink. These are so fragile they are seldom seen in stores. They are ideal for home gardens, however, and many fruit lovers regard the ripe yellow raspberry as the finest fruit in the world. A handful of them tossed together with a few red and black raspberries makes an elegant dessert.

Black raspberries have an unusual flavor that many people like very much, although others don't care for the slightly musky aroma and taste. Their growth habits differ from red raspberries in that, unlike the reds, they never produce suckers. Instead, they start new plants when their long canes bend over and the tips touch the soil, form roots, and grow into a new plant.

Purple raspberries, such as Sodus, are closely related to the blacks, with a similar flavor and growth habit. Other purple raspberries, such as Brandywine and Royalty, behave more like the reds and send up suckers the same way.

Classes of Blackberries

Blackberries come in three types: the *upright,* the *semi-upright,* and the *trailing kinds,* called dewberries. The growth habit of the upright is very similar to that of the red raspberry. Dewberries, however, resemble black raspberries in that they don't form suckers. Their canes grow long and vinelike, trail on the ground unless supported, and form new plants by tip layers. The semi-uprights share some of the characteristics of both the uprights and dewberries.

Hardiness

Many of the red and yellow raspberry cultivars are hardy far north in Canada. Others have been developed for zones 5 through 8. Black and purple raspberries are slightly less hardy, although some cultivars are suitable for zone 3. Most fall-bearing raspberries are winter-hardy, but in zones 3 and 4, many of them often fail to ripen their second crop before the early frosts.

Most blackberry cultivars have hardy roots. Their canes are not as hardy as raspberries, however, and are apt to die to the ground over the winter in cold climates. Few nurseries carry the older, hardy kinds anymore, so growers in cold areas may have trouble locating a blackberry that will produce fruit. Snyder, an old-time, hardy one, is still being sold, but, unfortunately, its size and quality are inferior to modern blackberries. Northern growers sometimes find some of the old cultivars on abandoned farms and transplant these to their gardens.

Trailing blackberries are even more tender, and most are suitable only in zone 6 and warmer climates. Lucretia, one of the hardier varieties, is worth a trial in zone 5, but like the other dewberries it needs a long growing season to properly harden its lush new growth before the first fall frost.

Planting Brambles

First, prepare the ground thoroughly, as described on page 164. Since red raspberries and blackberries sucker so badly, locate the planting where you can control the "volunteer" plants that spring from the vigorous roots. The upright blackberries need even more isolation from other plantings, because their long roots will send up suckers many feet from the parent plants. Separate black and purple raspberries from red and yellow raspberries by 100 feet or more, because the former often have a virus that can spread to the red and yellow cultivars, even though they may not noticeably bother the blacks and purples.

Mail-order plants are usually shipped bare-rooted and may be dry when they arrive. Unwrap them as soon as possible and soak their roots for several hours in a tub of water.

If you purchase your plants from a local nursery or garden center, they may be either bare-rooted or growing in small pots. The potted ones, although more expensive, will get off to a faster start because of their established root system. If you can find the kind you want in pots, therefore, these are worth the extra money, unless you are planting a large number of them.

Set raspberry and blackberry plants 2 feet apart, and, if you have more than one row, space the rows at least 6 feet apart. Set each plant to the same depth as it grew originally in the ground or pot. Soak the soil heavily with water to which you have added a weak solution of liquid fertilizer. Make sure that each plant sits in a muddy mixture and is free of any air pockets around the roots. Continue to water the newly set plants thoroughly every two or three days for three weeks unless it rains heavily, and, once a week, use the liquid fertilizer solution. Water is cheap fruit insurance.

If you use potted plants, no pruning at planting time is necessary. With bare-rooted plants, however, it is most important that you cut back the canes to 2 inches above the ground after you set them in. If you do not cut back the canes, the tops will start to grow, and there will not be enough corresponding root growth to support them. The result will then be a weak plant that is likely to give up entirely or take years to recover. Plants that have been cut back will not produce any berries the first year, but the idea is to develop a lot of canes that will produce heavily the third year.

Mulching

Grass and weeds can be one of the worst enemies of your brambles. They compete with the plants for nutrients, limit their growth, reduce production, and give the berry patch a messy, unkempt appearance. Since rototilling or hoeing can easily damage the bramble roots, heavy mulching is a better way to control grass and nourish your plants at the same time.

Thick layers of shredded bark, leaves, shavings, or wood chips are all excellent mulches for brambles. Sawdust packs too tightly and steals nitrogen from the soil. Several inches of mulch will provide enough shade to suffocate sprouting weed and grass seeds, yet the new berry canes will push through it easily.

Some gardeners lay black plastic, cardboard, newspapers, or sheets of old metal roofing or fiberglass between the rows and cover it with wood chips. This prevents the growth of sucker plants and weeds. Never use roofing paper, though, because the tar or asphalt isn't good for plants.

Support

As I said earlier, the trailing dewberries must be tied to a wire fence or some other support during the growing and fruiting season, but you can leave them on the ground over the winter, and mulch them if you fear winter damage.

You will probably also need to provide some means of support to keep raspberries and upright-growing blackberries from falling over. Some berry growers tie the canes to stakes or posts placed every 3 feet along the row (see page 171, top). Others put up a fence consisting of strands of smooth wire on each side of the row (see page 171, bottom). Still others never provide any support for the plants but simply cut back the canes to a height of 4 or 5 feet in late fall. The resulting canes are then stiff and less likely to bend over. Whether you give any support to your plants or not may depend on the growth habit of the kind you grow. The short- growing Newburgh raspberry is less likely to need staking than the taller-growing Royalty and Latham.

Pruning

If you neglect cutting out the old canes in your bramble patch each year, the planting will deteriorate rapidly. Both raspberries and blackberries have roots that are perennial, but their canes are biennial. The roots of these plants live for many years, but each cane sprouts and grows to its full height in one year, bears fruit the following year, then dies immediately. Neglected raspberries and blackberries become a jungle of dead canes after a few years, and both fruit size and quantity will suffer.

To keep your patch productive, cut each dead cane to ground level after it has finished bearing. You'll recognize the dead ones by their pallid color and brittle appearance. Hand-held clippers are ideal tools for this job, and you'll probably want to wear thick gloves to handle the thorny canes. Because insects and disease enjoy wintering over in the old canes, remove them to the local landfill or burn them as soon as possible.

As your berry patch ages, you will find that more pruning becomes necessary because the plants produce too many new canes each year. Cut off all the weak new canes when you remove the old ones, and thin out the strong, healthy canes, if they are closer together than 6 inches. Otherwise, the berries will be small and there will be fewer of them.

Keep the rows of red and yellow raspberries and upright blackberries no more than 2 feet in width, and those of black or purple raspberries and trailing

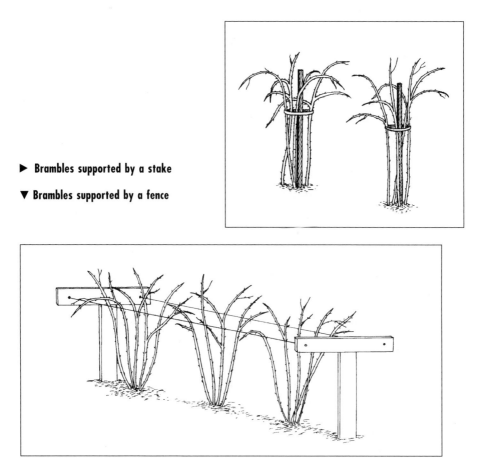

▶ **Brambles supported by a stake**

▼ **Brambles supported by a fence**

blackberries no more than a foot and a half wide. This permits easier harvesting and pruning, and also allows better air circulation, which reduces the chances of spur blight, mildew, and other diseases.

Harvesting

Raspberries ripen a few weeks before blackberries and the long ripening season of both lets you enjoy fresh picking every day for several weeks. If you want to extend the season even more, you can plant early, mid-season, and fall-bearing raspberry cultivars. Use only small pails for picking raspberries, because too many piled together will badly crush those on the bottom. For picking, we like to use a pail we can hang on our belts so we have both hands free. Avoid handling the berries any more than necessary, and move freshly picked berries out of the sun as soon as possible.

All kinds of raspberries and blackberries are delicious right off the bush. Eating them fresh as if they were candy is our favorite way to enjoy them. Some people prefer them with cream and sugar added, and, of course, nearly everyone loves berry pies, shortcakes, jellies, jams, and juice. Some of our friends swear that their homemade raspberry-rhubarb wine is the best there is.

Steps for Success in the Raspberry and Blackberry Patch

First Year
Prepare the soil carefully and plant the berries 2 feet apart. If you set out bare-rooted plants, cut the tops back to 2 inches above the ground after planting, but leave potted ones unpruned. Water both potted and bare-rooted plants thoroughly with a liquid fertilizer solution, and mulch.

Second Year
Spring. Cut back all plants that didn't make a strong showing the previous year to 2 inches above ground level. This encourages maximum cane growth for a big crop the following year. Add to the mulch, and apply a light helping of plant food.

Fall. Cut tops of plants back so canes are about 4 feet tall. This makes a stiff plant that doesn't fall over in winter's snow and wind. Install a fence or other support.

Third Year and Each Year Thereafter
Spring. Add fertilizer and fresh mulch. Trim out any broken canes. Spray with a fungicide if you spot any evidence of spur blight or anthracnose.

Early summer. Spray once more with a fungicide if any disease appears. Mow or pull out tips or sucker plants that are growing in the wrong places. Cut off and burn wilted tops as soon as they appear. Remove any sick-looking plants.

Late summer. Cut to ground level and remove all the canes that bore fruit. Cut out all weak canes, and thin remaining canes to 6 inches apart.

Late fall. Cut back canes to 4 or 5 feet in height for winter. Tighten wire supports, if necessary.

To Get the Biggest Fall Crop from Everbearers

If you are growing two-crop raspberries (everbearers) and want only a large fall crop, follow all of the procedures in the box above *except,* under "Third Year and Each Year Thereafter," add the following:

Spring. Cut *all* canes off to ground level. (This means there will be no summer crop, but the fall crop will be larger and will ripen earlier. It won't be necessary to prune off the old canes in late summer, because there won't be any.)

Diseases

Be on the lookout for the following diseases in your berry patch:

Anthracnose. This blight shows up on the cane bark as gray blotches with purple edges. Black raspberries are most susceptible. Fungicides control it.

Mosaic and other virus diseases. If you find that the leaves on your new canes are marbled green or have a greenish-yellow mottled look, a virus is likely the cause. Remove all such plants at once, because there is, as yet, no apparent cure, and both plant and fruit decrease in size each year until the bushes finally die.

Root (crown) gall. Fleshy growth on roots. Plant only certified plants in soil not previously infected with diseased plants. If the disease gets bad, dig out all the plants and start a new bed with new plants elsewhere.

Rusts. Several rusts, including orange rust, affect brambles, especially black-berries. Look for bright orange spores during the summer on the undersides of leaves and on the canes. Unfortunately, rusts are not easy to treat, and some nurseries sell infected plants. Many wild blackberries have the disease, too.

Spur blight. In the spring, when the berry patch sends out beautiful leaves that then suddenly turn yellow, and the canes die, the cause is likely to be spur blight. Since the disease affects only the old canes, new ones will replace them over the summer; but your crop for that year will be lost. The best control is to spray with a recommended fungicide in the spring just as the leaves appear, and spray again about a week later. Spray once more in late fall after you have cut out the old canes.

Verticillium wilt. The canes wilt suddenly and die, usually in midsummer. This same disease also strikes vegetable plants, maple trees, and many others. There's not much you can do about it, unfortunately, except remove the infect-ed canes and burn them. As a preventative, plant the brambles some distance from where you have grown potatoes, peppers, and tomatoes.

Insects

Although many insects may bother brambles, surprisingly few ever become serious in a home planting. The cane borer is one of the most common, and rare is the bramble grower who doesn't encounter it sooner or later. If the tops of your new canes suddenly wilt and fall over, this critter is at work. Inspection will reveal two complete circles near the top of the cane and if you open it at this point, you'll find the larva sitting there as though it had every intention of making this plant its summer career. If you leave it there undisturbed, it will bore down the cane, kill it and continue on to infect other canes, with increas-ing damage to your patch in future years. Happily, it is easy to control the borer without poisons. As soon as the wilted ends appear, simply cut them off below the bottom ring and burn them.

Aphids are spread by ants, and ants also eat berries. If you spot a nearby ant hill, soak it with an insecticide, and usually the damage will stop. Tree crickets, crown borers, sawflies, Japanese beetles, tarnished plant bugs, and raspberry beetles may attack brambles in certain areas of the country and can be especially troublesome to commercial growers. All-purpose orchard sprays control these pests when necessary, but, luckily, large bug colonies seldom show much interest in the tiny patches tended by us small-time berry growers.

Transplanting Wild Raspberries

Because the flavor of wild raspberries is so good, sometimes gardeners ask if it is practical to transplant these wild brambles to the garden. Actually, no. Native plants appear quickly in cut-over forests and provide shade for new tree seedlings to get started. The plants are apt to be short-lived, even if they are moved into a garden, mainly because they are nearly always infected with one or more of the virus diseases.

Even if they weren't infected, I feel that gardeners shouldn't pass up a century of fruit progress. It would be a shame not to take advantage of the wonderful, large, easy-to-pick cultivars, especially when the flavor of most of them is also superb. If you occasionally have a hankering for the wild ones, as my father-in-law does, you can always walk a few miles, climb over fallen logs and holes, and fight with the bears over them.

Cultivars

Raspberries

All are red, and hardy in zones 3–6, unless otherwise noted.

AMBER. Soft, pink-yellow, very sweet, high-quality fruit.
ANELMA. From Finland. Hardy, excellent-quality berries. Plants are vigorous and virus resistant.
BOYNE. Dark red, high-quality berry. Heavy bearer, vigorous.
CANBY. Thornless canes make this a favorite. Not hardy in zone 3.
CHIEF. Early variety, fairly good quality, small fruit. Recommended for Midwest.
DORMAN RED. A good raspberry for the South. Withstands heat and drought well.
HILTON. Strong canes need little support. Vigorous, productive.
LATHAM. Fairly good-quality. Susceptible to disease, so be sure to buy virus-free plants.
NEWBURGH. Good-quality. Productive and disease-resistant. Plants are short, so need little staking.
TAYLOR. Large, good-quality berries. Heavy bearer.
TITAN. Huge berries of high-quality. Of marginal hardiness in zone 3.

Two-Crop Raspberries

These are also called fall bearers and everbearers.

AUGUST RED. Good berry, but unfortunately for those in zone 3, not as early as the name implies.

Bababerry. Large, high-quality berries. Does well in the South.

Durham. Medium early, healthy, vigorous. Short canes.

Fall Gold. Good-flavored yellow.

Fall Red. One of the best two-croppers for areas with short growing seasons.

Heritage. One of the most popular cultivars for home gardens.

Indian Summer. Fair-quality, late.

Redwing. One of the best fall bearers. Early, moderately hardy, and productive.

September. Medium-early fall crop. Especially hardy plants.

Southland. High-quality, productive. Best planted in the South.

Black Raspberries

Allen. Sweet, high-quality, large berries. Vigorous plants.

Black Hawk. Early ripening, drought resistant, productive. Large berries. Good for freezing.

Bristol. Good-quality fruits. Productive, tall-growing plants, fairly resistant to mosaic.

Cumberland. A hardy old-timer, but subject to mosaic and anthracnose.

Dundee. Large, excellent-flavored fruit. Tall growing, productive.

John Robertson. One of the hardiest black raspberries, but fruit is fairly small.

Purple Raspberries

Brandywine. Tart, huge fruits with unusual flavor. Productive, hardy plants do not sucker.

Royalty. Large, high-quality fruits on vigorous, hardy plants.

Sodus. Good-quality berries. Tall-growing plants produce well and are moderately hardy.

Upright Blackberries

Darrow. Large fruits of good-quality. Tall plants produce heavily over a long season.

Early Harvest. Good-size, high-quality fruits. An old-time variety, popular in the Midwest.

Ebony King. Purplish black. A fairly hardy new variety. Good for wines as well as for eating fresh.

Snyder. Fruit small and of poor quality, but one of the hardiest.

Trailing Blackberries (Dewberries)

Boysenberry. Rich, full flavor. One of the largest dewberries. Grown commercially in the West.

Lucretia. Large, good-quality, early berry. Hardiest of the dewberries.

Marion. Large berries, heavy yielder. Vigorous, yet fewer canes make it easier to train than other dewberries.

Thornfree. Medium-size fruit with tart flavor, late. Semi-upright blackberry developed by the U. S. Department of Agriculture.

Thornless. Huge, purplish maroon berries, almost seedless. Similar to the boysenberry, but with no thorns. Vigorous grower.

Youngberry. High-quality, popular older cultivar. Heavy yields.

CHAPTER 24

The Strawberry
(Fragaria spp.*)*

During a Sunday service in our little church when I was a child, a visiting minister remarked that he was thoroughly sick of hearing about Heaven's pearly gates and golden streets. He visualized Heaven, he said, as a land where, among other pleasant happenings, juicy, red strawberries ripened eternally. It was one of the best sermons I'd ever heard. Probably lots of other people would agree, for it's hard to find anyone who doesn't like strawberries, even though there are those unfortunate folks who are allergic to them.

Like many gardeners, we have often risen in the dead of a late spring night, looked at the thermometer with half-opened eyes, and suddenly come wide awake in shock. Soon we are grabbing blankets, quilts, tablecloths, boxes, and anything else we can find to cover up the tender blossoms that ha' ~ foolishly opened just before the moon turned full and the temperature plun

Are strawberries worth fighting the frost, the bugs, the diseas and the quackgrass? Every strawberry lover will answer a boomir reward comes on a bright summer morning when you gaze at row in hungry anticipation and then pick the first, big, luscious r season. I find it's hard to break my childhood habit of one for t for the mouth.

The strawberry we cultivate in our gardens today is unique of the few fruits that originated in the United States. Today berries were all developed in fairly recent years in America an wild strawberry species that the early explorers found growin

While few claim that any of the modern berries comp tiny wild ones we picked among thistles and garter snakes tions, gardeners who have sought out the best-flavored them in rich, organic soil maintain that they come migh

Buying Plants

Because of the popularity of strawberries, a great man

developed since they have been in cultivation. There are now kinds that grow well all over the United States, as well as in parts of Alaska, Canada, and even the warmest sections of Florida. Because there is such a wide range of cultivars, be careful to choose the ones that are best adapted to your region.

Strawberries are troubled by diseases, and a few decades ago the plants were so infected it looked as if berry growing might be a thing of the past. Fortunately, horticulturists were able to develop disease-resistant strains, and presently most of the plants being sold are propagated by tissue culture, which guarantees they are disease-free. Look for these certified virus-free cultivars to save yourself distress later on.

Preparing the Soil

Choose the location on your property that is the most free from late frosts. Avoid the bottom of a slope, because cold air will settle there on quiet nights. Since your strawberry plants will be growing in the same spot for at least two years, it is important to prepare the soil thoroughly. The plants are small and shallow-rooted compared to other fruit plants, and must absorb all their moisture and nourishment from the top few inches of soil.

▲ Strawberries are nearly everybody's favorite. Not only are they a good home fruit, but they are also a good choice if one wishes to raise a few fruits to sell. *(USDA)*

► **Plant strawberries at the proper depth, with the crown at ground level. A is too shallow, B is just right, and C is too deep.**

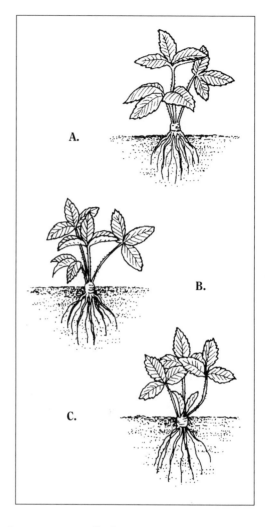

A.

B.

C.

The soil should be light, slightly acid (pH of 5 to 6), and rich in humus (manure, compost, or peat) that will hold moisture even during the driest spells of weather. Generally, soils that will grow good vegetables are also good for strawberries. In fact, it works best to plant them on land that has been used for cultivated crops for a year or more previously in order to get rid of the grass, weeds, and grubs. White grubs live in grass-covered soils, and because one of their favorite foods is strawberry roots, they are one of the plant's worst enemies. Well-prepared soil helps eliminate them. Grass and weeds shade the plants and compete with the shallow-rooted berry plants for nutrients and moisture. Frequent cultivation or a mulch will help keep the bed weed-free.

Never plant strawberries in soil that you know is infested with nematodes. These tiny root eaters are most prevalent in warm climates, but they are present in most other areas, as well. If you are sure you have them, sterilize the soil first. (Consult your Extension Service for information about soil sterilization.) Never replant strawberries in the same spot in nematode country without sterilizing it, and avoid planting in a spot where you have grown potatoes or tomatoes recently. Verticillium wilt often lurks in such soils and can infect a crop of strawberries months later.

Planting

Spring is usually regarded as the best time to plant strawberries, and the earlier, the better. Nothing seems to be gained by fall planting in the North, even if the plants survive — and many don't. I have always felt that if you plant anything in the fall you just have to weed it that much longer.

When you are ready to plant, you must make a decision, because you have two planting methods to choose from: the matted row or the lesser-used hill system. Whichever method you choose, be sure to set your plants at the correct depth (see page 179). If the crowns are buried under the soil, the plant will smother, and if they extend too high above the soil, they will dry out. In either case, they will die. If you cultivate or hoe the bed, never let soil pile up around the crowns as you would with corn or beans. Before you plant, pour a puddle of water into each planting hole. Then, water the plants every other day for two weeks, and once a week add liquid fertilizer to the water.

The Matted Row

Set the plants in a row, about 18 inches apart. If you plant more than one row, keep the rows at least 3 feet apart, or even wider if you plan to use a power tiller for cultivation. The plants, as they grow, will produce runners freely and form new little plants. Steer these runners so they will grow toward the adjoining plants and fill in the empty spaces to make a row "matted" with strawberry plants (see page 181, A).

In this system the plants are treated as biennials. For an ongoing bed, you must make a new planting each spring, which will be harvested the summer of the following year, and then plowed under. If you were to keep the bed for an additional year, so many new plants would develop that the bed would become greatly overcrowded and produce only a meager crop of small berries.

The Hill System

The hill system is not a method of planting in raised beds, as you might guess. The name comes from the appearance of the large plants. In this system, the plants are set from 12 to 15 inches apart in a bed consisting of three rows, each of which are also 12 to 15 inches apart. The bed can extend for as long as you like, but leave openings every 20 feet so you can cross over between the rows. If you set more than one bed, leave 3 or 4 feet of walking space between the beds.

The hill system takes more plants initially and requires more attention than the matted row. It saves the work and cost of annual replanting, however, and is ideal for home gardeners with little growing space. Anyone who likes to raise plants organically with a deep mulch also prefers it.

It is difficult to cultivate plants grown in the hill system, because after they have grown they will be close together. Some growers set the plants in slits cut in heavy black plastic, which they then cover with hay, shavings, or some other material to protect the plastic from deteriorating in the sun. Others use no plastic, but mulch with shredded bark, cocoa hulls, salt hay, or some other weed-free material, and they add to it each year. Unlike the matted row system in which you want runners to grow to fill the row, in the hill system you must cut off all runners as soon as they form and permit no new plants to grow (see page 181, B). In other words, treat the strawberry plants like the perennials they are. Since none of the plant's energy goes into producing runners and making new plants, both the plant and its berries get exceptionally large, and they will continue to produce for six years or more.

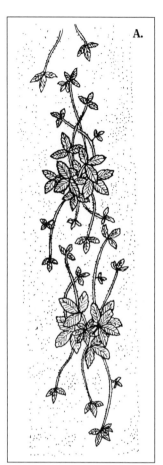
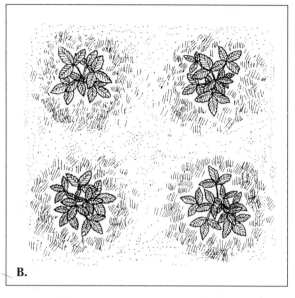

(A) The matted row method of growing strawberries and (B) the less common hill method

Rotate Your Crops

Although the hill system of growing strawberries has much to recommend it, most home gardeners prefer the matted row method. When you plant strawberries this way, you should rotate the crop with a cover crop between plantings. This helps keep diseases and insects from getting a start, and adds humus to the soil. In the spring set a row or more of plants alongside the vegetable garden, then mulch or cultivate them. The following spring, plant a second bed beside it or in another spot. That summer you can harvest berries from the first bed planted and, after picking, till under the entire bed and plant a crop of winter rye there. The following spring, till under the rye and plant a fresh bed of berries for the following year's crop.

It may be tempting to save money by digging extra plants from your old patch for replanting, but unless you are absolutely sure they are disease and insect free, it's safer to buy new ones each year.

Weed Control

An old Yankee saying warns that a man should never plant a bigger strawberry patch than his wife can keep hoed. These days such a statement might be regarded as sexist, but it is important that whoever has charge of weed control does it thoroughly and frequently. Weeds and grass can be a real problem among the shallow-rooted berry plants. Hand-weeding, power cultivation, and mulches, along with hoeing, are all ways to control the wily weeds. Some growers use preemergence herbicides to stop the germination of weed seeds that blow into their beds. Others keep geese to eat the grass and dandelions. Hoeing, cultivation, and mulching are the safest methods of weed control, however. Chemicals can be tricky to use, and geese are very dirty and not always selective about their diet.

Pick Off Blossoms the First Year

Whichever planting arrangement you choose, don't let any fruit develop on your strawberry plants the first year. Picking off the blossoms is time consuming, but very important. Growing and ripening even a single berry will weaken a new young plant so much that the following year's production will be drastically curtailed. Pick off all the blooms as fast as they form, even if it takes several pickings.

Everbearing strawberries are an exception to this rule, however. If you plant them, pick off all the blossoms until midsummer the first year, but from then on, allow the plant to flower and bear naturally. After midsummer, it should be well enough established to support its late summer crop.

Everbearing Strawberries

Everbearing strawberries bear a crop in early summer, then a few more fruits off and on throughout the summer, and another, usually light, crop in late summer or fall. They are ideal for vacation gardeners or others who preserve little fruit but like to pick a few fresh berries throughout the summer.

Everbearers are the ones to choose if you want to grow strawberries in pots, barrels, jars, window boxes, planters, or pyramids. Such plantings are hard to protect over winter, so if you live above the Mason–Dixon line, store your container-grown plants in a cold frame or other sheltered place, or mulch them heavily with some insulating material such as evergreen boughs.

Keep the runners cut off strawberry plants that are grown in containers, and water them often. Add fertilizer frequently, too, because waterings leach the nutrients rapidly from small containers.

Everbearers are a bit tricky to grow in some areas. Most kinds don't do well in the far South or where growing seasons are unusually short. That leaves zones 5–8 as their ideal growing spots.

Climbing Strawberries

Glowing ads in pulp magazines sometimes hail these berries as major miracles in the world of fruit gardening. With all the superlatives we old-time gardeners have learned to expect, we are told that climbing strawberry plants will produce amazing crops of large, tasty berries on beautiful, high-climbing vines.

According to the people we've talked with who have tried them, however, the best yield they ever got was a few small fruits resembling wild strawberries. So it is best to regard the climbing strawberry as an interesting novelty, but don't expect to see amazed tourists creating traffic jams as they gaze at it, nor make elaborate plans on how to dispose of your abundant surplus.

Strawberries from Seed

Like all fruits, strawberry cultivars don't come true from seed and must be started from parent plants asexually. *Fraises des bois* (Alpine strawberries), however, have been grown from seed for many years, often as edible borders for flower beds. The berries are small, like wild strawberries, with wonderful flavor, and seeds of both the native kinds and a few cultivars are sold in catalogs. One cultivar, Mignonette, produces good crops of fruits somewhat larger than the wild species. Another, Sweetheart, is an everbearer that will often bear a few fruits the first year, if you start it indoors. Its berries are even larger and very sweet, and the plants bear good crops.

Strawberry seeds are small, so plant them in an artificial growing mix available from farm and garden stores. Barely cover them with a layer of perlite, and keep them in a cool place. Don't let them dry out, but don't overwater them, either. The seeds germinate slowly, so be patient. After two leaves have developed, transplant them to a flat or to small pots, and plant them outside in the spring after danger of frost is over.

Keep the blossoms picked off for the first part of the summer, and after midsummer, treat them like other everbearers.

Winter and Frost Protection

Even though strawberry plants vary considerably in hardiness, in almost every spot north of the Mason–Dixon line — and in some of the South — it is necessary to protect them over the winter in order to get good yields. It is the fruit buds, rather than the plants themselves, that are most vulnerable to frost damage, and this can occur even before the buds begin to show in the spring. The prominence of the word "straw" in the name suggests that the value of covering the plants has long been recognized. Straw was once cheap, fairly weed-free, and plentiful, so gardeners buried their plants beneath thick layers of it before winter. When they uncovered them in the spring, the leftover straw provided a nice mulch that conserved moisture and kept the ripening berries free from dirt. Straw is still an excellent winter cover, although it is hard to find nowadays. Shavings, wood chips, leaves, salt hay, and commercial plant insulation, are all good covers; but because we have plenty of evergreen boughs, we use them as coverings.

Cover the plants in the fall about the time hard frosts start to freeze the ground slightly. Leave the covering on in the spring until you are sure all medium-hard frosts (28°F or under) are finished. Remove the coverings on a cloudy or rainy day, if possible, or late in the afternoon, so bright sunlight won't hit the tender new white shoots before they have had a chance to "green up."

Strawberry blossoms are also sensitive to frost, and some years you will probably need to protect them when late spring frosts occur at blooming time. This is the time, as I mentioned before, to cover the plants with Reemay polyester plant covers, old quilts, blankets, sheets, or burlap bags. If you are sure a frost is coming, cover your plants in late afternoon while the soil is still warm. Some gardeners set out kerosene flares or turn lawn sprinklers on their beds. Commercial growers use irrigation for frost protection, and some of our friends use a string of Christmas tree lights under a low plastic tent.

Whatever method you use, listen to weather forecasts at blooming time, and watch the thermometer closely, especially on clear nights. The temperature can be a balmy 60°F at dusk and plunge to well below 30°F by 2 A.M. No one wants to work all year and then lose the crop a few days before it's ready to pick. You may want to invest in a frost alarm, for extra insurance.

Insects and Diseases

Some manuals on growing strawberries list dozens of bugs and diseases that devastate them. If we started out by reading those bulletins, most of us would never have the courage to plant strawberries at all. Fortunately, very few of these pests are likely to become problems in a backyard garden. They are more likely to target large plantings grown on the same land for years. If you buy virus-free plants, and don't plant them where you recently raised potatoes or tomatoes that might have been diseased, you will have good insurance against leaf spot, leaf scorch, verticillium wilt, red stele, and other such diseases. If you do get unlucky, however, the spray program in Chapter 9 should control most of your problems.

As for insects, you are likely to encounter at least a few, including Japanese beetles, aphids, thrips, leafhoppers, slugs, grasshoppers, spittlebugs, and leaf rollers. Both organic and chemical insecticides are available that should take care of all of them. Some strawberry growers plant a marigold between every plant to help repel certain insects. Since marigolds are annuals, they never become weedy and they dress up the patch as well.

Three other pests are fond of strawberry plants:

White grubs. These root-eating pests can devastate a new planting in short order. They develop into those big May (or June) beetles that bang on the windows and buzz around lights on early summer nights. Since they live mostly in sod, the best prevention is to plant your berries on ground that has been cultivated the previous year.

Cyclamen mites. These small, hard-to-see insects also bother delphiniums, houseplants, and other ornamentals, causing their leaves and buds to curl tightly. It is difficult to find safe sprays to use on this pest. Parasitic insects often offer the best control.

Weevils. Weevils are one of the most serious problems for many growers. They lay their eggs in the bud cluster, partly severing it from the plant. Insecticides can control them, but you must be careful to use one that can be washed off later, and spray before the blooms open so you won't kill any pollinating bees. Pyrethrum and rotenone, both organic insecticides, wash off the fruit easily, but frequent applications may be necessary if the pests persist.

Harvesting

Your strawberries will have the best flavor and vitamin content if you pick them on the day they ripen, which usually means daily picking during the peak of the season. Overripe fruit spoils quickly, whether on the vines or off. In the early morning, while the air is still cool and just after the dew has evaporated, is the best time to pick. Put the berries in a cool place immediately after picking them so they will stay fresh longer. Even in a refrigerator, however, it is hard to keep strawberries more than a few days. Don't wash them until just before using; wet berries spoil faster.

Nobody needs to be reminded of the delightful taste of fresh, ripe strawberries and cream, or strawberry shortcake, milk shakes, and ice cream. Furthermore, they are good for you. The fruit contains a healthy amount of vitamin C and so do the leaves, which some people use for making strawberry tea. The berries freeze very well raw, either whole or mashed with sugar, and in our home, a great many of them go into jam.

Cultivars for Special Regions or Purposes

Because of the huge numbers of cultivars, the beginning grower can get badly confused as to the best kind to choose. It is most important to buy the ones that are right for your climate, of course, but if there is room, many people like to experiment with a few plants of several different kinds, in order to find out what ones grow best and taste best. Also, by choosing early, midseason, and late cultivars growers can enjoy fresh fruit for much of the summer. Here are some suggestions:

FOR AREAS WITH LITTLE FROST

FRESNO, POCAHONTAS, TIOGA

HARDIEST (ZONES 3 AND 4)

CATSKILL, CRIMSON KING, DUNLAP, EMPIRE, FAIRFAX, PREMIER, ROBINSON, SPARKLE

Everbearers

Gem, Ogallala, Ozark Beauty, Tribute, Tristar

Excellent flavor

Albritton, Cardinal, Dunlap, Earliglow, Empire, Fletcher, Sparkle

Best for home freezing

Earlidawn, Midway, Pocahontas, Red Glow, Sparkle

Largest fruit

Atlas, Catskill, Guardian, Jerseybelle, Sequoia, Tioga

Most resistant to late spring frosts

Catskill, Earlidawn, Midway

Earliest

Atlas, Blakemore, Dunlap, Premier, Sequoia, Sunrise, Surecrop

Midseason

Apollo, Catskill, Empire, Fairfax, Fresno, Guardian, Marshall, Midway, Raritan, Red Chief, Robinson

Latest

Albritton, Hood, Jerseybelle, Ozark Beauty, Sparkle, Tennessee Beauty, Vesper

CHAPTER 25

Bush Fruits —
Currant, Gooseberry, Jostaberry, Elderberry, and Saskatoon

For many years we had a large gooseberry bush in our front yard that "belonged" to the boys in my 4-H club who frequently visited us. It was mutually agreed upon that they could eat freely from that one if they would ignore those in the back garden. The bush produced so lavishly year after year that it always supplied more than their needs, even though it was not unusual to find several boys sitting around it eating with both hands. I'm sure every berry on that bush got squeezed at least twice, as the impatient teenagers waited for them to ripen.

Like the brambles, the bush fruits come in many colors. There are the red, white, and black currants; the green, amber, pink, and red gooseberries; the blueberries; and the wine-dark jostas, elderberries, and saskatoons. They all furnish a tremendous amount of good eating in return for the small amount of time and money you need to spend on them. They begin to bear at an early age, bear big crops each year, and add exciting variety to any home grower's fruit collection. If climate, space, and government regulations (see pages 189-90) will permit, we hope you will consider including some of them in your plantings.

Every section of North America has its own native bush fruits, including beach plums, buffalo berries, bearberries, chokecherries, sand cherries, highbush cranberries, huckleberries, and juneberries. Some are delicious eaten right off the plant, some are best only if they're cooked, and still others are enjoyed only by wildlife or those who have grown up with them and learned to like their unusual flavors.

Horticulturists have domesticated and produced outstanding cultivars of several of these native bush fruits — blueberries, currants, elderberries, gooseberries, and saskatoons. The Europeans have developed several new fruits, including the jostaberry, a hybrid between the gooseberry and black currant, which is now becoming popular in this hemisphere.

Getting Started

If you are just starting out with small fruits, it is best to buy disease- and insect-free plants from a nursery. Potted plants may be set any time the ground isn't frozen, and because every root is intact, they get off to the fastest start. Plant bare-rooted stock in early spring for best results.

If you decide to beg a plant or two from a neighbor who has exactly what you want, you can often sever a small offshoot from a large bush in early spring with a quick thrust of a sharp spade. Be sure the fledgling plant has good roots, leave the soil around it intact, and plant it in your own garden as soon as possible. Currants and gooseberries are self-fertile, so one bush usually produces abundantly with no partner. Hybrid elderberries and saskatoons bear better if two different cultivars are planted, or if there are wild ones nearby that bloom at the same time.

Planting and Culture

The culture of all the bush fruits is much the same. Set the plants 5 or more feet apart, unless you want them to grow into a tight hedge, in which case set them slightly closer together. In the North they do best in full sun, but in zones 5 and warmer, all will tolerate some light shade. Most bush fruits like well-drained soil. An exception is the elderberry, which prefers a moist location. All thrive in soil rich in humus.

Growth habits of the various bush fruits differ considerably. Gooseberries and red and white currants are well behaved and will stay quite within bounds for many years, but black currants and jostaberries are likely to become spreading. Elderberries, unless controlled, often spread all over the lot, so plant them in a spot by themselves and keep them confined by frequently mowing off all the persistent sucker plants.

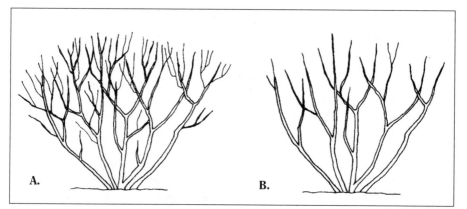

▲ Bush fruits require less pruning than most other fruits and berries but need to be thinned every few years. (A) Before pruning; (B) after pruning.

Since the bush fruits are really small trees, you don't need to plant them in soil that is as carefully prepared as that required for strawberries and brambles. Simply dig a large hole, mix an equal amount of well-rotted manure or compost with the soil you remove, and fill the hole with water. Set in the plants, as you would a fruit tree, at the same depth they grew originally in the pot, or, if bare rooted, before they were dug. Keep grass and weeds from choking them, and water them heavily two or three times a week for the first few weeks. Feed them with a liquid fertilizer solution once a week for the first month.

Although currants and gooseberries are often found growing and bearing on abandoned farms where they're choked with grass and receive no care, they produce much better when they get a little attention. Apply a 2-inch mulch of bark or wood chips around the bush at planting time, and add to it each year. Each spring, too, put a shovelful or two of manure or compost under the mulch, or add a small amount of complete fertilizer. Keep a watchful eye out for insects and diseases, and be ready to keep them in check.

After the bushes are four or five years old, do a light pruning every year to get rid of old wood and to thin out branches that are too thick.

Currants and Gooseberries *(Ribes* spp.*)*

One time, years ago, when I was visiting friends in New York City, some of us were discussing our favorite pies. I voted for gooseberry, and a hush fell over the group. The city folk had finally met an honest-to-goodness country boy. Poor souls! I felt sorry for them. Even though acid fruits have gained favor as health foods in recent years, lots of Americans still apparently regard rhubarb and gooseberries as suitable for low country humor rather than the healthful delicacies they actually are. In Europe, however, currants and gooseberries have long been not only respectable, but taken seriously as gourmet foods. Many of our best cultivars have been developed there or in Canada.

Although their poor public image is gradually improving in the United States, the gooseberry and its cousin the currant have another major obstacle to being widely grown. Just as blueberry growing is restricted by its fussiness about acid soil, and peach growing by its insistence on a mild climate and light soil, the members of the *Ribes* group are denied admittance to some areas because they can't always get along with their neighbors. The plants can be alternate hosts to a disease, blister rust, that infects and kills the native white pine *(Pinus strobus)*. They are, unfortunately, one of the Typhoid Marys of the plant world.

Blister rust seldom noticeably affects the *Ribes* plants, but the spores travel back and forth between them and nearby white pines. First, only a few limbs on the pine die, but ultimately the whole tree succumbs. Curiously, the disease does not spread from one pine tree to another, but always through one of the "host" plants. Although blister rust may be present in other members of the currant-gooseberry clan, most horticulturists feel that nearly all of the pines' trouble comes from the European black currant, which is now naturalized in many parts of North America, and the native wild gooseberry, which is equally

◀ Gooseberries are a dependable fruit, ripen early, and are an excellent source of juice. Unfortunately, they are a "forbidden fruit" in many areas. *(USDA)*

widespread. Many of the newer cultivars of the red, white, and black currant, jostaberry, and gooseberry, are resistant to blister rust. Nevertheless, laws in some states still require that all *Ribes* be planted at least 900 feet from any white pine and other five-needled pines, such as Swiss pine, and even farther from a nursery raising white pine seedlings. No restrictions limit plantings near mugho pine, Austrian pine, jack pine, Japanese pine, or Norway (red) pine. The vulnerable species are always light green in color and have five needles in each clump.

Canada has no laws prohibiting the planting of cultivated *Ribes,* and the federal regulations have now been repealed in the United States. Most state laws are seldom enforced, but it is still important to check out your own area before you write out an order for *Ribes* plants. Otherwise, you could kill some of your own prized trees or perhaps find yourself at odds with the local constabulary and an unhappy group of neighbors who have carved their dead white pines into war clubs.

Because pines don't grow naturally in our alkaline soil, we never have any problems growing all of the *Ribes* plants we want, and are excited about the introduction of the new European cultivars. Horticulturists have not only developed cultivars that are mildew- and rust-resistant and those that produce larger and more flavorful fruits, but they have also recently given us two new hybrids: the jostaberry, a hybrid between the black currant and gooseberry; and the worcesterberry *(Ribes divaricatum),* a small, purple, currantlike berry already popular in England for jam making.

If you are interested in knowing more about these new fruits, consider joining the International Ribes Association (see Appendix for address). This group was formed to encourage importing, propagating, growing, and using all kinds of currants and gooseberries. Contact them for more information.

Culture

Although *Ribes* will grow and produce in light shade, and were at one time planted between fruit trees in orchards, they have fewer diseases when they have plenty of sun and good air circulation.

Young *Ribes* plants need little or no pruning, and even after they begin to bear heavily, the only pruning they need is the removal of broken branches and wood that is over three years old. Be sure to use heavy gloves when you tackle the thorny gooseberries! If mildew is a problem, thin out even more of the branches so sun and air can better dry out the interior of the plant.

The vigorous-growing black currants and jostaberries all need heavier pruning, both for the best production and to keep them under control. You should also prune the large-fruited gooseberry cultivars more heavily than the smaller-fruiting ones so the berries will grow to their ultimate size.

Diseases and Pests

Both **American mildew** and **powdery mildew** often attack the more susceptible cultivars of *Ribes*. The former starts out as a white powdery growth over the leaves and fruit, but later it turns brown. Powdery mildew is a white powdery growth that covers twigs, leaves, and fruit, making it inedible. Both can be difficult to control, especially during a warm, humid summer. Plant mildew-resistant cultivars, when possible, and set them in a sunny location where the air can circulate freely around them. Prune them heavily, if necessary, to further aid air circulation, and don't let the plants crowd each other. If either disease becomes serious, ask your garden store to recommend a suitable fungicide.

Anthracnose, a less common disease, shows up as leaf discolorations. Keep weeds and grass out of the planting, provide good ventilation, and cut back any plants that show signs of infection. Spray the plants with a fungicide two or three times about a week apart if the disease becomes more than cosmetic.

Leaf-eating **sawflies** or **currant (gooseberry) worms** may attack *Ribes* in early summer. These can be easily checked by using an organic insecticide such as rotenone. You may need to give the plants the same treatment if natural predators fail to keep **aphids** or **currant fruit flies** under control.

Harvesting

The red currant is a bit tart, and best when cooked, although as a boy I liked to eat them fresh off the bush. They are a good source of vitamin C and high in pectin until they become overripe, which makes them ideal for jelly making. Red currant jelly has long been a gourmet treat used to accompany meat dishes as well as desserts. Black currant jelly and jam is just as tasty, and I'll never forget our first jar of "Confiture de Cassis," which we picked up on a trip to Montreal — a treat that made me want to start growing them right away. Some people make black currants into juice and wine, or dry them.

We don't pick currants and gooseberries when they first turn color, because both get better flavored if they stay on the bush a while. Watch them closely, though, because birds like them, too. The noted Nova Scotia fruit gardener and writer Jo Ann Gardner advises using a mixture of ripe and half-ripe red currants for jelly, ripe ones for jam, and slightly overripe ones for juice and wine. She prefers black currants to be slightly underripe for jelly, and a bit more ripe for jam. She feels the dead-ripe ones are best for juice.

Gooseberries, although smaller than kiwis, resemble them in texture and flavor. The different cultivars vary widely in size, color, and sweetness. When fully ripe they are soft, and many are delicious right off the bush. Some people prefer to pick them when they are slightly underripe for tart sauce and pies. They also are delicious in jam, jelly, and a real treat — gooseberry fool. Traditionally, the cook "tops and tails" the berries before using, but for most recipes this painstaking job is unnecessary. (See recipes in Chapter 30.)

Gooseberries can be a bit tricky to pick on some of the more thorny cultivars. I wear a leather glove on my left hand to hold up the branches while I pick the fruit with my right. Currant and jostaberry bushes are not thorny. The fruits are soft, and we prefer to pick the red and white currants by the cluster like grapes and strip them off later when we are ready to use them.

Cultivars

Both currants and gooseberries are cold-weather plants and aren't likely to grow well in the warm parts of North America. Those listed are suitable for most of zones 3 through 5, although the GLENDALE gooseberry does well in Virginia and Arkansas.

RED CURRANTS *(RIBES SP.)*

CHERRY RED. A large-fruited, old-time cultivar that is quite mildew resistant.

JONKEER VAN TETS is a new, mildew-resistant cultivar from Holland that is rapidly gaining popularity.

RED LAKE. This popular cultivar is very hardy, but susceptible to powdery mildew.

REDSTART is a new English cultivar that is becoming popular in the U.S. and Canada. It grows into an upright bush and produces heavy crops of medium-size fruit late in the season.

WILDER is a heavy bearer, but the berries are rather small.

WHITE CURRANTS *(RIBES SP.)*

WHITE GRAPE and WHITE IMPERIAL, the most popular kinds grown in North America, are quite similar.

WHITE VERSAILLES, a sweet, yellow-fruiting cultivar, is a favorite in Europe and available in Canada and the States.

BLACK CURRANTS *(RIBES SP.)*

Canadian originations CONSORT, CORONET, and CRUSADER are blister rust-resistant and rich in vitamin C. WILLOUGHBY, an older cultivar is ornamental enough for landscaping, and has fragrant flowers. Plant it only where there are no white pine trees, however, since it is not completely rust-resistant.

Many European black currant cultivars are being tested in North America, including the following:

BEN LOMOND, a large-fruiting, disease-resistant variety.

BEN NEVIS, a hardy, tall-growing bush is vigorous and has flowers that are quite frost-resistant.

BEN SAREK, a shorter plant, good for small gardens.

BROADTORP BLACK. From Scandanavia, this is one of the best black currants for drying.

GREEN'S BLACK has long clusters of large berries and is excellent for jelly.

LAXTON GIANT has early-ripening, very large, sweet fruit, but is susceptible to spring frosts.

MALLING JET grows too large for most gardens, and produces small berries and only moderate crops.

WELLINGTON XXX is an older variety that bears large crops of good-flavored berries. It blooms early, however, so late frosts sometimes ruin the crop.

GOOSEBERRIES *(RIBES* SP.*)*

Gooseberry plants grow from 3 to 5 feet tall. Older kinds include

DOWNING, a yellow-green, very thorny plant.

POORMAN has wine-red fruits.

OREGON CHAMPION has high-quality, green fruits. It is a good plant to use as a prickly hedge barrier against wildlife.

PIXWELL is most often found in catalogs. Medium-size green berries that ripen to a pale pink. The thorns on its stems are shorter than those on most other gooseberries.

WELCOME has few thorns and bears sweet, deep red fruits.

Newer varieties include

CANADA 0-273. Red, good-flavored, pear-shaped fruits. Nearly thornfree bush, but not a heavy bearer.

CAPTIVATOR. A European-American hybrid. Large, pink, good-flavored berries, but bears light crops.

CLARK. A heavy-bearing cultivar. Red fruits with red flesh. Dessert quality.

INVICTA. Resistant to American mildew. Bears large, pale green fruits best suited for culinary use.

JUBILEE. Large, greenish yellow dessert-type fruits on a compact bush.

LEEPARED. Disease-resistant plant with dark, translucent fruit.

LEVELLER. Very large, greenish yellow, highly flavored fruits.

SYLVIA. A heavy bearer of large, sweet, green berries with a red blush. Developed in Canada.

WHINHAM'S INDUSTRY. A favorite dark red, all-purpose gooseberry.

JOSTABERRIES *(RIBES* HYBRIDS*)*

A recent addition to the *Ribes* world, the josta or jostaberry was developed in Germany as a cross between the European black currant and a North American dessert-type gooseberry. These bushes are thornless and resistant to both blister rust and mildew; they need heavier pruning, however, than either gooseberries or currants. Jostas lack the musky flavor and fragrance of black currants, and even though the flavor does not appeal to everyone, their advocates declare that preserves made from the berries are superior to the fruit of other *Ribes*. Like currants, the vitamin C-rich, smooth-skinned fruits have no tails, and their size is between a currant and gooseberry. The jostas are becoming increasingly popular, and commercial plantings are already being made in North America. Various cultivars have black or dull red skin, but the flesh is usually greenish. They are such vigorous growers that the usual 5-foot spacing between bushes is not enough; 8 feet is recommended.

Although many josta cultivars have been developed, not many, other than the original hybrid, are yet offered for sale in North America. Among those you may find are: BAUER BLACK, one of the original developments, and four of Swiss origin: SWISS RED, JOSTINA, JOSTAKI, and JOSTAGRANDA.

ORVIS 8, another new *Ribes,* from Oregon, is probably a gooseberry-black currant cross, also. It resembles the gooseberries, and bears medium-size, dark purple fruits. The bush has some thorns and is quite disease resistant. Raintree Nursery sells it (see nursery list in the Appendix).

Elderberries *(Sambucus canadensis)*

The elderberry is extremely hardy, gets along well with pine trees, grows in almost any soil that is somewhat moist, and needs almost no care. So what's wrong with it? Not much, though it is perhaps a bit *too* easy to grow, so it spreads rapidly, both by seed and root suckers.

Fortunately, we have plenty of room, and by keeping the grass mowed all around the bushes, we keep them under control. Furthermore, they let us make use of land that even though it is not swampy, is too wet for other fruits. In fact, they don't do well on light, dry soils. Our two rows of 6- to 7-foot-high bushes are each about 20 feet long and 3 feet wide, and produce gallons of highly flavored fruit each year.

The flavor of elderberries is somewhat like that of blackberries, but richer. The fruit is fun to pick because the bushes have no thorns, there's no bending over, and the hybrids which are usually about the size of chokecherries, are much larger than the wild berries. Elderberry juice is reputed to be one of the most healthy drinks, and it is likely that the elderly ladies of bygone days who had their glass of elderberry wine each afternoon "for medicinal reasons" knew exactly what they were doing.

I am not including cultural directions, because I don't know any. Elderberries require the least work of any of the cultivated fruits and make it on their own with little attention. We cut out any winter-killed branches, however, and are never alarmed even if there are a lot of them, since the fruit is produced on the new growth each year. Our plants have never been bothered by bugs or disease.

Our biggest problem with elderberries is that birds love them as much as we do. Every year they try to grab all the fruit, usually by picking it a day or two before I think it is ready. To make matters worse, the heavy birds occasionally

▲ Elderberry blooms have nearly as many tasty uses as the fruit.

break off whole clusters by perching on them. Since the tall bushes are impossible to cover, and the birds difficult to scare away, we usually resort to picking the fruits a day or two before they are completely ripe, and let them finish ripening in a warm room. Fortunately, we've also found that in our climate some of the new hybrids ripen so late that many berry-eating birds have already gotten sick of wild elderberries and headed south before the fruits of the cultivars turn color.

Since elderberries are ready to harvest in early fall when we're up to our necks processing the apples, cider, plums, and vegetables, we've found it works well to pick them and freeze them immediately without processing. Later in the season or in the winter, when time isn't quite so precious, we cook them into syrups that we freeze for delicious drinks, or make them into jellies, pies, and juice. The vitamin C-loaded juice mixed with orange juice, cider, or ginger ale is our winter health tonic to ward off colds and flus.

The clusters of tiny, white elderberry blossoms are also tasty in many ways and can be made into wine or vinegar. We like to fry them in batter for a special treat or make them into an unusual soft drink — elderberry blow. We put a few bunches of the freshly picked flowers into a gallon jar along with a little sugar, lemon juice, and enough water to fill the jar. We place the jar, tightly capped, in the sun for a day, and then strain and chill.

It is possible that if you grow elderberries you may get some undeserved attention for your horticultural abilities. The leaves have a distinctive shape, and late one night while we were transporting some husky, potted elderberry plants in our car, we were stopped by a county sheriff, who took an unusual interest in our load. It took nearly half an hour before he was completely convinced that the plants were not marijuana and he finally let us go on our way. Naturally, we got lots of kidding later about our potted "pot."

Cultivars

ADAMS. Large crops of medium-size, early-ripening berries. Especially good for areas that have early fall frosts.

JOHNS. Large berries come a bit later than Adams, but the bush is not as productive.

NEW YORK 21. One of the best of the new hybrids. Large berries, medium-size bush. Ripens midseason, productive.

NOVA. Heavy bearer of large fruit. Fairly early.

YORK. Large, productive bushes, good-size fruit. Ripens late.

The Saskatoon *(Amelanchier alnifolia)*

The saskatoon is one of the few fruits that not only survives in the sub-zero temperatures of the prairie provinces and northern states but also produces tremendous crops. Few gardeners in the East are familiar with this relative of the wild shadbush that blooms early in the spring, however.

Although commonly called a berry, the fruit of the saskatoon is actually a small pome, like an apple or pear. Most wild bushes produce fruits of ¼ to ⅜ inch in diameter, although the improved kinds are much larger. Both resemble blueberries in appearance and flavor. The bushes grow from 3 to 16 feet or more in height and produce 6 or more quarts of fruit per bush. Plantings of some of the improved cultivars in western Canada have yielded as much as 6 tons per acre.

The bushes are very hardy, but like the shad, the flowers come early, so late spring frosts sometimes damage the crop. To avoid frost damage, plant them in a spot where air drainage is good. Delay the blooming for a few days by using a thick mulch to help hold winter's frost around the roots. Saskatoons do best in well-drained soil with plenty of organic matter, and a pH between 5.6 and 6.5. Set them about 6 feet apart, and if you plant more than one row, space the rows at least 10 feet apart.

Keep the plants weed-free by mulching or mowing. Mechanical cultivation is likely to damage their tender fibrous roots, which are close to the surface. Your new plants should begin to bear within three or four years.

Wild plants produce well with no pruning, but the cultivars do best if you prune away all the old wood from time to time. Don't cut out too much of the young growth, however, because unlike elderberries, the fruit is produced on wood that grew during the previous season. Prune in early spring after the coldest part of the winter is over, but before the buds swell.

Because birds love the ripening fruits, some growers plant a hedgerow of wild saskatoons nearby hoping birds will get their fill on these, and leave the cultivated fruits alone. Because fruit maggots occasionally attack saskatoons, some years you may need to spray them with an insecticide. Mildew and mummy fruit, a form of rust, are diseases that can affect the saskatoon, so a fungicide may be necessary. See Chapter 9.

Saskatoons grow in clusters and all ripen at once, so you can harvest the whole crop at one picking. Fruit that is overripe has less vitamin C and is not as good for freezing and preserving. You can use saskatoons in the same way as blueberries. Native Americans used to pound them into their pemmican, a form of dried meat.

Cultivars

Most saskatoon cultivars are selections from seedling plants, but a few were developed by hybridizing. FORRESTBURG, PEMBINA, and SMOKEY are widely grown commercially in the prairie provinces. FORRESTBURG produces the largest fruit, but the quality is not quite as good as that of Pembina and Smokey. ALTAGLOW has sweet berries, and the bush is considered a good ornamental. HONEYWOOD produces very large crops, and MOONLAKE has large fruits, as does THIESSEN.

CHAPTER 26

Blueberry
(Vaccinium spp.*)*

I wouldn't be surprised to hear the expression, "As American as blueberry pie," sometime soon. It makes sense, because the treat is becoming one of the most popular desserts in restaurants. Furthermore, blueberries are a North American fruit, while the apple tree is an import.

Although several species of wild blueberries grow in different sections of the United States and Canada, until the 1950s few were being grown in home gardens. Both highbush and lowbush berries were harvested and processed commercially, but the lowbush were most common. Since then, hundreds of large-fruited cultivars have been developed, and except for those who live in the tropical tip of Florida, gardeners nearly everywhere can grow blueberries.

Three species are commonly grown in North American gardens:

Hardiest of the three, the lowbush, *Vaccinium angustifolium,* are the blueberries everyone loves to pick from the wild. Native Americans dried the berries and pounded them into "moosemeat," an ingredient they used to make pemmican. Wild lowbush blueberries are grown commercially in some northern states, including Maine. Gardeners who grow wild blueberries in their backyards can expect about a pint of berries for each foot of row.

The highbush, *V. corymbosum,* is the most popular blueberry plant both for home gardeners and commercial growers. The bushes grow from 6 to 15 feet high, and produce large berries in midsummer and later. Although less hardy than the lowbush, some cultivars do well in zone 3 when planted in a spot sheltered from the wind. Crosses between highbush and lowbush blueberries have resulted in several hardy, large-fruiting plants. Yields vary widely among the cultivars, but most gardeners can expect from 5 to 15 pounds per bush.

The rabbit-eye blueberry, *V. ashei,* cannot stand low winter temperatures, so the plants are suitable only for the southern United States. They need a chilling period, however, so cannot be grown in tropical climates. Rabbit-eyes grow on drier soils than the highbush kinds will tolerate, but in hot climates most need some type of irrigation. They are usually more productive than the highbush, and a yield of 20 pounds of fruit per bush is not unusual.

All types of blueberries are extremely fussy about soils. They do best at a soil pH of from 4.5 to 5, which is so "sour" that most garden plants do not grow well in it. If you decide to invest in blueberry plants and are uncertain about the pH, make a soil test first. Sometimes the vegetation that grows naturally in the area will give you a clue about your soil type. Pines, hemlocks, and wild blueberries all indicate an acid soil, but if goldenrod and white cedar trees flourish, the soil is probably far too alkaline for blueberries. This is not always a certain method, because acid and alkaline soils often lie in close proximity to each other.

Even if your soil tests from 5.5 to 6, you can probably grow blueberries if you mix *sphagnum* peat moss with the soil around the plants. Cottonseed meal, composted pine needles or oak leaves, or compost made from pine, oak, or hemlock bark also help acidify the soil. After planting, mulch your plants with pine needles, oak leaves, or shavings from oak, pine, or hemlock to help maintain the soil's acidity. If you use chemical fertilizers, ammonium sulfate supplies both nitrogen and acidity. Aluminum sulfate, formerly prescribed for lowering acidity, is toxic to the soil and noticeably changes the flavor of the fruit. Like many home gardeners, I feel that organic methods for lowering soil pH are safer and their acidifying effects last much longer.

If your soil test indicates that the pH is higher than 6.2, it is likely that the subsoil contains lime that will percolate into the topsoil with each rain. To lower the acidity of such soil and maintain it may not be not worth the trouble and expense. One day a gardening friend who lives in a lime pocket showed us her beautiful, giant-sized bushes, heavily laden with blueberries. "Do you like them?" she asked. "I estimate that the berries on those bushes have cost about a dollar each."

Planting and Care

Blueberry plants may start to bear a few fruits the second year after planting, but they are slow growers and take many years to reach full production, so it is best to start with two- or three-year-old plants. After you have made sure the soil is acid enough for blueberries, and added manure and humus, till it thoroughly. Blueberries are shallow rooted and have no root hairs, so the soil must be loose for them to start growing well. Unlike deep-rooted plants, they must find all the moisture and nutrients they need in the top several inches of soil.

Blueberries need cross pollination, so plant at least two different cultivars. It is even better to plant three different ones not only to ensure pollination, but so that in case one dies, two will still be left. Blueberry blossoms are not especially fragrant and therefore not as attractive to bees as most other flowers, so always mix up your plantings and keep the different cultivars close to each other. If you set 20 Jerseys in one block and 20 Earliblue in another some distance away, the same bee may not find both kinds.

You can plant potted blueberry bushes almost any time that the ground isn't frozen, but plant bare-rooted kinds only in the spring in the North, and in spring or fall in the South. Set highbush and rabbit-eye blueberries 5 feet apart, and space the rows 7 to 9 feet apart. Unlike lowbush plants, these do not spread by underground rhizomes. Set lowbush plants 1 foot apart in rows 3 or more feet apart. Since these spread by underground rhizomes, they will quickly make a low, thick hedge.

Water the small bushes directly after planting, with water to which you have added a small amount of liquid fertilizer, such as manure tea, fish emulsion, or soluble chemical plant food. Continue to water every other day, and add the liquid fertilizer once a week for the next three or four weeks. This will help the plants get over their transplanting shock and encourage them to grow rapidly. Add a mulch to protect the roots, and check weed growth.

Apply a cup of cottonseed meal, soybean meal, dried or rotted manure, or a complete fertilizer such as 5–10–10 around each plant in the spring, and add more mulch. Use larger amounts as the plant grows. Blueberries need lots of nitrogen, so make sure the plant food you choose contains this element. Stunted growth and yellow or reddish leaves often indicate that nitrogen is lacking.

You can easily damage the shallow roots by hoeing or cultivating, so pull out any weeds that penetrate the mulch. Even with a mulch, the shallow-rooted blueberries are apt to dry out in prolonged spells of dry weather, so you may have to water them often. With care, your blueberry plants should produce well for several decades.

Unlike most bush fruits, it is not easy to start additional highbush blueberry plants from the ones you have, because well-rooted offshoots and suckers seldom form around them — one reason why blueberry plants usually cost more than other small fruits.

Pests

One of the nice things about blueberries is the small number of insects and diseases that bother them. Large commercial plantings are more vulnerable, but home gardeners have far less to worry about and may never encounter any serious diseases or harmful insects. The *blueberry maggot* and *cherry fruit worm* are the most common troublesome insects, but if you clean up all the old fruit each year before winter, it should discourage them. *Wasps* and the *plum curculio* may also show up, and if these or any other insects persist, rotenone dust should control them quite effectively.

Blueberry diseases tend to be the most common in the South but may occasionally show up elsewhere. Cut away any abnormal-looking growth as soon as it appears. Three diseases are most prevalent: *Mummy berry* causes the fruit to rot and fall, but you can prevent it by keeping the berries picked so the disease cannot overwinter on the ground; *stem canker* may cause cracks in the canes; and *botrytis tip blight* kills new growth. Check with your garden store to see what fungicides are available for treatment if your plants become infected.

Virus diseases such as *stunt* are the most difficult to control, and invariably result in the gradual deterioration of the plant. When you buy plants, choose cultivars that have been tissue cultured and are virus-free.

Animals seldom bother blueberries, although birds are unusually fond of them. Unless you are very lucky or skillful at bird repulsion, you may need to cover the bushes with very tight netting before the berries begin to ripen.

Pruning

Highbush and rabbit-eye blueberries need annual pruning after they reach 5 or 6 feet in height in order to produce large crops of big fruits. A mild day in late winter or early spring is a good time to get out there with your clippers. For the first few years, prune the bush only as necessary to get it into a sturdy upright shape, but after it begins to produce good crops, cut out all wood that shows signs of age, and thin out any of the branches that are crowding each other. Whenever the twiggy ends of the canes appear too thick, thin them out. Cut back the tops of any plants that are growing too high. This pruning will open up the bush and let sunshine in so the berries will ripen better, and allow you to harvest them more easily.

Different cultivars grow in different ways, so prune them according to the needs of each individual bush. You can easily determine when older canes should be cut back completely to the ground, and when they should be cut back to a main trunk. Bushes sometimes set more fruit buds than is good for the plant. When this happens, thin out some of them so you will get fewer but larger berries. On dormant plants you can easily distinguish between the fat fruit buds and the thinner leaf buds.

In the North, highbush blueberries grow more slowly than in warmer climates, and they don't ever get as tall as in the South, so they require a different type of pruning. In zones 3 and 4, any heavy cutting back, such as you would do in zones 5 and 6, is likely to result in greatly reduced production for several years. For best results, thin only the twiggy ends of the branches each year, and cut out broken or winter-damaged branches. Eventually it will become beneficial to gradually renew the plant by removing some of its older wood but only after the bush is twelve to twenty years old.

Growers who manage hundreds of acres of wild lowbush blueberries eliminate the weeds and renew their bushes by burning over different sections of their plantings each year. New plants sprout from the roots and begin to bear after a year or two. This method is rather impractical for us home gardeners, to say the least. We should prune our lowbush blueberries only to remove old and injured branches and to thin out any growth that is too thick.

Harvesting

The fruits of different cultivars become various shades of blue when they are completely ripe, so color is not a good indication of ripeness. For the best flavor, don't pick them until they have developed a rich bloom; then taste a few to determine exactly when they are at their peak. Fortunately, blueberries ripen over a long season, so there is no need to pick them daily, like strawberries and raspberries. The fruit will stay in good condition for several days after picking if you keep it cool and dry. Cooks never run out of ways to use blueberries in season. They are a treat on our morning cereal and in muffins, pies, puddings, and other desserts. They make wonderful jams and conserves, and are easy to freeze for winter feasts. We just wash them and put a cupful in a plastic bag, so no measuring is necessary when we use them later.

Cultivars

Lowbush Blueberries

Several lowbush cultivars that produce larger berries and heavier crops than the wild kinds include Augusta, Bloodstone, Bluehaven, Brunswick, Chignecto, Putte, and Top Hat.

Highbush Blueberries

Atlantic. Heavy bearer of high-quality, large, light blue berries.
Avonblue. Large berries on 5-foot bush. Does best in southern locations.
Berkeley. Large, sweet berries. Midseason. Moderately hardy.
Bluecrop. Moderately hardy, reliable bush. Light blue berries are a bit tart.
Bluegold. Heavy producer of good-flavored, late-ripening berries.
Bluejay. Fruit resists cracking well. Pleasant, tart flavor.
Blueray. Early ripening, firm, sweet fruit on fairly hardy bush.
Bluetta. One of the few blueberries that is self-fruitful. Heavy bearer of light blue berries of fair quality.
Burlington. Best in mild climates. Vigorous bush, firm and crack-resistant berries.
Coville. Large berries on vigorous bush. Tart until fully ripe.
Earliblue. 4- to 6-foot, moderately hardy bush; fruit ripens early.
Herbert. Heavy crops of large, flavorful berries in midseason.
Ivanhoe. Big crops of early ripening, light blue, good-flavored berries.
Jersey. Popular, large, fair-quality berry. Ripens midseason.
Meader. Heavy bearer of large berries. Moderately hardy.
November Glow. 5- to 6-foot plant with leaves that turns a brilliant red in the fall.
Rubel. Heavy producer of small berries. Good for processing.
Sharpblue. Large berries, good bearer.
Sierra. Early to midseason ripening. A vigorous bush that produces heavy yields.
Spartan. Vigorous, moderately hardy cultivar. Exceptionally large fruit.
Weymouth. Older cultivar that ripens very early.

In the Pacific Northwest, Darrow, Elliott's Blueberry, and Olympia are popular.

Hardy Hybrids

Numerous crosses between highbush and lowbush species have resulted in several hardy, large-fruiting kinds that are being grown in zone 4 and sheltered spots of zone 3. They grow from 18 to 36 inches in height, so are easy to cover with bird-proof netting. These include

Early Bluejay. Vigorous, early-bearing bush also bears early in life.

Northblue. Heavy bearing, superhardy plant. High-quality fruit.

Northcountry. Good-size fruits with wild blueberry flavor. Early, productive. Best where snow cover is reliable.

Northland. Early ripening fruit on 4-foot, spreading bush.

Northsky. Fine wild blueberry flavor. The fruit is not as large as most other hybrids.

Patriot. Large, early-ripening, rich-flavored fruit. Four-foot bush.

Rabbit-eyes

These cultivars need a mild climate, grow rapidly to from 10 to 25 feet in height, and may yield up to 20 pounds of fruit per bush. Cultivars include

Aliceblue. Early-ripening, medium to large fruit.

Beckyblue. Medium to large, light blue fruit. Upright grower.

Bluebelle. Extra-large fruit in midseason.

Bluegem. Large fruits on vigorous, heavy-bearing bush.

Bonita. Vigorous grower. Medium-large, light blue fruits. Early.

Briteblue. Sweet, late-ripening, frosty-blue berries of fine flavor. Vigorous bush.

Centurion. Large, dark blue fruits on upright, productive bush.

Chaucer. Large fruits, vigorous bush, bears early. Sensitive to frosts.

Choice. Dark blue, medium-size fruits. Late ripening.

Climax. Vigorous plant, medium-size, early-ripening berries.

Powder Blue. Heavy producer of large, dark blue fruits. Late.

Premier. Large, early-ripening fruits on spreading bushes.

Southland. One of the hardiest rabbit-eyes.

Tifblue. Good-quality, sweet berries. A popular cultivar.

Woodard. Early-ripening, large, good, but slightly tart fruits.

CHAPTER 27

Vine Fruits —
The Grape *(Vitis* spp.*)*
and the Kiwi *(Actinidia* spp.*)*

According to Aesop's ancient fable, a fox once found a beautiful bunch of grapes growing on a vine just out of his reach. He leaped at it a couple of times and then backed up and took several running jumps, all to no avail. He just couldn't reach the grapes. Finally, he trotted off muttering, "They're probably too sour to eat anyway." Aesop not only gave us the worthwhile and oft-used expression "sour grapes," but he probably helped name the wild North American fox grape as well.

This story is only one of thousands about the grape, one of the most ancient and romantic fruits. Almost everyone wants to grow them. Growers may be motivated by the old legends, or perhaps dream of the day when each man will sit under his own fig tree and vine as the Bible promises. But more likely, they just love grapes.

Grapes are one of the world's oldest cultivated fruits. The Egyptians made wine as early as 3,000 B.C., and at the beginning of Western civilization in the Fertile Crescent of the Mediterranean, tables were piled high with the fresh fruit, and wine making and selling were important industries. Ruins of ancient cities and ships sunk millenniums ago always contain vast numbers of wine jars. Much later, the grape and its wine continued to be interlaced with European history. The wine-producing areas of Italy, France, Spain, and Germany became world famous, and when the early settlers came to America they brought the European vines with them. Unfortunately, most of their plantings were doomed to failure, because the highly developed Old World grapes could not adapt to the climate of eastern North America, or its diseases and insects.

Eastern America already had several native grapes, however. Among them were the fox *(Vitis labrusca)* and the frost *(V. riparia),* both of which grew wild in the Northeast; they were probably the grapes the Vikings found when they named the country "Vinland." The muscadine *(V. rotundifolia)* grew from Maryland to Florida, and west as far as Kansas.

Persistent horticulturists kept a few of the European grapes alive long

▲ A mature grape vine can produce 15 or more pounds
of fruit annually, and in a small space. *(USDA)*

enough to cross them with the native species, hoping to develop high-quality
hybrids that would withstand the growing conditions of the New World. The
Concord, developed at Concord, Massachusetts, in the mid-1800s, was the most
famous of the new grapes. Ephraim Bull, a gold beater by trade, abandoned his
occupation to devote full time to his experiments with grapes. His discovery of
the Concord was not an accident or a simple stroke of luck, since he is said to
have grown over 22,000 seedlings before he developed the vine that ushered in
the American grape industry.

Nearly a century and a half later, the Concord and its hybrids are still the
leading grapes grown in northeastern United States and southern Canada. They
adapt easily to many different soils and produce an abundance of quality fruit for
eating, juice, and wine. Furthermore, the vine is vigorous, hardy, and propa-
gates easily from cuttings. Crosses of these with the muscadine grapes have
produced many muscat grape cultivars.

Even the southern European grapes, *Vitis vinifera*, eventually found a North
American home to their liking in California where, thanks to a good climate,
irrigation, and careful culture, nearly every year is a "vintage" year. Crosses

made with native grapes and other hybrids have provided us with hundreds of red, white, and blue cultivars, many of which are suitable for home culture.

Climate is still a limiting factor in growing grapes in northern home gardens, and commercial growers would never plant them where there were fewer than 150 continuous frost-free days during the growing season. Most, in fact, prefer to have an even longer growing season. This effectively rules out zones 3, 4, and part of zone 5 as prime grape-growing country. Nevertheless, we home gardeners in the cooler zones are not left without grapes to grow. Horticulturists have developed a number of cultivars that require fewer than 120 warm days to ripen their fruit. Several can be grown successfully even in the short seasons of the Dakotas, Minnesota, northern New England, and Canada.

Grapes are one of the easiest fruits to propagate. Hardwood cuttings taken in early spring (see Chapter 13) root easily and become husky, well-developed plants by fall. The following spring you can transplant the cuttings to their permanent home, and begin picking fruit in a couple of years. Grapes can also be started by layering and by softwood cuttings. On the other hand, grape seeds are likely to produce mostly wild-type plants with little value.

When you buy them, select the largest grade of the one-year-old vines. Two-year-old plants are likely to have been grown from weak, leftover plants from the previous year. Choose your cultivars according to both your climate and whether you want them for table use, juice, or wine making.

If you garden in zones 6–8 you'll probably have little trouble growing most of the grapes offered by nurseries, and most certainly you will want to take advantage of this healthful and delicious fruit. If grape culture sounds a bit involved at first glance, don't worry. It actually is not much more complicated than staking peas.

In zones 3 or 4, plant your grapes in heat pockets. The best locations are where buildings, walls, or hills form coves or corners that face southeast, protect against the cooling north wind, and trap the warm sunshine in spring and fall. Grapes prefer light, sandy soils that warm up fast, too.

In the cold regions of northern Vermont where the climate is often compared with that of the Arctic, we know of a steep southerly slope that drops sharply to a small lake. It is protected by woods and hills and gets all the morning and mid-afternoon sun. Here, year after year, the late-ripening Concord has found a perfect home. It is completely protected from the wind, tilts toward the sun, and is warmed by the gentle air currents from the lake on cool fall nights.

Because there are few such spots in zones 3 and 4, you may need to create your own heat trap. Fiberglass fences, plastic tents, and other artificial structures can be used to intensify and hold heat for sun-worshiping grapes. It also helps to mulch them with clear plastic or crushed rock, both of which attract and hold heat better than organic mulches.

The easiest way for beginners to manage a backyard vineyard is on a two-wire fence using a method called the Kniffin System (see page 207, B). Later on, as you get more proficient, you may want to try other methods, but vines grown on latticework, arbors, and trellises are particularly hard to prune. It is neces-

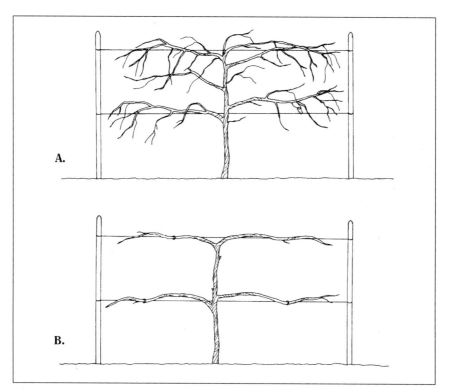

▲ **(A) A grapevine in need of pruning (B) A well-pruned grapevine trained to the Kniffin System**

sary to keep them in control, even if you feel that appearance is more important than productivity.

Pruning is a very important part of grape culture, and one that must not be neglected. Because of the grape's tendency to grow vigorously, after it reaches maturity a lot of wood must be cut away each year. Unpruned grapevines become so overgrown and dense that the sun cannot reach into the areas where fruit should form, and the further the grapes are produced from the main stem, the smaller the crop is likely to be.

First Year

In most of North America, spring planting is best because grapes need an abundance of heat and sunlight to get established before winter. They are one of the last fruit plants to start growth in the spring, and they blossom much later than any of the tree fruits. The soil for grapes should be slightly sandy so it will warm up fast and stay warm. It should also not be excessively fertile, or they will grow too fast and not bear well. Too much fertilizer will not only cause possible winter injury, but also delay the coloring and ripening of the fruit. Grapevines have deep roots and can go searching for their nourishment better than most other small fruits.

Plant the vines about 8 feet apart, with a post midway between each plant and one on each end of the row. If you have more than one row, keep the rows at least 8 feet apart. String two strands of smooth 9-gauge wire on the posts; the first one should be 2 feet above the ground, and the second, about 2 feet higher.

If you bought your vines bare-rooted, cut them back directly after planting so each is only 5 or 6 inches long and contains just two or three fat buds. This pruning will encourage the roots to start growing rapidly and help them to keep up with the top growth. If you plant potted vines, omit this cutting back.

Water the vines frequently and allow them to grow freely, without further pruning the first year.

Second Year

Very early in the spring, when the plants are dormant and before the buds start to swell, cut the vine back to a single stem with no branches. This treatment will encourage faster growth as the vine hurries to replace its lost canes.

During the year, allow four side branches to grow (two in each direction) and train them along the wires, which they will grasp with their tendrils. Pinch off all buds that start to grow in other directions.

By the end of the second year, if growth has been good, the space along both wires should be filled. These vines should then bloom and produce a few grapes the third year.

Third Year

During the year, allow only four more canes to grow from buds along the main stem. Train these to grow along the ground, parallel to the four on the wires so that they can replace them later.

In late winter following the third growing season, cut off the canes that produced that year and tie the new canes to the wires. Trim off all other growth except the four new canes.

With this type of training, each mature vine should produce from 12 to 15 pounds of grapes (30 to 60 bunches) per year. If more bunches than that form, remove the surplus before the grapes develop, to avoid overbearing and thus weakening the vine. In this way, the vines are constantly being renewed, and should go on producing for fifty years, or even longer.

Keep the vines weed-free either by cultivation or mulching. Cultivation works best in cool climates, because grapes need a warm soil to grow well and ripen. Like peaches, even the hardy varieties sometimes have trouble terminating their rapid growth in time to harden up before an early frost. Because of this characteristic, apply fertilizer only when the vines appear to need it, and then only very early in the season.

Pollination

Most grapes are self-fruitful, so cross pollination is seldom necessary. Brighton is an exception, and one of the few common varieties that is not self-pollinating, so it needs a partner to bear fruit. Nursery catalogs will usually state when a pollinator is needed for any cultivar.

Harvesting

Ripe grapes have brown seeds, full color and bloom, and the clusters separate easily from the vines. Don't pick your grapes early because, unlike many other fruits, they will not continue to ripen after they have been picked. If you intend to use them for jelly, you can harvest them while they are slightly "green," but for eating or for juice, leave them on the vines until they are sweet and juicy. Don't let them freeze, though. Pick them on a dry day, because wet grapes do not keep well.

Grapes keep in a refrigerator for many weeks if they are dry and the temperature is set at just above freezing. Drying grapes into raisins is possible if you use the right varieties, but the process is not easy for home gardeners.

Home grape growing has many advantages. You will be using far fewer chemical sprays than commercial growers are likely to apply. The fruit is delicious when eaten fresh from the vine, and made into juice, jelly, and wine. The seedless kinds are also good in pies. The by-products are useful too. Grape leaves, picked in early summer, are often used in Eastern Mediterranean cooking, and the dormant vines (those you prune away) can be used to make wreaths.

Diseases

Grapes have collected nearly as many pests as apples over the centuries, but, fortunately, vines in isolated home gardens usually escape most of the diseases that large growers must cope with. You can't count on missing them all indefinitely, however, so sooner or later one of the following may show up. Most can be controlled by fungicides.

Anthracnose. Anthracnose, or bird's-eye rot, will appear as spots on the fruit. It also affects leaves and the new sprouts.

Black rot. This disease turns the fruit black, rotten, and shriveled, and covers the leaves with brown spots and black pimples.

Dead arm. If left unchecked, this fungus disease gradually kills the plant. Fungicides applied early in the season may help, but usually cutting off and burning the infected parts is more effective.

Downy mildew. This is an especially serious disease in the East. It covers leaves, new shoots, and fruit with a gray down. Bordeaux mixture or powdered sulfur were often used to control mildew in times past, but modern fungicides work better.

Insects

Hundreds of insects attack grapes in different parts of North America, and even isolated vines may be visited by some of them. Some, such as the Japanese beetle, are familiar names to growers of other fruits. Some bother only the grape.

Keep the grapes picked, and remove all the prunings to prevent overwintering of insect larvae. Encourage birds and use insect traps whenever possible to avoid spraying, but if chemicals seem the only solution, follow the grape-spraying schedule in Chapter 9.

Here are some insect pests to watch for:

Curculio attacks the fruit, much as a similar insect attacks plums.

Cutworms feed on opening buds at night.

Flea beetles attack the vine and leaves.

Grape berry moths are the main source of wormy grapes. Their larvae eat the pulp.

Phylloxera are small sucking insects, similar to aphids. They attack European grapes.

Rootworms are small, grayish-brown beetles that attack leaves. Their larvae eat the grapevine roots.

Rose chafers eat blossoms, buds, newly formed fruit, and leaves. Usually they are most troublesome to vines grown on sandy soil.

Thrips are sucking insects that also attack other small fruits.

Other Pests

In spite of Aesop, I have never heard of foxes actually eating grapes, but in regions where birds steal the fruits, you may need either netting or other protective measures.

Cultivars

Many nurseries feel they need to introduce new fruits every year, so they won't be branded old-fashioned. But newer doesn't always mean better — at least for the home gardener. Why not start out with one or two of the old reliable Concords if your season is long enough — Beta if you live where it's cold, or one of the muscats if you live in the South? Add others one by one, as your skill improves, and then, who knows? You may one day become known as the Bacchus on your block.

Probably even the apple has fewer named cultivars than the grape. In millenniums of culture, thousands of kinds have appeared and disappeared, but at present there are more than 5,000 named cultivars. The following are usually available for home gardeners in various parts of the country:

DESSERT GOLD OR WHITE TABLE GRAPES

GOLDEN MUSCAT, HIMROD, INTERLAKEN, LAKEMONT, NIAGARA, REMAILY

BLUE GRAPES

ALDEN, BETA, BUFFALO, CONCORD, FREDONIA, GLENORA, SCHUYLER, STEUBEN, VAN BUREN, WORDEN

RED GRAPES

BRIGHTON, CATAWBA, DELAWARE, RELIANCE, SUFFOLK RED

WINE GRAPES

AURORA, BACO-NOIR, CASCADE, CATAWBA, CAYUGA, DE CHAUNAC, DELAWARE, DUNKIRK, FOCH, STEUBEN

EARLIEST

ALPHA, BETA, ONTARIO, SENECA, VAN BUREN

NEXT EARLIEST

BRIGHTON, BUFFALO, FREDONIA, WORDEN

HARDIEST

ALPHA, BETA, CONCORD, DELAWARE, EDELWEISS, KAY GRAY, VAN BUREN, SWENSON'S RED, VALIANT, WORDEN

SEEDLESS

CONCORD SEEDLESS, HIMROD, INTERLAKEN, MARS, REMAILY, SUFFOLK RED, VENUS

FOR ZONE 9

BLACK SPANISH, BLUE LAKE, CHAMPANEL, DAYTONA, STOVER, SUWANNEE, and the Muscadine grapes — COWART, DIXIE, JUMBO, MAGOON, ROANOKE, and SUGARGATE

The Kiwi *(Actinidia* spp.)

In recent years there has been much interest in the kiwi, also called the Chinese gooseberry. Kiwis originated in China but were imported to New Zealand where they were improved and renamed after one of the native flightless birds. Kiwi fruits ripen in late summer on vigorous vines, which need some kind of support. The fruits have thin skins and vary from the size of a large gooseberry to that of a good-size plum. They can be stored up to three weeks in a refrigerator.

The flesh of kiwis resembles that of gooseberries and grapes in texture, color, and flavor. The vines are ornamental, with small, white blossoms, and can be grown over arbors like grapes or allowed to trail over walls or fences. They are propagated by cuttings or by layering the plants. (See Chapter 13.)

The male and female flowers of most kiwis are borne on separate plants, so at least one of each sex is necessary to get fruit. *A. chinensis,* the Chinese kiwi, has large fruits and most are hardy only in zones 7–9. Many cultivars of this species are available. CALIFORNIA and MONTY are two female cultivars; MATSU and Tomuri are males.

Arctic Beauty *(A. kolmikta)* is a fairly hardy kiwi, but it is less vigorous than *A. chinensis,* so it is better for smaller lots. It also has smaller fruits.

Issai *(A. arguta)* is popular, not only because it is one of the hardiest, but also because the male and female flowers are borne on the same plant. Its fruits are about 1½ inches long and rich in vitamin C. The vines not only bear heavily but also at a young age. When mature, a vine may produce up to 100 pounds of fruit a year.

Plant kiwis 10 feet apart in full sun in ordinary garden soil — they don't like wet soil — and give them something to climb on or trail over. The plants are relatively pest-free. Prune occasionally to keep them under control, and to thin out the older canes.

Kiwi plants are still relatively expensive, but if you already have vines you can start new plants by layering. Most gardeners will want to plant them as an experiment only, but it may be one you will find fun to try.

CHAPTER 28

Nuts for the Home Garden

Nearly every region in America once had an abundance of wild nut trees, and it used to be an annual event for country folks to take burlap bags into the woods on a crisp, fall day and race the squirrels to the tasty treats hidden among the newly fallen leaves. Back home they'd dump out their sticky treasures on the attic floor to dry for winter cracking. Unfortunately, blights, weather, and heavy cutting of the nut trees for their valuable lumber have taken their toll. Nutting, as it was called, is mostly a thing of the past.

People still love nuts, though, and gardeners are planting nut trees in increasing numbers in their backyards, even though most get too large for a small suburban lot. They are logical companions to fruits, but unlike fruits, you can easily store them for months or even years without processing. Nuts are an excellent source of protein and other nutrients. Various recently developed cultivars are hardier, bear younger, and best of all, produce nuts that are larger, tastier, and crack more easily than their wild ancestors. If you like nuts and have the right climate and enough space, consider planting a nut tree or two.

Eating nuts is one of the most enjoyable ways to use them, of course, but they also have other uses. The shells are made into ornaments and jewelry, or burned to make a fragrant smoke used for smoking meat and to make activated charcoal, a product used in filters and gas masks. Wood from nut trees is among the most prized in the world. Windmill propellers used to be made from butternut, one of the strongest lightweight woods known. Gun stocks, fine furniture, and many other products are made from black walnut. Hickory, known for its great strength, is used for skis, tool handles, and much more. Even before the chestnut blight struck America, most of the great chestnut forests of the East had already been cut for their fine lumber.

Improved Cultivars

Nut breeding has progressed less rapidly than fruit and berry development, both because there has not been as much interest in improving them and because they take such a long time to bear. The most progress has been made with almonds, filberts, pecans, Persian walnuts, and other nuts grown commercially. Recently, however, some excellent cultivars of butternuts, black walnuts, chestnuts, and hickories have been developed. Still, many of the nut trees being sold are simply seedlings from ordinary wild trees.

Your Tree in a Nutshell

If you like the idea of raising wild nuts and are not in a hurry, you might as well grow your own. It's easy — just imitate the squirrels. Practically all the great nut forests in this country were planted by these active little creatures as they stashed away huge numbers of nuts and then forgot where they hid them. Like the squirrels, all you need to do is dig a small hole and bury your nut an inch or so deep. Either plant it where you want the tree to grow permanently, or plant a bed of seeds and transplant them after they have grown for two or three years.

Fall is the time that the squirrels do their planting, and it's the best time for us, too. Most nuts sprout well only if they have been frozen for a few days first, so if you forget to plant them in the fall, you can do it in the spring after freezing each nut for a week inside a teacup of water in your freezer. They may not sprout quite as fast as if the shells had softened in the ground during the winter, however.

Whenever you plant, protect the nuts with a wire screen or a scattering of mothballs, particularly if you have squirrels or chipmunks around. They may forget where they've hidden their own nuts, but they'll have no trouble finding yours and hauling them away.

Don't worry if your new little tree doesn't appear the same week the dandelions bloom, or even with the first sprouts of corn. It may be midsummer before it finally bursts through the soil. As soon as it does pop up, it will grow rapidly, however, and may be 2 or 3 feet tall within six or eight weeks. The nut itself carries enough nutrients to get the tree off to a good start, so don't feed it anything or it may keep growing too late in the season and be winter-killed. For aftercare of seedlings, see Chapter 13.

If you transplant nut trees, don't wait until they get large. Most grow tremendous taproots that head speedily toward the center of the earth, so don't attempt to move them after they get much more than 3 or 4 feet tall. If you should break or bend the taproot in the process of transplanting, the tree is likely to die. The best time to transplant is in early spring.

Planting and Culture

Since some of the new cultivars are as superior to wild nuts as named apples are to wild, sour ones, if the cultivars will grow in your climate, consider planting them rather than seedling trees. Planting a nut tree is much the same as planting a fruit tree (see Chapter 6.) When you are choosing a location, however, keep in mind the eventual size of the tree. Filberts remain nicely within fruit tree dimensions, but most other species become 50 or more feet tall, and nearly as wide. Give them enough room, and don't plant them beneath overhead wires, or too close to your house. The falling nuts can become a nuisance, too, so plant away from streets, sidewalks, roofs, and any lawns that will be mowed in late fall. Nuts are hard on mowers.

Nut trees grow best in well-drained, deep soil. After the first year they benefit from annual spring applications of fertilizer that is rich in nitrogen. To imitate the conditions of the lush forest floor, apply a thick, organic mulch when the tree is still young. Grafted cultivars take much less time to produce their first crop than do seedling trees, which may require eight years or more to bear their first nut.

Because even a hybrid nut tree still closely resembles its wild relatives, it needs no special care. For a strong tree, prune it to have one central trunk with no branches for the first 8 feet. Diseases and insects seldom infest backyard nut trees. This is fortunate, because spraying such large trees is not easy.

Pollination

Although a single black walnut or butternut tree can produce nuts, there is general consensus among horticulturists that they benefit from having a companion. Most other nut trees definitely need a partner, and to be compatible, the partner must be of the same species. The two should be within a hundred feet of each other, because nearly all nuts are pollinated by wind instead of bees.

If you are planting all cultivars rather than seedlings, plant two different cultivars or a few seedling trees of the same species to pollinate them. In other words, if you plant a Royal Filbert, plant another filbert hybrid, such as Graham or Skinner, or some wild filberts to pollinate it. Two Royal Filberts would not pollinate each other, because they both originated from the same tree. Each seedling tree is different, however, so they will pollinate any other seedling or hybrid of the same species.

Harvesting

When the nuts begin to fall off the tree they are mature and ready to pick. Squirrels don't always wait for them to fall, however, so it is best to begin collecting as soon as the squirrels do. If you are careful not to damage the limbs, you can shake most nuts from the trees. In fact, walnuts are often harvested commercially by mechanical shakers. The entire crop of most nut trees can be gathered at one time, although some, like walnuts, may need several pickings. Don't let nuts stay on the ground for any length of time after they fall because they deteriorate rapidly.

Nuts need to be dried thoroughly before their meats ripen enough to eat. Spread them out, one layer deep, on benches in a greenhouse or garage, on warm attic floors, or, best of all, on raised screens where the air can circulate all around them. Turn them occasionally so they will dry on all sides. On our attic floor the playful kittens turned them for us.

After drying the nuts completely, store them in burlap bags, boxes, or barrels in a cool place, making sure the storage area is squirrel-proof.

It would be wrong not to mention some of the bad habits of nut trees. Some kinds are not the best trees to plant as close neighbors to other plantings. Both black walnut and butternut roots give off a toxic substance that eliminates their competition by killing certain nearby plants, especially evergreens. They don't have this poisonous effect on grass and many other plants, however.

Nut Species

I include here only the nut trees that home gardeners usually grow. The planting zones listed indicate the areas where the trees appear to do best and are most widely grown, although they may succeed in other zones under the right conditions.

Black Walnuts *(Juglans nigra)*
Zones 4–7

The native black walnut grows well throughout most of zones 5 through 8, and hardier strains survive in zones 3 and 4. Most cultivars have nuts that crack easier, and have larger and better flavored meats than the wild kinds, but the trees are less hardy. Not everyone cares for the black walnut's unusual flavor, but their fans use them to flavor cakes, ice cream, and other desserts.

In addition to the different strains of seedlings that vary widely across the country, the following cultivars are among those being sold by nurseries: Bowser, Cornell, Elmer Meyers, Emma Kay, Kwik-Krop (Stark), Ohio, Patterson, Ridgeway, Snyder, Sparrow, Stabler, Stambaugh, Thomas Black, Thomas Meyers, Vandersloot, Victoria, and Weschcke. Patterson and Weschcke are among the most hardy.

The Butternut *(Juglans cinerea)*
Zones 3–7

Like dried corn, beans, and smoked meat, butternuts were one of the staple foods that helped the Iroquois Indians live well through the hard northern winters. The early settlers soon learned to store and use them too, and they have been a winter treat in the Northeast ever since. There's no solid evidence that Native Americans ever mixed butternuts with maple sugar to make what I consider one of the most delicious confections in the world — maple butternut fudge. But since they used both products, I like to think that they made and enjoyed it, too. (For recipe, see page 241.)

The butternut is one of the hardiest nut trees and its oily meats are one of the most flavorful nuts. New hybrids and selections of native trees produce nuts that are larger and easier to crack than the wild ones. Even the wild ones crack easily if you pour boiling water over them, let them stand for fifteen minutes, and then drain. With one easy hammer blow you can then pop the halves apart intact.

Butternut blooms are easily damaged in late spring frosts, and even if they are not harmed, the trees are likely to bear abundantly one year, and then take a few years off, so it is lucky for us butternut lovers that the nuts store well.

Some improved varieties now being sold are: AYERS, BOUNTIFUL (STARK), CHAMBERLIN, CHAMBERS CORNER, CRAXEZY, CREIGHTON, GEORGE ELMER, KENWORTHY, MITCHELL, VAN SYCKLE, and WESCHCKE. Ayers has very large nuts; Mitchell begins to bear at an early age; Chamberlin and George Elmer are among the most hardy.

The buartnut tree, a cross between the Japanese heartnut and the butternut, combines the hardiness and good flavor of the latter with the easy cracking, high yields, and disease resistance of the former. Several hybrids are now on the market. Among them are COBLE'S NO. 1, CORSAN, DUNOKA, FIOKA, HOPKINS, and WALLICK.

THE CHESTNUT FAMILY (CASTANEA)
ZONES 5–9

The American chestnut *(Castanea dentata)* was an important part of North American life during its developing days. Its lumber was greatly prized for paneling and for export to Europe. During cold winter nights, the nuts popped in many a Colonial fireplace, and holidays were never complete without chestnut dressing for the turkey or goose. In New England there is still a belief that a blacksmith shop should stand "under a spreading chestnut tree."

▲ **Nearly wiped out by the blight, chestnuts have made a big comeback.** *(USDA)*

When the blight of the early 1900s wiped out nearly every chestnut tree, a search began for blight-resistant varieties. Trees were introduced from China, Japan, Manchuria, and Spain, and some were successfully crossed with the few remaining American species. Many of the resulting new hybrids are now producing quality nuts in American backyards.

The Chinese chestnut *(Castanea mollissima)* is frequently sold in nurseries and garden centers. It is less hardy than most peaches, however, and the grafted cultivars appear to be even less hardy than the seedling trees. As with the peach, you must fertilize them carefully when the trees are young or they will grow too rapidly and get winter injury.

Many chestnut cultivars available today are improved Oriental species. Others are hybrids of the Oriental and American species. Among them are: Crane, Douglass, Dunstan, Eaton, Heritage, Layeroka, Meader, Meiling, Nanking, Myoka, Revival, Skookum, and Willamette.

The Filbert and Hazelnut *(Corylus)*
Zones 5–9

The round filbert *(Corylus avellana)* is familiar to everyone who has ever bought a bag of mixed nuts for the holidays. It is a native of southern Europe, probably originating in Italy. Most of North America's commercial filbert production is in the Pacific Northwest, with Barcelona, Daviana, and Duchilly the leading cultivars. They seldom do well in the rest of the continent, however.

An American cousin of the filbert, the hazelnut *(Corylus americana)* grows wild in hedgerows all over the northern U.S. and southern Canada. The small nuts are favorites of chipmunks and squirrels, and as children we used to gather them, too. It always seemed to me that it was hardly worth the effort to take off the prickly burrs and dry and crack the nuts to get the tiny sweet meat.

Filbert trees have the advantage of maturing to a size that fits well into most home landscapes. The trees grow from 10 to 15 feet tall or about the size of semi-dwarf apples. Plant them about 20 feet apart. Unlike most other nut trees, they don't have a long taproot so they are easy to transplant. Soils suitable for fruit trees usually suit the filbert, too, but fertilize them only lightly so they don't grow too fast.

Filbert trees root easily from layers and root suckers, so even cultivars are seldom grafted. If you buy a tree, you may want to propagate it in this way to increase your plantings. The following European filberts are worth a trial in zones 6–8: Butler, Cassina, Contorted, Daviana, Duchilly, Ennis, Hall's Giant, and Royal.

Many catalogs list cultivars of the American filbert (hazelnut) that are hardy in zones 4–7, although they have smaller nuts than their European cousins. Walter and Winkler are two improved cultivars.

Some crosses have been made between the European filbert and the hardy wild American hazelnut. These so-called "filazels" are hardy in zones 5–8 and include Gellatly, Minnesota F2, Peace River Cross, and the Fred Ashworth Crosses, which are reputed to be among the hardiest.

The Hickory and Pecan (Carya spp.)
Zones 5–9

As the botanical name shows, hickories and pecans are closely related, even though they grow in different climatic zones. The relationship, however, has permitted some worthwhile hybrids between them to be developed.

Of the two, hickory trees are hardy over a wider area, from zones 5 to 8. Although they are seldom offered commercially, they are much enjoyed by those lucky enough to live in the same habitat. The shagbark hickory, the best of dozens of native hickories, has the disadvantage of a very tough shell and a small meat that usually breaks in cracking. Many new cultivars, which are selections of these wild trees, are now available. These bear nuts at a younger age, and the nuts are larger and easier to crack. The hardiness of the new kinds isn't always known for sure, however, and thus far not many are being grafted and offered for sale. Davis, Grainger, Neilson, Porter, Weschecke, and Wilcox are some that are available.

Shellbark hickory cultivars are slightly less hardy than shagbarks. They include Abundance, Anderson, Eureka, Henry, Kaskaskia, Missouri Mammoth, and Richmond Furnace.

Pecans need a long season to develop their nuts, so the trees are limited mostly to southeastern United States and Mexico. Unlike most North American trees, the pecan has been cultivated commercially for many years.

Pecans keep for only a few months in ordinary storage, but store well for a year or more at temperatures below freezing. Some pecan cultivars currently being grown are Apache, Barton, Cape Fear, Choctaw, Major, Missouri, Nutcracker, Pawnee, Rocket 800, Schley, Sioux, Starking Hardy Giant, Stuart, and Surecrop (Stark). Paper-shell pecans include Cheyenne, Mohawk, Peruque, Schley, and Stuart.

In an effort to combine the flavor of pecans with the hardiness of hickories, horticulturists have created hybrid "hicans." Among them are Burlington, Burton, Gerardi, Henke, Jackson, Pleas, and Underwood. All can be grown further north than pecans but the different cultivars vary widely in hardiness.

The Walnut (Juglans regia)
Zones 5–8

Persian walnuts (Juglans regia) are often called English walnuts because they have been grown in Great Britain for centuries. They were considered far too tender for all of North America except the warm regions of the West Coast until a missionary, Reverend Paul Crath, discovered a strain growing wild in the cold mountains of Poland. He brought several thousand seeds to Ontario in the 1930s and found they grew well there. They succeeded so well, in fact, that within only a few years the Carpathian strain he introduced was being grown in zones 5 and 6, and hardier strains will survive in favored parts of zone 4.

Walnuts are without doubt the most popular of all nuts both to eat out of the shell and to enjoy in countless appetizing desserts. Unfortunately, a few people get canker sores in their mouths from eating walnuts and have to

▲ Introduction of the Carpathian walnut has increased the walnut-growing area of the United States and Canada by many times. *(USDA)*

sacrifice a real delicacy. Perhaps a variety without this unpleasant side effect will someday be developed, so all of us can enjoy this delicious nut.

Persian walnuts suitable for zones 7–8 include these cultivars: Champion, Kentucky Giant, Kwik Krop Stark, Lockport, Serr, Spurgeon, Sunland, and Super. In California, Franquette and Hartley are widely grown commercially.

Most nurseries offer only seedling trees of the Carpathian walnut, but those that specialize in nut trees have some good cultivars available. Some of these are Ambassador, Ashworth (one of the hardiest), Broadview, Chopaka, Fately, Gurney, Hansen, Lake, McKinster, Russian, and Somers.

Your Extension Service or Agriculture Canada can supply information on the nut-growing prospects in your locality. See the Appendix for a partial list of the nurseries that sell nut tree seedlings and cultivars.

CHAPTER 29

Fun Experimenting
with Fruits

In addition to growing the best fruit in the world and saving money while doing it, home orchardists can have a good time experimenting with their trees and plants. You may feel like searching for a superior new kind of fruit or berry, or perhaps creating your own dwarf fruit trees. You may get a kick out of multiple grafting, or use surgery to help your trees bear fruit at an earlier age. For some of us fruit addicts, fooling around with fruits is almost as much fun as eating them.

Searching for Superior Fruit

The perfect apple, peach, plum, pear, cherry, berry, grape, and nut has yet to be developed, so you still have a chance. Don't assume that you cannot compete with the big experiment stations, because most of the best fruits we have today were accidentally discovered by individual growers and small orchardists. In fact, of all the leading apple cultivars being grown now, only one, the Cortland, was developed by scientific methods.

If you would like to be a local Luther Burbank, there are any number of improvements yet to be developed in existing fruits. For instance, how about everybody's dream apple? It could have the flavor of a Northern Spy, color of a Double Red Delicious, size of a Wolf River, shape of a Lodi, make as good pies as a Duchess, ripen as early as a Yellow Transparent, keep in ordinary storage all winter, and grow on a tree that needs little pruning. We could use fruits of all kinds that are insect and disease resistant, and dwarf trees that will produce nuts.

How about developing some plums that need no cross-pollination? Grapes, nectarines, peaches, sweet cherries, and walnuts that are hardy in zones 3 and 4, and not fussy about soils? Wouldn't it be nice to have blueberries that don't need acid soil, thornless gooseberries and bramble fruits, seedless raspberries for denture wearers, blackberries with smaller cores, and strawberries with frostproof buds and blooms? You can think of more.

Among the many ways you can begin to search for unusual and superior fruit characteristics is to be on the lookout for accidental seedlings or sports that have some of these outstanding characteristics.

Accidental Seedlings

The search for superior seedlings can be a hobby as fascinating as hunting for intact bottles in old dumps, searching out first editions at book sales, or panning for gold in mountain streams. Begin your search when the fruits are ripening by looking where seedling trees are likely to be growing — in old orchards around abandoned farms, along country roads, and even farther out in the wilds where birds, deer, picnickers, or hunters may have dropped seeds that sprouted. Look for fruit with especially fine appearance and taste or any other superior characteristic. Finding a fruit that is just "good" is not enough. There are already lots of good fruits.

You can also plant seeds, the way that Johnny Appleseed did, if you don't mind being patient. People have told me that one out of every ten seeds in an apple would grow into a tree that would be exactly like the one that produced it. Actually the odds are not nearly that good, and most seeds, if planted, would grow into trees that produced fruit that was good only for cider. Only one in hundreds could compare favorably with the parent, and only one in many thousands would be superior.

Although it takes time to grow seedlings, it always surprises me how fast a small seed can grow into a sizeable tree. It can be frustrating to wait for it to bear fruit, however. I suspect that a lot of good trees have been cut down because the experimenters thought there was no merit in a tree that took eight or nine years to produce its first crop. This timespan is not unusual and is called the "youthful factor" of the tree. Grafted trees always bear in a much shorter length of time, often within two to four years.

Since seedling trees take so long to bear, another way to test their fruiting quality much earlier is to graft limbs from dozens of different seedlings onto one large tree so you can compare the fruits of many different seedlings years earlier and in much less space.

Hybridizing

Since casually planting seeds leaves a lot to chance, hybridizers who are sure about their goals are more scientific in their research and try to combine qualities from many different fruits into what they hope will be a winning combination. Rather than just planting the seeds from good fruits with no knowledge of what tree furnished the pollen, they try to double their chances for success. They make sure that both the flower that supplies the pollen and the flower that receives it are on trees with some of those characteristics they want in their new fruit. You can do this, too.

Put a bag over a flower bud cluster on both of your chosen trees a few days before the blooms open. This will keep out any ambitious bees that might mess up your plans before you get to work. After the blooms have opened, remove the bag from the blossoms on the pollinator tree, and collect some of the yellow pollen. Transfer it to the blossoms of the tree you want to bear the fruit, as described in Chapter 7. Pick off all blossoms in the cluster except the ones you are pollinating and mark the limb carefully, so you can easily find the fruit in the fall. Keep a written record of all your activity, too.

When the fruit is ripe or slightly overripe, pick it and plant the seeds. Then await the results. Hopefully, your selected seedling will be something special, but keep Mendel's law of heredity in mind, too. You may have to wait another generation or two for the elusive characteristics that you want to show up.

Don't lose your records while you are awaiting the first fruits of your new baby. If an exciting new variety appears, horticulturists will want to know all about its ancestors.

Berry Improvement

If you think fruit trees take too long to bear and you want to work with plants that show faster results, experiment with small fruits such as grapes and berries. They will often produce results within only three or four years from seed. Use the same hand-pollination procedure you would for fruit trees, and be just as careful that the bees don't beat you to it. Plant berry seeds quite shallow in the soil, mulch them lightly, and keep them moist. Even if your discovery doesn't make a big splash nationally, you may have something of local interest. Horticulturist George Aiken, who later became a prominent U.S. Senator, developed the Green Mountain strawberry that became a popular variety for many years in the Northeast.

We have developed some very good seedlings of gooseberries, black currants, and elderberries, but none of them are outstanding enough to register. Other small fruits that we feel are worth hybridizing are raspberries, blackberries, currants of all colors, blueberries, saskatoons, kiwis, and grapes.

Sports

Another way to achieve fame and fortune in the fruit world is to find a superior sport or mutation growing on a fruit tree. A sport is a limb that suddenly begins to bear fruit that is noticeably different from that on the rest of the tree. A sport can produce fruits that are worse as well as better, and appearances can be deceiving. A nice-looking fruit doesn't always taste great, and a rather plain-looking one might taste super. The great sports of fruit history have produced trees that bore fruits that were superior in color, size, or uniformity or perhaps had better ripening habits than their parents. These are important, but look for fruit quality, as well as appearance.

Sports are not only exciting to find but they can be profitable to the finder. In 1963 the Stark Brothers Nursery paid Elon Gilbert of Yakima, Washington, the sum of $51,000 for the rights to a sport that appeared in his orchard. It became the Starkspur Golden Delicious apple.

Sport hunters roam through orchards, both large and small, at harvest time looking for the magic limb that big nurseries will eagerly buy and propagate. Isn't it fun to know that there is always a chance it could sprout in yours or mine?

Nut Selection

Because far less hybridizing has been done with nuts than with tree fruits, nut cultivars are not nearly as numerous, so there are opportunities galore for new discoveries. We need nut trees that will bear heavy crops of high quality that crack easily. The trees should begin to bear at an early age, and annually. The common nuts aren't the only ones worthy of improvement. Horticulturists are also working to develop larger beechnuts, edible acorns, and higher-quality pine nuts.

Both professional horticulturists and hobbyists search forests every fall for that special one-in-a-thousand tree that nature has hybridized; or they make their own crosses and wait patiently for many years to see the results. Unless you can find blossoms on some of the lower branches, pollinating a nut tree is not easy, however, and instead of worrying about beating the bees to the blooms you have to beat the wind.

Your Own Multiple Grafts

Although I don't usually advise buying the 3–in–1 or 5–in–1 trees advertised in fruit catalogs, I think it is fun to create your own orchard on a single tree. Follow the grafting instructions in Chapter 13, and you can have early, midseason, and late apples all together, or a combination of red, yellow, and green. And how about grafting one limb of a red-flowering crab to sit amidst all the white blooms of an apple tree?

You can graft a pear on an apple tree, too, but the graft is likely to be short-lived. Pears and quinces can be grafted interchangeably upon each other. Several different cultivars of grapes can also be grafted on the same vine, but pruning it will be a real headache.

You can also make a collection of stone fruits all on the same tree. Plums, cherries, peaches, apricots, and nectarines can all be grown on a plum or peach tree, to make a delicious curiosity.

As I mentioned earlier, multiple grafts pose a problem at pruning time. You must have a good memory, or be able to mark the limbs in some way so you don't lop some of them off when it comes time to prune.

Dwarfing Fruit Trees by Surgery

Another way to play tricks on nature is to make a full-sized fruit tree into a dwarf by some surgery. This is useful for those who want small trees but live where the commonly used Malling rootstocks aren't hardy. It is only practical when the tree is still young, with a trunk diameter of less than 1½ inches. In early spring when the bark slips easily, remove a strip of bark exactly 1 inch wide from the tree by cutting through the bark completely around the trunk, but not into the wood, about a foot from the ground. Make a vertical cut on the strip so it can be removed. Then, turn the bark upside down and put it back on the tree, with the same side out, of course. Be sure that the upside-down bark fits tightly, and then cover the whole thing with grafting wax, tree dressing, or rubber (not plastic) electrical tape. You'll need an extra sharp knife to make your cuts exact enough for a tight fit.

The inverted bark will slow down the growth of the tree for many years, keeping it small, and even forcing it to bear at an earlier age. Unfortunately, all the cells will readjust eventually, and the tree will then grow large. If you sell your property in the meantime, this unusual spurt of growth will probably puzzle the new owner no end.

Making Trees Bear

Sometimes fruit trees grow heartily year after year without blooming or producing. This may happen if the soil is too rich and the tree is growing too fast. It could be a slowpoke because it is missing a necessary nutrient, or possibly it is a cultivar like the Baldwin or Northern Spy apple that takes its own sweet time to bear — sometimes ten years or more.

Orchardists have long known that a tree can be made to bloom by slowing down the sap movement. One old-timer told me he used to wound such a tree with an axe. Others claimed they drove a few nails into the trunk here and there. I am not sure how effective either technique was.

The method I have used is to cut a slit through the bark on two or three limbs in early summer. I cut nearly but not quite all around the limb, through the bark, but not into the wood. This supposedly builds up the nutrients in those limbs and forces the formation of fruit buds that will produce fruit the following year. If you try it, experiment with only a tree or two, because *ringing,* as it is called, is hard on a tree and should be done only if absolutely necessary.

What's Ahead?

In the last half of the twentieth century, we have seen the introduction of a great many new fruits, nuts, and berries, as well as an amazing array of machines, tools, fertilizers, pest controls, and other aids, including gene-splitting and tissue-cultured plants. Very likely we "ain't seen nothin' yet!" We can expect to see even more virus-free trees and berry plants propagated, more disease- and insect-resistant cultivars developed, and more fruits created especially for us small growers. Trees will be available that need less pruning and fruits that need little thinning. The growing range of many species will be extended so that gardeners in the hot southern states and the cold northern regions can grow a larger variety of fruits and nuts. Pest controls will be safer to use and more efficient.

It is fun to imagine what's ahead, but there is no certainty that fruit growing in the distant future will be any more enjoyable or the fruits more beautiful or tasty than they are right now.

CHAPTER 30

Treats from
Nancy's Winter Kitchen
by Nancy Hill

Fruit tastes best, of course, plucked fresh from your own vine, tree, or berry patch. But since our love for fruits continues far beyond their prime season, each year we hoard any surplus. The following are some of the favorite recipes we use so that we can enjoy homegrown produce year-round. You will find a separate index for the recipes on page 264.

Apples

Each fall, in addition to the large number of apples we store in the root cellar, we freeze an extra supply of raw cooking apples by peeling, slicing, and packing them tight in plastic bags. To prevent darkening of the fruit, before packing, dip the slices in a solution of ascorbic acid, such as Fruit Fresh. Whenever the recipe calls for "fresh apples," the frozen ones can be substituted. We thaw them in a microwave oven just enough to break them apart. Duchess and Beacon are our favorite early apples for baking and sauce.

APPLE UPSIDE-DOWN CAKE
SERVES 9

Mother's recipe is a long-time favorite of Vermonters.

2 CUPS SLICED APPLES	1¼ CUPS ALL-PURPOSE FLOUR
3 TABLESPOONS SHORTENING	1½ TEASPOONS BAKING POWDER
1 TABLESPOON BUTTER OR MARGARINE	¼ TEASPOON GROUND CINNAMON
½ CUP BROWN SUGAR, FIRMLY PACKED	¼ TEASPOON GROUND NUTMEG
2 TABLESPOONS MILK	¼ TEASPOON GROUND ALLSPICE
¼ CUP SHORTENING	½ CUP MILK
¾ CUP GRANULATED SUGAR	MAPLE SYRUP AND ADDITIONAL MILK
1 EGG, BEATEN	FOR TOPPING

Preheat oven to 350°F.

Spread the sliced apples in bottom of buttered 8"x8" pan.

Melt together the 3 tablespoons shortening and the butter. Add the brown sugar and the 2 tablespoons milk to the shortening mixture and spread over apples.

Cream the ¼ cup shortening and the granulated sugar thoroughly in bowl, and add the beaten egg. Sift together the flour, baking powder, cinnamon, nutmeg, and allspice. Add the ½ cup milk to the egg mixture alternately with dry ingredients. Spread this batter over the apple mixture.

Bake for approximately 1 hour. Serve warm with maple syrup and milk.

DUCHESS APPLE PUDDING
SERVES 9

This easy recipe, from Una Lou Richardson's vintage collection, has also come down to us through several generations.

2 CUPS ALL-PURPOSE FLOUR	*SAUCE*
3 TEASPOONS BAKING POWDER	¾ CUP GRANULATED SUGAR
2 TABLESPOONS SHORTENING	1 TEASPOON BUTTER
1 EGG	¼ TEASPOON SALT
¾ CUP MILK	¾ CUP BOILING WATER
3 OR 4 LARGE DUCHESS APPLES,	2 TEASPOONS CORNSTARCH
PEELED AND SLICED AS FOR PIE	2 TABLESPOONS COLD WATER
⅓ CUP GRANULATED SUGAR	1 TEASPOON VANILLA EXTRACT
¼ TEASPOON NUTMEG OR CINNAMON	

Preheat oven to 375°F.

Sift together the flour and baking powder. Cut the shortening into the dry ingredients. Beat together the egg and milk, and add to shortening mixture. Spread the dough in a greased 9"x9" pan and cover with the sliced apples.

Mix together the ⅓ cup sugar and the nutmeg or cinnamon, and sprinkle the mixture over the apples. Bake 20–25 minutes.

For the sauce, mix the ¾ cup sugar, butter, salt, and boiling water in a saucepan. Dissolve the cornstarch in the cold water and add to saucepan; cook until thick. Cool slightly. Stir in the vanilla. Serve the pudding warm, cut into squares and topped with the sauce.

APPLE CROW'S NEST
SERVES 9

Newcomers to Vermont are often surprised by the name of this dish, but everyone loves it. My grandmother's recipe calls for nothing but 5 or 6 large apples, peeled and sliced into a 9-inch-square, greased baking dish, topped with ordinary sweet biscuit dough, and baked at 375°F for ½ hour or until the apples are soft. The crowning glory is a pitcher of rich milk with pure maple syrup and a pinch of nutmeg added. The sweetened milk is poured over the "nest," and is it good!

FRESH APPLE CAKE
SERVES 16

*Our frequent contribution to potluck suppers. Add a dollop of whipped cream
or ice cream to each piece for an extra-special treat.*

1¼ cups safflower oil	1 teaspoon baking soda
1 cup granulated sugar	2 teaspoons ground cinnamon
¾ cup light brown sugar	¼ cup milk
2 eggs	1 cup raisins
1 teaspoon vanilla extract	1 cup chopped nuts
3 cups all-purpose flour	3 cups peeled, chopped apples
1 teaspoon salt	

Preheat oven to 350°F.

Mix well the oil, sugars, eggs, and vanilla. Combine the flour, salt, soda, and
cinnamon. Add dry ingredients to oil and sugar mixture. Stir in the milk. Add
the raisins, nuts, and apples. Pack into a 9"x13" greased cake pan. Bake at 350°F
for ½ hour; then reduce heat to 325°F, and bake for ¼ hour more.

APPLE MACAROON
SERVES 4

*When time is too short to make a full-fledged apple pie, this is a superb
substitute.*

Approximately 4 large, tart apples	½ cup all-purpose flour
½ cup granulated sugar	½ teaspoon baking powder
Ground cinnamon to taste	1 tablespoon melted butter
1 egg	Whipped cream (optional)
½ cup granulated sugar	

Preheat oven to 375°F.

Arrange apples, peeled and sliced as if for pie, in bottom of 8-inch pie plate.
Sprinkle ½ cup sugar and cinnamon to taste over apples. Stir together the egg,
the remaining ½ cup sugar, the flour, baking powder, and melted butter, and
pour over apples. Bake for 40–45 minutes. Serve warm, with or without whipped
cream.

APPLESAUCE

We freeze lots of thick, sweetened applesauce each fall, which we later thaw and use to make Aunt Margaret's delicious Applesauce Deluxe, or bake in cookie, cake, or tea bread recipes. Lewis says I married him for his applesauce! His simple method is to peel and quarter the apples and place them in a saucepan in a small amount of boiling water. Cover and cook them only until they are soft but still slightly lumpy. His secret for good flavor is not to overcook the fruit, and since the time allowed depends upon the apple variety and its ripeness, it is essential to watch the pot carefully. When the apples are soft, stir in granulated sugar to taste and remove the pan from the heat.

APPLESAUCE DELUXE
SERVES 8

5 TABLESPOONS BUTTER
4 TABLESPOONS GRANULATED SUGAR
APPROXIMATELY 1½ CUPS FINELY
   CRUSHED GRAHAM CRACKER CRUMBS
   (OR CRUSHED MACAROONS OR
   BREADCRUMBS)

4 CUPS SWEETENED APPLESAUCE
WHIPPED CREAM
RASPBERRY OR CURRANT JELLY

Melt butter and add sugar. Add crumbs to butter mixture, which should be rather dry. Just before serving, spread half the applesauce on the bottom of an 8"x8" pan; sprinkle with one-half of the crumbs. Repeat these two layers, ending with crumbs on top. Decorate with whipped cream, and top with dots of jelly. Can also be assembled in individual dishes.

This recipe is easy to increase or decrease by adjusting the proportions of the other ingredients according to the amount of applesauce you have on hand.

APPLESAUCE COOKIES
YIELD: 3–4 DOZEN

These flourless cookies make a nutritious snack with herbal tea on a winter afternoon.

⅔ CUP SAFFLOWER OIL
1 CUP BROWN SUGAR
¼ TEASPOON VANILLA EXTRACT
¼ TEASPOON SALT

1¼ CUPS SWEETENED APPLESAUCE
½ CUP RAISINS OR CHOPPED DATES
½ CUP CHOPPED NUTS
4 CUPS QUICK-COOKING ROLLED OATS

Preheat oven to 350°F.

Blend together the oil, sugar, vanilla, and salt. Add the applesauce, dates, nuts, and rolled oats to the oil mixture. Drop by rounded teaspoonfuls onto greased cookie sheet and press flat with spoon. Bake approximately 15 minutes, or until slightly browned. Cool on sheet.

APPLESAUCE CAKE
SERVES 16

2 SCANT CUPS GRANULATED SUGAR
1 CUP BUTTER OR MARGARINE
2 EGGS
3 CUPS ALL-PURPOSE FLOUR
1 TABLESPOON BAKING SODA
1 TABLESPOON GROUND CINNAMON

1 TEASPOON GROUND CLOVES
1½ TEASPOONS GROUND NUTMEG
½ TEASPOON SALT
2½ CUPS SWEETENED APPLESAUCE
2 TABLESPOONS DARK CORN SYRUP
1 CUP RAISINS

Preheat oven to 300°F.

Mix sugar and butter with pastry blender. Beat the eggs, and then beat them into sugar mixture. Sift together the flour, baking soda, cinnamon, cloves, nutmeg, and salt. Mix together the applesauce and corn syrup, and add to sugar mixture alternately with dry ingredients. Add raisins to batter. Pour into 9"x13" pan, and bake for 1½ hours.

APPLESAUCE TEA BREAD
YIELD: ONE 9" x 5" LOAF

1⅔ CUPS SIFTED ALL-PURPOSE FLOUR
1¼ CUPS GRANULATED SUGAR
1 TEASPOON BAKING SODA
½ TEASPOON BAKING POWDER
½ TEASPOON SALT
1 TEASPOON GROUND CINNAMON

1 CUP SWEETENED APPLESAUCE
2 EGGS, BEATEN
½ CUP SHORTENING
⅓ CUP WATER
½ CUP NUTS AND/OR ½ CUP
    RAISINS (OPTIONAL)

Preheat oven to 350°F.

Sift together the flour, sugar, baking soda, baking powder, salt, and cinnamon. Mix together the applesauce, beaten eggs, shortening, and water. Add dry ingredients to applesauce mixture, beating only until moistened. Add nuts (and/or raisins). Bake in a wax-paper-lined 9"x5" loaf pan for approximately 1 hour. Cool in pan 10 minutes and then remove to cooling rack.

SPICED APPLE PICKLES
YIELD: ABOUT 12 PINTS

Here's the Hill family heirloom recipe. Substitute cooking pears for apples if you wish.

APPROXIMATELY 9 POUNDS DUCHESS OR OTHER COOKING APPLES	1 CUP PURE MAPLE SYRUP
WHOLE CLOVES (APPROXIMATELY 3 OUNCES)	1 QUART CIDER VINEGAR
2 POUNDS LIGHT BROWN SUGAR	4 CUPS WATER
1 CUP GRANULATED SUGAR	2 TEASPOONS SALT
	EIGHT 3-INCH STICKS CINNAMON

Wash, quarter, and core apples, but don't peel them. Stick 1 clove in each piece. Bring to a boil the sugars, maple syrup, vinegar, water, salt, and cinnamon (allow cinnamon sticks to float freely). Place apple pieces in the spiced liquid, one layer at a time, and simmer. Watch closely for doneness; they should be tender but not mushy.

As soon as they are cooked, using cooking tongs, pack immediately into hot, sterilized pint jars, and pour liquid over them to fill jars to within ½ inch of top. Process in a boiling-water bath for 10 minutes. Wait at least 2 months before eating these, so that they will have developed a spicy flavor.

SPICED CRAB APPLES
YIELD: TWO ½-PINT PLASTIC CONTAINERS

These give a festive touch to holiday meals.

15–20 RIPE BUT FIRM, DOLGO RED CRAB APPLES (OR OTHER LARGE CRAB APPLES)	½ CUP WATER
	8 WHOLE CLOVES
⅔ CUP GRANULATED SUGAR	ONE 3-INCH STICK CINNAMON
	LARGE STRIP LEMON PEEL

Remove blossom ends of crab apples, but leave stems on. Prick each apple with a darning needle or fork (at least twice). Mix together the sugar, water, cloves, cinnamon, and lemon peel in a medium-size saucepan and bring to a boil. Reduce the heat, then place the apples in a single layer upright in pan and cover loosely. Simmer slowly for 10 minutes over very low heat without stirring; do not overcook. The skins will crack open slightly but stay intact. Remove from heat, and cool in liquid.

Pack crab apples into an airtight plastic freezer box, so that the second layer fits between the stems of the first layer. Pour the strained juice over the apples. Let stand overnight in refrigerator, and then freeze.

Plums, Pears, and Peaches

TART PLUM COFFEECAKE
SERVES 9

This coffeecake can be made with fresh, canned, or frozen plums. We like to freeze plums, too, by washing and halving them, removing the pits, and then packing them raw in airtight freezer bags.

¼ CUP SHORTENING
1¼ CUPS GRANULATED SUGAR
2 EGGS
1½ CUPS ALL-PURPOSE FLOUR
1 TEASPOON BAKING POWDER
¼ TEASPOON BAKING SODA
¼ TEASPOON SALT

½ CUP BUTTERMILK
8 MEDIUM-SIZE PLUMS, HALVED AND
   PITTED (FRESH OR FROZEN AND
   THAWED)
¼ CUP BROWN SUGAR
¼ TEASPOON GROUND CINNAMON

Preheat oven to 375°F.

Cream together the shortening and sugar. Beat the eggs well, and add them to the sugar mixture. Sift together the flour, baking powder, baking soda, and salt. Add the buttermilk to the sugar mixture alternately with the dry ingredients, mixing well.

Pour batter into a well-greased 8"x8" pan, and top with the plums, skin-side down — they'll sink! Sprinkle plums with the brown sugar and cinnamon. Bake for approximately 45 minutes.

BAKED PEARS MERINGUE
SERVES 4

Pears that have been stored in the root cellar are excellent in this dish.

4 PEARS
4 TEASPOONS GRANULATED SUGAR (USE
   BROWN SUGAR WITH SECKEL PEARS)

2 TEASPOONS BUTTER
2 EGG WHITES
3 TABLESPOONS GRANULATED SUGAR

Preheat oven to 300°F.

Cut pears into halves, and scoop out the cores. Place in a 9-inch Pyrex pie plate, and fill each pear cavity with ½ teaspoon sugar and ¼ teaspoon butter. Bake in 300°F oven until tender but still firm (about ½ hour). When the pears are done, beat the egg whites until stiff and sweeten them to taste; spoon meringue over pears. Raise oven heat to 400°F, return pears to oven, and bake until the meringue is brown (about 8 minutes).

STREUSEL FRUIT CUSTARD
SERVES 8

We make this favorite with either fresh or canned peaches.

6–8 MEDIUM-SIZE FRESH PEACHES OR
  1 QUART JAR CANNED PEACHES,
  DRAINED
¼ CUP GRANULATED SUGAR
¼ SCANT CUP ALL-PURPOSE FLOUR
1 CUP DAIRY SOUR CREAM
2 EGGS, BEATEN

1 TEASPOON VANILLA EXTRACT
¼ CUP BUTTER OR MARGARINE
¾ CUP ALL-PURPOSE FLOUR
½ CUP BROWN SUGAR
½ TEASPOON GROUND CINNAMON
WHIPPED CREAM OR ICE CREAM

Preheat oven to 350°F.

Slice peaches and arrange them in the bottom of an ungreased 8"x8" pan; peaches should cover the bottom of the pan. Blend the ¼ cup sugar, the ¼ scant cup flour, the sour cream, beaten eggs, and vanilla extract until smooth, and pour over fruit. Cut the butter into the remaining flour, brown sugar, and cinnamon until crumbly. Sprinkle over the fruit mixture. Bake for 30–45 minutes. Serve warm with whipped cream or ice cream.

Berries and Cherries

COUNTRY STRAWBERRY SHORTCAKE
SERVES 6

No dessert can surpass a good strawberry shortcake. "Good" to farm families means a rich biscuit dough instead of angel-food cake mix.

2 CUPS ALL-PURPOSE FLOUR
⅓ CUP GRANULATED SUGAR
2 TEASPOONS BAKING POWDER
¼ TEASPOON SALT
½ SCANT CUP SHORTENING
1 EGG

APPROXIMATELY ⅓ CUP MILK
1 QUART STRAWBERRIES, CRUSHED AND
  SWEETENED TO TASTE
1 CUP HEAVY CREAM, WHIPPED AND
  SWEETENED TO TASTE

Preheat oven to 425°F.

Sift together the flour, sugar, baking powder, and salt. Cut the shortening into sifted mixture. Beat egg, and add to flour mixture. Stir in the milk, a little at a time, adding only as much as is needed to make the dough stick together. On a floured pastry board, roll dough lightly into size that fits into a lightly greased 9-inch-round cake tin. Bake for 12–15 minutes. Cool slightly.

While biscuit is still warm, split it into two layers, and cover bottom layer with crushed, sweetened, fresh or thawed berries. Replace the top layer, turning it upside down so that the soft side is up. Cover it with another layer of berries. Shortcake should be assembled long enough before eating so that the juice will soak in well. Cover with thick, sweetened whipped cream.

BLUEBERRY BUCKLE
SERVES 9

Blueberries (frozen raw, straight from the bush) often go directly from our freezer into blueberry buckle. We eat it warm, with milk poured over it, for dessert or as a rich coffeecake.

¼ CUP MARGARINE	2 CUPS ALL-PURPOSE FLOUR
½ CUP GRANULATED SUGAR	2 TEASPOON BAKING POWDER
⅓ CUP ALL-PURPOSE FLOUR	½ TEASPOON SALT
½ TEASPOON GROUND CINNAMON	½ CUP MILK
1 EGG	1 TEASPOON VANILLA EXTRACT
¾ CUP GRANULATED SUGAR	2 CUPS BLUEBERRIES
½ CUP MARGARINE	

Preheat oven to 375°F.

Cut the ¼ cup margarine into a mixture of ½ cup sugar, ⅓ cup flour, and cinnamon; set aside for topping.

Cream together the egg, the ¾ cup sugar, and the ½ cup margarine. Sift together the 2 cups flour, baking powder, and salt. Add the milk and vanilla extract to the creamed mixture alternately with the dry ingredients. Fold the blueberries into the batter. Pour into a greased 9-inch-square pan, and cover with topping. Bake for approximately 45 minutes.

RED GOOSEBERRY PIE
YIELD: ONE 9-INCH PIE

A corner of our freezer is always reserved for several bags of gooseberries (frozen raw) to go into this dish.

4 CUPS RED GOOSEBERRIES	¼ TEASPOON GROUND CINNAMON
1¾ CUPS GRANULATED SUGAR	PASTRY FOR 9-INCH DOUBLE-CRUST PIE
3 TABLESPOONS QUICK-COOKING TAPIOCA	1 TABLESPOON BUTTER

Preheat oven to 400°F.

Thaw berries partially, and grind them by giving them a few whirls in a food processor. Mix the sugar, tapioca, and cinnamon, and add mixture to the berries.

Line a 9-inch pie plate with pastry and fill with fruit mixture. Dot with the butter, and cover with top crust. Bake at 400°F for 10 minutes. Reduce heat to 350°F, and bake for 35 minutes longer.

BLUE-RIBBON RASPBERRY PIE
YIELD: ONE 8-INCH PIE

In Vermont's Annual Farm Show competition, Marion Urie won a well-deserved blue ribbon for this simple, scrumptious recipe.

3 CUPS RASPBERRIES (FRESH OR
   FROZEN AND THAWED)
1¼ CUPS GRANULATED SUGAR

3 TABLESPOONS CORNSTARCH
PASTRY FOR 8-INCH SINGLE-CRUST PIE

Preheat oven to 400°F.

If using frozen berries, thaw and drain them, and reserve the liquid. Place berries in medium-size saucepan and add sugar. Combine cornstarch with enough berry liquid to make a paste, and stir into berries in saucepan. (If using fresh berries, place them in saucepan with sugar and 3 tablespoons water. Simmer gently until juice flows. Pour out 3 tablespoons juice and mix with cornstarch. Return to pan.) Cook over low heat, stirring frequently, until filling looks clear. Cool.

Preheat oven to 400°F. Line 8-inch pie plate with pastry. Pour berry mixture into crust. Bake for 30–40 minutes.

BLUEBERRY PIE DELUXE
YIELD: ONE 9-INCH PIE

We always make this favorite during the berry season and again in the cold months when we have access to a pint of fresh berries. The delightful texture and flavor that results from the combination of raw and cooked berries makes this pie superior to all others, we feel. The recipe lends itself to creativity, too. Our editor, Gwen Steege, poured the cooked blueberry filling over fresh red raspberries, blackberries, and blueberries, and her family loved it.

¾ CUP GRANULATED SUGAR
3 TABLESPOONS CORNSTARCH
⅛ TEASPOON SALT
2 CUPS BLUEBERRIES (FRESH OR
   FROZEN AND THAWED)
¼ CUP WATER

1 TABLESPOON BUTTER
1 TABLESPOON LEMON JUICE
2 CUPS FRESH BLUEBERRIES
WHIPPED CREAM (OPTIONAL)
BAKED 9-INCH PIE SHELL

Combine the sugar, cornstarch, and salt in a medium-size saucepan. Add the 2 cups fresh or frozen and thawed berries and water. Cook over medium heat, stirring constantly until mixture boils, thickens, and clears. Remove from heat and stir in butter and lemon juice. Cool.

Place the 2 cups fresh berries into the baked 9-inch shell and top with cooked mixture. Chill. Serve with whipped cream.

WASHINGTON'S BIRTHDAY CHERRY PIE
YIELD: ONE 9-INCH PIE

In February we look forward to this special cherry pie.

Approximately 4 cups pitted, frozen
  or canned pie cherries
⅓ cup cherry liquid
2 tablespoons and 1 teaspoon
  quick-cooking tapioca
1 teaspoon lemon juice
¼ teaspoon almond extract

¼ teaspoon salt
1 cup granulated sugar
Pastry for a 9-inch double-crust
  pie
¼ cup sugar
1 tablespoon butter

Preheat oven to 425°F.

Drain cherries and save liquid. Mix together the ⅓ cup cherry liquid, tapioca, lemon juice, almond extract, and salt. Stir in 1 cup sugar and the cherries. Let stand while making pastry.

Line a 9-inch pie plate with pastry. Fill with cherry mixture. Sprinkle with ¼ cup more sugar and dot with butter. Moisten rim with water and top with lattice crust, fluting edges high.

To keep edges from browning too much, fold a strip of aluminum foil loosely around the edge of pie. Bake at 425°F for 10 minutes, and then reduce the heat to 350°F and bake for approximately 20 minutes longer.

VERENA'S ELDERBERRY SOUP WITH APPLES AND ICEBERGS
SERVES 4

Our German niece gave us this tasty and beautiful dessert soup recipe, which she says can be found in most general cookbooks in Germany. "Holundersuppe mit Apfeln und Schneebergen" is a feast for both the eye and the palate. We've used it as a dinner party appetizer as well as for dessert.

3½ cups ripe elderberries
½ cup sugar
1 small piece lemon peel
1-inch piece of cinnamon stick
2 cups water

2 apples, peeled, cored, and sliced
Juice of 1 small lemon
1 tablespoon cornstarch
1 large egg white
2 tablespoons sugar

In a medium-size saucepan, boil together the elderberries, ½ cup sugar, lemon peel, cinnamon stick, and water until the elderberries are soft. Strain the juice through a sieve, add water, if necessary, to make 3 cups of liquid, and return liquid to saucepan, reserving 2 tablespoonfuls. Mix the reserved liquid with the cornstarch, and then stir this mixture into the liquid and elderberries in the pan. Add the apples and lemon juice, and bring the mixture to a boil. Cool and refrigerate.

For the "icebergs," beat the egg white until stiff. Add 2 tablespoons sugar. Refrigerate. When ready to serve, take off pieces of the beaten egg white with a tablespoon and let them float on the soup.

RASPBERRY ICE CREAM
YIELD: ½ GALLON

Occasionally, we go on a calorie binge and, even in the winter, indulge in this home-cranked raspberry ice cream, a recipe perfected by our neighbors, the Jaffin family.

APPROXIMATELY 2 QUARTS BERRIES
(FRESH OR FROZEN AND THAWED)
2¾ CUPS GRANULATED SUGAR

4 CUPS HEAVY CREAM
1 TEASPOON SALT

Mash fresh or frozen and thawed berries, and sprinkle with sugar. Allow to rest for ½ hour.

Strain berries to remove seeds. Juice yield should be 3½ cups. Add heavy cream and salt to juice and pour into can of crank freezer. Process as you would any ice cream.

Jams and Jellies

Much of our surplus fruit goes into preserves for the pantry. Among our favorites are thick plum jam, rich elderberry jelly, and uncooked raspberry or strawberry jam that we store in the freezer. (Freezer jam keeps the extraordinary fresh berry taste.) We ignore any exotic directions for making them, and have good luck with the simple instructions on the pectin box or bottle.

RASPBERRY JAM CAKE
SERVES 8

There is no tastier way to enjoy jam in any season than spread in a piece of old-fashioned jam cake. In berry season, we not only use the jam but also sprinkle fresh berries over the whipped cream topping.

⅓ CUP UNSALTED BUTTER
¾ CUP GRANULATED SUGAR
2 EGGS
2 TEASPOONS LEMON ZEST
1⅓ CUPS SIFTED ALL-PURPOSE FLOUR

1½ TEASPOONS BAKING POWDER
¼ TEASPOON SALT
6 TABLESPOONS MILK
¾ CUP RASPBERRY JAM
WHIPPED CREAM (OPTIONAL)

Preheat oven to 350°F.

Beat butter until light, and gradually add sugar. Add eggs one at a time, then lemon zest. Sift together the flour, baking powder, and salt. Add dry ingredients to butter mixture alternately with the milk, ending with dry ingredients.

Bake in a buttered and floured 9-inch cake pan for 25–30 minutes. Cool on rack.

With a long serrated knife, cut cake in half horizontally to make two layers. Spread jam carefully over bottom layer. Replace the top layer, and cover with whipped cream.

GOOSEBERRY TEA CAKE
SERVES 6–8

Although other jams and jellies can be used in this simple tea cake, we prefer gooseberry. Served warm, it is reminiscent of afternoon tea in the English countryside.

½ CUP BUTTER
½ CUP LIGHT BROWN SUGAR
½ TEASPOON VANILLA EXTRACT
1½ CUPS ALL-PURPOSE FLOUR
¼ TEASPOON SALT

1 CUP QUICK-COOKING ROLLED OATS
¾ CUP GOOSEBERRY JAM
WHIPPED CREAM OR VANILLA ICE CREAM
  (OPTIONAL)

Preheat oven to 350°F.

Cream together the butter and sugar. Add the vanilla. Sift the flour and salt together, and add to the creamed mixture, along with the oats; use your fingertips to crumble everything together. Press half of the oat mixture into a greased 8-inch springform pan. Spread the jam over it, and top with the remaining oat mixture. Bake for 30–40 minutes. Cool for 15 minutes, release from pan, and serve as is, or with whipped cream or ice cream.

ELDERBERRY SCONES
SERVES 8

Teatime, after skiing, is extra-special with these rich, hot scones filled with homemade elderberry jelly. We sometimes make them with dried currants, too, and strawberry or raspberry jam.

2 CUPS ALL-PURPOSE FLOUR
2 TEASPOONS BAKING POWDER
½ TEASPOON SALT
1 TABLESPOON GRANULATED SUGAR
½ CUP SHORTENING

½ CUP MILK
2 EGGS, BEATEN
1 CUP ELDERBERRIES (FRESH; OR
  FROZEN, THAWED AND DRAINED)
¾ CUP ELDERBERRY JELLY

Preheat oven to 400°F.

Sift the flour, baking powder, salt, and sugar together. Cut in the shortening. Combine the milk and beaten eggs. Add mixture to dry ingredients along with elderberries. Mix lightly only until ingredients form dough.

Divide dough in half. On a floured board, roll each section into a flat circle to fit a greased 8-inch-round cake pan. Place one circle in pan, pressing the dough slightly up the sides. Spread jelly over it, and cover with the other circle. Cut into eight wedges. Bake about 20 minutes. Serve warm.

Beverages

Several years ago we began to question why we were drinking so much tropical fruit juice when our own New England fruits were so good. We have since remedied that situation by freezing lots of apple juice and cider, as well as berry juices, such as elderberry, raspberry, strawberry, and black currant. Crab apple, plum, and even rhubarb juice are also delicious. We either use a juice steam extractor (see Appendix for source) or cook the fruit briefly, as if for making jelly, and strain it through a jelly bag or wire strainer. We then chill the juice quickly and pour it into plastic freezer containers, leaving plenty of headroom for expansion as it freezes. During the winter we drink the thawed juices "straight," or combine them with orange juice or cider. (Orange juice and cider provide natural sugars, making it unnecessary to add other sweetening.) For a sparkling Christmas punch we combine the juices with ginger ale or club soda. If we are too busy to make juice during the harvest season, we sometimes freeze the raw fruit and make it later.

GRAPE JUICES

This recipe is the easiest we've found, and makes delicious juice.

Fill sterilized quart jars half full of fresh, ripe grapes. Pour boiling water over the grapes to fill each jar, leaving ¼ inch headroom. Seal, and process in boiling water bath (190°) for 30 minutes. After storing for several months, open, strain, and serve over crushed ice.

The following, more standard recipe, is a fine way to use surplus grapes, and a treat for nonimbibers.

YIELD: 1 GALLON

> APPROXIMATELY 10 POUNDS GRAPES   3 POUNDS GRANULATED SUGAR
> 1 CUP WATER

Heat grapes and water in saucepan until pulp and stones separate. Strain through jelly bag. Add sugar to juice and heat to boiling. Freeze, or bottle by pouring into hot, sterilized jars, leaving ¼-inch headroom. Adjust lids and process in boiling-water bath for 15 minutes. Dilute with equal amount of water before serving.

RASPBERRY SHRUB
YIELD: 1 QUART

This tingly drink was enjoyed by the local farmers when haying in summer days gone by. We find it delicious year-round and make it with frozen berries as well as fresh.

1 CUP WHITE VINEGAR
1 CUP WATER
1 QUART RASPBERRIES (FRESH OR FROZEN)

APPROXIMATELY 3 CUPS GRANULATED SUGAR

Combine the vinegar and water, and pour enough of the mixture over the berries to cover them, but not enough to let them float. Let stand for 24 hours, and then squeeze through strainer or cheesecloth. Measure the juice, and add an equal amount of sugar. Boil for 20 minutes. Cool, and either freeze or bottle. Dilute to use, adding approximately 3 tablespoons to a glass of water, orange juice, lemonade, iced tea, or ginger ale. We use it as a punch base, too.

RED LAKE CURRANT SHRUB

The favorite drink of one of our gourmet neighbors.

CURRANTS
WATER

GRANULATED SUGAR

Mash currants, and strain juice through strainer or cheesecloth. Measure juice, and add an equal amount of water and half as much sugar. Chill, and serve with chipped ice.

FRUIT SHAKES

Frozen strawberries, raspberries, and blackberries make superb milkshakes. We like to freeze some of our berries each year on a jelly-roll-type cookie sheet before placing them in plastic bags. They then separate easily for snacks and milkshakes. We toss a handful of whole, raw berries (it's not necessary to thaw them) into the blender along with a cup of milk. Add ice cream or sugar if you have a sweet tooth, or use skim milk and no sweeteners if you are watching your weight and cholesterol count.

Miscellaneous

MAPLE BUTTERNUT FUDGE

We refuse to count the calories in the best candy we've ever eaten.

3 CUPS PURE MAPLE SYRUP
1 CUP MILK

½ CUP CHOPPED BUTTERNUTS OR WALNUTS

Boil the maple syrup and milk in a large saucepan to soft-ball stage (when ½ teaspoon dropped into a cup of water can be shaped into a soft ball with your fingers), or about 236°F. Remove from heat and cool. When mixture is lukewarm, beat until it is creamy. Add the nuts to the maple cream, and spread the mixture in a buttered 8-inch-square pan. Mark it into 16 squares and, if you wish, place one nutmeat on top of each.

SPICED GOOSEBERRIES
YIELD: 3–4 PINTS

2 QUARTS RED OR GREEN GOOSEBERRIES
1 CUP CIDER VINEGAR
4½ CUPS GRANULATED SUGAR
JUICE OF 1 ORANGE

½ TEASPOON GRATED ORANGE RIND
½ TEASPOON GROUND CINNAMON
½ TEASPOON GROUND CLOVES

Remove stems and bottom ends of berries. Add remaining ingredients to gooseberries, and let stand for several hours. In an enamel kettle, bring mixture slowly to a boil and simmer about 2 hours, or until mixture becomes thick; stir frequently. Taste, and add more sugar, if needed. Pour into hot, sterilized glass jars, leaving ½-inch headroom, seal immediately, and process in a boiling-water bath for 10 minutes.

Appendix

Botanical Names of Fruits and Nuts

This list may be useful for determining the different families of fruits for budding, grafting, plant breeding, and pollination.

		GENUS	SPECIES
	Apple	Malus	sylvestris
	Apricot	Prunus	armeniaca
	Cherry, Sour	Prunus	cerasus
TREE FRUITS	Cherry, Sweet	Prunus	avium
	Nectarine	Prunus	persica
	Peach	Prunus	persica
	Pear	Pyrus	communis
	Plum, American	Prunus	(various)
	Plum, Damson	Prunus	insititia
	Plum, European	Prunus	domestica
	Plum, Japanese	Prunus	salicina
	Quince	Cydonia	oblonga

		GENUS	SPECIES
	Blackberry	Rubus	(various)
	Blueberry	Vaccinum	(various)
	Elderberry	Sambucus	canadensis
BERRIES	Grape, American	Vitis	(various)
	Grape, European	Vitis	vinifera
	Kiwi	Actinidia	(various)
	Raspberry	Rubus	(various)
	Saskatoon	Amelanchier	alnifolia
	Strawberry	Fragaria	(various)

		GENUS	SPECIES
NUTS	Butternut	Juglans	cinerea
	Chestnut, Chinese	Castanea	mollissima
	Filbert	Corylus	avellana
	Hazelnut, American	Corylus	americana
	Hickory	Carya	ovata
	Pecan	Carya	illinoinensis
	Walnut, Black	Juglans	nigra
	Walnut, English	Juglans	regia

Government Agencies — United States and Canada

AGRICULTURAL EXTENSION OFFICES (US)

STATE	CITY	ZIP CODE	STATE	CITY	ZIP CODE
Alabama	Auburn	36830	Montana	Bozeman	59715
Alaska	College	99701	Nebraska	Lincoln	68503
Arizona	Tucson	85721	Nevada	Reno	89507
Arkansas	Fayetteville	72701	New Hampshire	Durham	03824
California*	Berkeley	94720	New Jersey*	New Brunswick	08903
Colorado	Fort Collins	80521	New Mexico	Las Cruces	88001
Connecticut	Storrs	06268	New York*	Ithaca	14850
Delaware	Newark	19711	North Carolina	Raleigh	27607
Florida	Homestead	33030	North Dakota	Fargo	58102
Georgia	Athens	30601	Ohio*	Columbus	43210
Hawaii	Honolulu	96822	Oklahoma	Stillwater	74074
Idaho	Moscow	83843	Oregon	Corvallis	97330
Illinois*	Urbana	61801	Pennsylvania	University Park	16802
Indiana	Lafayette	47907	Rhode Island	Kingston	02881
Iowa	Ames	50010	South Carolina	Clemson	29631
Kansas	Manhattan	66502	South Dakota	Brookings	57006
Kentucky	Lexington	40506	Tennessee	Knoxville	37901
Louisiana	University	70803	Texas	College Station	77840
Maine	Orono	04473	Utah	Logan	84321
Maryland	College Park	20740	Vermont	Burlington	05405
Massachusetts*	Amherst	01002	Virginia*	Blacksburg	24061
Michigan*	East Lansing	48823	Washington*	Long Beach	98631
Minnesota	St. Paul	55101	West Virginia	Morgantown	26505
Mississippi	State College	39762	Wisconsin	Madison	53706
Missouri	Columbia	65201	Wyoming	Laramie	82070

*States marked with a star are leading producers of fruit and have excellent bulletins on the subject.

United States
Publications Division
Office of Communication
U.S. Department of Agriculture
Washington, DC 20250

Canada
Information Services
Agriculture Canada
Sir John Carling Building
Ottawa, ON KAI 0C7

Books and Magazines for Fruit and Nut Growers

American Fruit Grower (37733 Euclid Ave., Willoughby, OH 44094)
■ *Monthly magazine for orchardists*

Backyard Fruits and Berries, by Diane E. Bilderback and Dorothy Hinshaw Patent (Rodale Press, Emmaus, PA, 1984)
■ *Excellent book on organic fruit growing*

Brooklyn Botanic Garden booklets (for list, write to Brooklyn Botanic Garden, 1000 Washington Ave., Brooklyn, NY 11225)

Cold-Climate Gardening, by Lewis Hill (Garden Way Publishing, Pownal, VT, 1987)
■ *Fruit- and berry-growing tips for northern gardeners*

The Complete Book of Edible Landscaping, by Rosalind Creasy (Sierra Club Books, San Fransisco, 1982)
■ *Much useful information for home gardeners*

Designing and Maintaining Your Edible Landscape Naturally, by Robert Kourik (Metamorphic Press, Santa Rosa, CA, 1986)
■ *Good information, and a complete appendix of information*

Fruit, Berry, and Nut Inventory, edited by Kent Whealy (Seed Saver Publications, Rural Route 3, Box 239, Decorah, IA 52101, 1989)
■ *Very complete list of cultivars and who sells them*

Good Fruit Grower (11 South Fifth Avenue, Yakima, WA 98901)
■ *Information for western fruit growers*

The Old-Fashioned Fruit Garden, by Jo Ann Gardner (Nimbus Publishing Limited, Halifax, Nova Scotia, Canada B3K 5N5, 1989)
■ *Cultural directions and recipes for small fruits*

Organic Gardening and Farming (33 East Minor St., Emmaus, PA 18049)
■ *Monthly magazine of gardening information*

Plant Propagation: Principles and Practices, by Hudson T. Hartman and Dale E. Kester (Prentice Hall, Englewood Cliffs, NJ, 1990)
■ *Detailed methods of propagation for serious gardeners*

Pruning Simplified, by Lewis Hill (Garden Way Publishing, Pownal, VT, 1985)
■ *Easy-to-follow instructions for pruning almost everything*

Secrets of Plant Propagation, by Lewis Hill (Garden Way Publishing, Pownal, VT, 1985)
- *Easy way for beginning gardeners to start lots of plants*

Sweet and Hard Cider, Making It, Using It, and Enjoying It, by Annie Proulx and Lew Nichols (Garden Way Publishing, Pownal, VT, 1980)
- *Methods, best kinds of fruits to choose, much more*

Fruit Organizations

American Pomological Society, 103 Tyson Building, University Park, PA 16802
- *Information on old and new varieties*

International Ribes Association, 18200 Mountain View Rd., Boonville, CA 95415
- *Information on importing, propagating, growing, and using currants and gooseberries*

New York State Fruit Testing Cooperative Assn., Geneva, NY 14456
- *Information about old and new varieties; also trees for sale*

North American Fruit Explorers, c/o Robert Kurle, 10 South 55 Madison Street, Hinsdale, IL 60521
- *Exchange of fruit-growing ideas*

Northern Nut Growers, 4518 Holston Hills Rd, Knoxville, TN 37914
- *Excellent source of nut-growing information*

Dwarfing Rootstocks Used in Propagating Fruits

Many catalogs now give their readers a choice of dwarf rootstocks as well as fruit cultivars. This information is given to help you decide which kind is best for your location. Heights are approximate, since they will vary according to soil and climate as well as the cultivar that is grafted upon them.

APPLE DWARF ROOTSTOCKS

The most common dwarf rootstocks used in propagating dwarf apples have been developed in England at the Malling experiment station. They are identified by numbers and the letters EM (East Malling) or MM (Malling Merton).

EM 2. Semi-dwarfing to 10 feet. Does well on loams but not on clay soil. Does not anchor tree as well as some, so may need staking.

EM 4. Early bearing, heavy producer, widely used in Europe. Tends to root one-sided and therefore may lean in later years.

EM 7. Widely used semi-dwarf stock, 8 feet. Anchors the tree well and suckers very little. Tolerates heavy soils and is early bearing.

EM 9. Very dwarf (about 6 feet). Good for espaliers, living fences, and small areas. Susceptible to aphids and fire blight. Staking is recommended in windy areas as wood is very brittle.

EM 26. Slightly larger growing than EM 9, but smaller than EM 7. [Often gets winter injury.] Needs staking.

EM 27. Most dwarfing of all, even more than EM 9. Patented. Hardier than most Mallings but susceptible to fire blight. Needs well-drained soil.

MM 13A. Semi-dwarf. Productive but tends to take longer to bear than many dwarfs. Does fairly well in wet soils.

MM 104. Semi-dwarf. Vigorous but cannot tolerate wet soils. Grows to 11 feet. Not early bearing.

MM 106. About 9 feet. Resistant to aphids but may have trouble with collar rot in the Northwest. Sometimes is damaged by early autumn freezes. Needs well-drained soil.

MM 109. Semi-dwarf, well anchored, nonsuckering. A good producer.

MM 111. Vigorous, drought-resistant, productive. Aphid-resistant. Does especially well in warmer climates. Widely used in commercial plantings.

Antanovka. Very hardy Russian stock that does not sucker, but produces a full-size tree. Vigorous.

Budagovski. Also from Russia, (various) strains of these are used to produce trees varying from quite dwarf (Bud. 491) to three-quarter-size (Bud. 118).

Ottawa. Hardy dwarf rootstock from Canada.

Plum, Peach, and Cherry Dwarf Rootstocks

The stone fruits are usually grafted on one of these:

Prunus americana. Native American plum. Hardy and vigorous, but it suckers badly. Good for moist soils.

P. besseyi. This is the native western sand cherry. It produces a tree only about 6 feet tall, and they often begin to bear at about half that size. Especially good for tiny yards, large tubs, planters, roof gardens, and espaliers.

P. fruticosa. European dwarf ground cherry. Dwarfing stock. Several cultivars are available, including G. M. 9, G. M. 61, and G. M. 79.

P. tomentosa. The Nanking cherry grows about the same size and shape as the *besseyi* but is hardier and less vigorous. It would probably be selected if only hardiness were a factor.

P. fruticosa. The native ground cherry is used occasionally for dwarfing cherries, particularly the sweet varieties.

Mail-Order Nurseries and Sources of Orchard Supplies

The names of companies, nurseries, books, magazines, and organizations in this section and elsewhere in this book are listed to save the reader time and inconvenience. In no way does their inclusion represent an endorsement or recommendation of the companies or products. Write to the firms that supply the items you are interested in, study their literature carefully, check any available consumer guides, and then make your own decisions. *The Complete*

Guide to Gardening by Mail is available from The Mailorder Association of Nurseries, Dept. SCI, 8683 Doves Fly Way, Laurel, MD 20723. Please add $1.00 for postage and handling.

For a complete list of nurseries in any state, write to the state Department of Agriculture, which is usually located in the capital city. There is often a small fee for such a list.

NURSERIES

Some of the following companies may charge a small fee for their catalogs.

Adams Nursery, Inc., P.O. Box 108, Aspers, PA 17304
- *Fruit trees on a variety of rootstocks*

Ahrens Strawberry Nursery, R.R. 1, Huntingburg, IN 47542
- *Berry plants*

Allen Co., P.O. Box 1577,. Salisbury, MD 21801
- *Strawberry plants*

Aldrich Berry Farm and Nursery, 190 Aldrich St., Mossyrock, WA 98564
- *Blueberry plants*

Bear Creek Nursery, P.O. Box 411, Northport, WA 99157
- *Hardy fruits and berries*

Bigelow Nurseries, P.O. Box 718, Northboro, MA 01532
- *Fruits, berries*

Bluebird Orchard & Nursery, 429 E. Randall St., Coopersville, MI 49404
- *200 apple cultivars, SASE for list*

Burgess Seed and Plant Co., 905 Four Seasons Rd., Bloomington, IN 61701
- *Fruits, berries, nuts*

Buckley Nursery, 646 N. River Ave., Buckley, WA 98321
- *Fruits, berries, nuts*

C&O Nursery Co., P.O. Box 116, Wenatchee, WA 98807
- *Fruit trees on a variety of rootstocks*

Country Heritage Nursery, P.O. Box 536, Hartford, MI 49057
- *Fruits, berries, nuts*

Cumberland Valley Nurseries, P.O. Box 471, McMinnville, TN 37110
- *Fruits on a variety of rootstocks, pecans*

Edible Landscaping, P.O. Box 77, Afton, VA 22920
- *Fruits, berries*

Farmer Seed and Nursery Co., Reservation Center, 2207 East Oakland Ave., Bloomington, IL 61701
- *Fruits, berries*

Fedco Trees, P.O. Box 340, Palermo, ME 04354
- *Fruits, berries*

Henry Field Seed and Nursery, Shenandoah, IA 51602
- *Fruits, berries, nuts*

Finch Blueberry Nursery, PO Box 699, Bailey, NC 27807
- *Rabbit-eye blueberries*

Forest Farm Nursery, 990 Tetherow Rd., Williams, OR 97544
- *Fruits, berries, nuts (catalog $2.00)*

Foster Nursery Co., Inc., 69 Orchard St., Fredonia, NY 14063
- *Grapevines*

Louis Gerardi Nursery, 1700 E. Highway 50, O'Fallon, IL 62269
- *Persimmons, nuts (send stamped envelope for list)*

Girard Nurseries, P.O. Box 428, Geneva, OH 44014
- *Blueberries, nuts*

John Gordon Nursery, 1385 Campbell, Blvd., N. Tonanwanda, NY 14120
- *Nuts*

Grootendorst Nurseries, 15310 Red Arrow Hwy., Lakeside, MI 49116
- *Fruit rootstocks for grafting and budding*

Gurney's Seed & Nursery Co., Yankton, SD 57079
- *Fruits, berries, nuts*

Johnson Orchard and Nursery, R.R. #5, Box 325, Ellijay, GA 30504
- *Fruits for the South*

Jung Seeds and Nursery, 335 S. High St., Randolph, WI 53957
- *Fruits, berries*

Kelly Nurseries, 19 Maple St., Dansville, NY 14437
- *Fruits, berries, nuts*

Lawyer Nursery Inc., 950 Hwy. 200 W., Plains, MT 59859
- *Fruits, nuts, berries*

Lennilia Farm Nursery, Rte. 1, Box 683, Alburtis, PA 18011
- *Grafted nut trees, fruits*

Henry Leuthardt Nurseries, P.O. Box 666, East Moriches, Long Island, NY 11940
- *Fruits, berries*

Makielski Berry Nursery, 7130 Platt Rd., Ypsilanti, MI 48197
- *Berries*

Earl May Seed and Nursery, Shenandoah, IA 51603
- *Fruits, berries, nuts*

Mellinger's, Inc., 2340 West South Range Rd., North Lima, OH 44452-9731
■ *Fruits, berries, nuts, country living items*

Miller Nursery, 5060 W. Lake Rd., Canandaigua, NY 14424
■ *New and old apples, other tree fruits, grapes, berries, nuts*

Nebraska Nut Growers Assn., 207 Miller Hall, Lincoln, NE 68583
■ *Nuts*

New York State Fruit Testing Assn., P.O. Box 462, Geneva, NY 14456
■ *Wide assortment of new tree fruits and berries*

North Star Gardens, 19060 Manning Trail, N. Marine, MN 55047
■ *Raspberries, currants, gooseberries, jostaberries*

Nolin River Nut Tree Nursery, 797 Port Wooden Rd., Upton, KY 42784
■ *Nut trees, persimmons*

Nourse Farms, Inc., P.O. Box 485, S. Deerfield, MA 01373
■ *Berries*

The Nursery Corporation, P.O. Box 578, Hartford, MI 49057
■ *Fruit trees*

Oikos Tree Crops, 721 N. Fletcher, Kalamazoo, MI 49007
■ *Nuts*

Oregon Rootstock, Inc., 10906 Monitor-McKee Rd. N.E., Woodburn, OR 97071
■ *Large number of dwarf rootstocks*

Pony Creek Nursery, Tilleda, WI 54978
■ *Fruits, berries*

Raintree Nursery, 391 Butts Rd., Morton, WA 98356
■ *Fruits on a variety of rootstocks, berries, nuts*

Rayner Bros., Inc., P.O. Box 1617, Salisbury, MD 21801
■ *Blueberry and strawberry plants*

Rocky Meadow Orchard and Nursery, Rte. 1, Box 104, New Salisbury, IN 47161
■ *Fruits on a variety of rootstocks*

F. W. Schumacher Co., 36 Spring Hill Rd., Sandwich, MA 02563
■ *Fruits, berries, nuts, tree seeds*

Southmeadow Fruit Gardens, Lakeside, MI 49116
■ *Old and new fruits and berries*

Stark Bros., Hwy. 54, Louisiana, MO 63353
■ *Fruit trees, berries, nuts*

St. Lawrence Nursery, Rte. 2, Potsdam, NY 13676
■ *Extra-hardy, old and new fruits, berries, and nuts*

Turkey Hollow Nursery, R.R. 2, Box 31, Cumberland, KY 40823
- *Scions and budwood of old apple cultivars*

Van Well Nursery, P.O. Box 1339, Wenatchee, WA 98801
- *Fruits on a variety of rootstocks, berries, nuts*

Whitman Farms Nursery, 1420 Beaumont NW, Salem, OR 97304
- *Fruits, berries, nuts*

Yakima Valley Nursery, 6461 W. Powerhouse Rd., Yakima, WA 98908
- *Fruits*

Canadian Nurseries

Beaverlodge Nursery Ltd., P.O. Box 127, Beaverlodge, Alberta, Canada, TOH 0C0
- *Saskatoons, extra hardy fruits and berries*

McConnell Nurseries, Inc., Port Burwell, Ontario, Canada N0J 1T0

W. H. Perron Co. Ltd., 515 Labelle Blvd., Chomedey Laval, Quebec, Canada H7V 2T3

Teolum River Fruit Trees, Box 68, Merville, BC, Canada EOA 2HO
- *Apples, other fruits (catalog $2.50)*

Windmill Point Farm and Nursery, 2103 Perrot Blvd, N.D, 16 Perrot, Quebec, Canada J7V 5V6
- *Antique apples, other fruits, nuts, scion wood; also does custom grafting*

Apples for Tasting

Applesource, Route One, Chapin, IL 62628

Equipment

Gardener's Supply Co., 128 Intervale Rd., Burlington, VT 05401
- *Gardening supplies, natural pest controls*

Good Nature Products, Inc., P.O. Box 866, Buffalo, NY 14240
- *Cider mills and presses*

Kemp Co., 160 Koser Road, Lititz, PA 17543
- *Shredders, chippers*

Mantis Manufacturing Co., 1458 County Line Rd., Huntington Valley, PA 19006
- *Tillers, sprayers, shredders*

Osmo Heila, Mehu-Maija Products, 6383 Podunk Rd., Trumansburg, NY 14886
- *Juice extractor*

Orchard Equipment and Supply, Conway, MA 01341
- *Cider mills and presses*

State College Laboratories, 840 William Lane, P.O. Box 13848, Reading, PA 19612-3848
- *Deer and rabbit repellent*

Troy Built Mfg. Co., 102nd St. and 9th Ave., Troy, NY 12180
- *Tillers, mowers, chippers*

ORCHARD SUPPLIES

Department stores, garden centers, nurseries, hardware stores, and even general stores are possible places for you to buy supplies and equipment for your orchard. If you cannot locate a local source, the following firms may be of help.

Agway Farm Stores have retail outlets in many cities and towns
- *Tools, fertilizers, spray and spray materials, weed killers, etc.*

Day Equipment Corporation, 1402 East Monroe, Goshen, IN 46526
- *Commercial cider-making equipment*

Friend Manufacturing Corporation, Gasport, NY 14067
- *Commercial orchard equipment of all kinds*

Holland Organic Garden, 8515 Stearns, Overland Park, KS 66214
- *Organic sprays, fertilizers, and beneficial insects*

K. C. Biological Co., P.O. Box 148487, Lenexa, KS 66215
- *Supplies for tissue culture propagation*

A.M. Leonard Company, P.O. Box 816, Piqua, OH 45356
- *Tree paint and sealers, grafting supplies, pruning tools, sprayers, electric bug killers, soil test kits, and harvesting equipment (catalog)*

The Necessary Trading Co., New Castle, VA 24127
- *Supplies for organic gardeners, including biological pest controls, beneficial insects*

Pollen Products, 255 East Milgeo, Ripon, CA 95366
- *Pollen*

MANUFACTURERS OF ORCHARD CHEMICALS

These companies can supply information on the various fertilizers, insecticides, fungicides, and herbicides they make or distribute, and can suggest where you can purchase them locally.

Agway, Inc., Fertilizer Chemical Division, Syracuse, NY 13201

American Cyanamid Co., Box 400, Princeton, NJ 08540

Chemagrow Agriculture Division, Mobay Chemical Corporation, Box 4913, Kansas City, MO 64120

Dow Chemical, Ag Organics Dept., Midlands, MI 48640

E.I. Dupont de Nemours and Co., Inc., Bio Chemical Division, Wilmington, DE 19898

F.M.C. Corporation, Agricultural Chemical Division, Middleport, NY 14105

Merck Chemical Division, Agricultural Products, Rahway, NJ 07065

Rohm and Haas, Philadelphia, PA 19105

Stauffer Chemical Co., Agricultural Chemical Division, Westport, CT 06880

Uniroyal, Inc., Chemical Division, 59 Maple Street, Naugatuck, CT 06770

Index

Page numbers in *italics* indicate illustrations or tables.

Recipe Index

Blueberry Buckle, 234
Fresh Apple Cake, 228
Gooseberry Tea Cake, 238
Raspberry Jam Cake, 237
Tart Plum Coffeecake, 232
Candy:
Maple Butternut Fudge, 241
Cherries:
Washington's Birthday Cherry Pie,
236
Cookies:
Applesauce Cookies, 229
Country Strawberry Shortcake, 233
Crab apples:
Spiced Crab Apples, 231

D
Desserts:
Apple Crow's Nest, 227
Applesauce Deluxe, 229
Baked Pears Meringue, 232
Country Strawberry Shortcake, 233
Duchess Apple Pudding, 237
Streusel Fruit Custard, 233
Duchess Apple Pudding, 237

E
Elderberry Scones, 238

F
Fresh Apple Cake, 228
Fruit Shakes, 240

G
Gooseberry Tea Cake, 238
Grape Juices, 239

I
Ice Cream:
Raspberry Ice Cream, 237

J
Jams and Jellies:
Elderberry Scones, 238
Gooseberry Tea Cake, 238
Raspberry Jam Cake, 237

M
Maple Butternut Fudge, 241

P
Peaches:
Streusel Fruit Custard, 233
Pears:
Baked Pears Meringue, 232
Pickles and Preserves:
Spiced Apple Pickles, 231
Spiced Crab Apples, 231
Spiced Gooseberries, 241
Pies:
Apple Macaroon, 228
Blueberry Pie Deluxe, 235
Blue-Ribbon Raspberry Pie, 235
Red Gooseberry Pie, 234
Washington's Birthday Cherry Pie,
236
Plums:
Tart Plum Coffeecake, 232
Puddings:
Duchess Apple Pudding, 227

R
Raspberry Ice Cream, 237
Raspberry Jam Cake, 237
Raspberry Shrub, 240
Red Gooseberry Pie, 234
Red Lake Currant Shrub, 240

S
Soups:
Verena's Elderberry Soup with
Apples and Icebergs, 236
Spiced Apple Pickles, 231